# Cohabitants

# Cohabitants

*Fourth Edition*

Stephen Parker LLB, PhD

*Solicitor, England and Wales*
*Barrister and Solicitor, Australian Capital Territory*
*Barrister, Queensland*
*Professor of Law, Griffith University, Queensland*

John Dewar, BCL, MA

*Barrister, England and Wales*
*Professor of Law, Griffith University, Queensland*

LAW & TAX

ISBN 075200 0861

*Published by*
FT Law & Tax
21–27 Lamb's Conduit Street
London WC1N 3NJ

A Division of Pearson Professional Ltd

*Associated offices*
Australia, Belgium, Canada, Hong Kong, India, Japan, Luxembourg, Singapore, Spain, USA



A CIP catalogue record for this book is available from the British Library.

Printed in Great Britain by Hartnolls, Bodmin, Cornwall

# Contents

# Preface

The previous three editions of this work, written by Stephen Parker, were entitled *Cohabitees*. For reasons explained more fully in chapter 1, this new edition goes under the name *Cohabitants* and it is the joint work of Stephen Parker and John Dewar (formerly a Fellow of Hertford College, Oxford and now a fellow emigre). We hope that the new title, new authorship and revised text will continue the book's usefulness to its readership of legal practitioners, teachers and students in England and Wales.

There have been some significant changes to the law concerning cohabitants since the third edition was published in 1991. Some of the few remaining income tax advantages that cohabitation had over marriage have been removed. Very significantly, a new Family Homes and Domestic Violence Bill was introduced in 1995 and the whole of chapter 6 has been rewritten on the assumption that the Bill becomes law (but *see below*). Case law has appeared in the aftermath of the House of Lords decision in *Lloyds Bank Plc v Rosset* concerning the troublesome area of informally created ownership rights. The Children Act 1989, newly in force at the time of the last edition, has now been the subject of considerable litigation. Finally, the Child Support Act 1991 has been brought into force, accompanied by volumes of regulations and not a little controversy.

Despite these changes, it is clear that the legal system in England and Wales has so far failed to come to terms with an apparently intractable fact. Unmarried cohabitation is here to stay. Sooner or later some general legislation is going to be needed that deals with the regulation of ownership, occupation and maintenance. In several Australian jurisdictions there is now statutory provision for the adjustment of property interests and the award of limited maintenance on the breakdown of what is called there a *de facto* relationship. After an uncertain start, the case law on the leading measure, the De Facto Relationships Act 1984 in New South Wales, indicates that the Act is being used to chart a middle way between treating unmarried couples as complete legal strangers, on the one hand, and treating them as *de jure* spouses, on the other. Interestingly, the use of cohabitation contracts, which are expressly provided for in that Act and which allow the couple to opt out of the court's discretionary powers, seems to have been minimal. For the purposes of providing a succinct statement of the law in England and Wales, we have omitted regular references to other jurisdictions. Nevertheless, there is much that this country could now learn from family law elsewhere. At the time of writing, the Law Commission is enquiring into cohabitants' property issues, and its enquiry may branch out into domestic co-ownership issues generally, but proposals for legislative change are presumably some way off.

The law on cohabitation in England and Wales is often derivative from other parts of the law. It draws, for example, on contract, licences, estoppel and trusts and there is relatively little that can be described as exclusively about cohabitants. Whilst we have tried to give an introduction to the basic principles of these other areas, some familiarity with them has had to be assumed. Similarly, some understanding of family law as it affects married couples is assumed in parts. Although a few express comparisons between the law affecting spouses and cohabitants are included in the text, this is usually for the purpose of showing how different the two can be.

Our treatment of the subject is very much confined to legal rules. We are dealing with the law on the books, not the law in action. Stephen Parker has elsewhere tried to place the legal treatment of informal marriage in some kind of historical and theoretical context (see *Informal Marriage, Cohabitation and the Law, 1750–1989*, Macmillan, 1990).

The citations in the text are primarily to the Family Law Reports (FLR) and only if a decision is not reported there are other series cited. The All England Reports are used for modern cases. Whilst this reverses the order of conventional authoritativeness, it is intended to reflect the access that readers will have. Of course, many of the major cases are reported in various series.

In the Preface to the third edition it was noted that the number of little Parkers seemed to grow in line with the editions of the book, although a wish was expressed that that was pure coincidence and now over. The presence of a little Dewar has maintained the parallel development of children and editions and John Dewar can now assume sole responsibility for continuing the tradition. Stephen Parker owes thanks to Rhian for her continued support and holding of the fort whilst he was collaborating on this edition in England. John Dewar likewise owes grateful thanks to Henrietta Dewar. Both authors thank the Fellows of Hertford College,

Oxford, whose hospitality in the early part of 1995 ensured timely completion of the manuscript. The work of Kylie Burns, Research Assistant at Griffith University, is gratefully acknowledged.

The manuscript was prepared on the assumption that the Family Homes and Domestic Violence Bill, as amended by the Special Bills Committee, would be enacted without further substantial amendment. We now know that this was an optimistic assumption. The failure of the Bill in early November 1995 left us with a difficult decision. In the end, we decided to go ahead with the manuscript as we had prepared it. There seemed little point in updating the old law, given that the Lord Chancellor intends to reintroduce an amended Bill as soon as possible. Equally, there seemed little to be gained from waiting for the revised Bill, since it should be obvious where the new Bill will differ from the old. Besides which, there is a great deal of new law contained in this book that is unaffected by the Bill.

We have tried to cite the law as at 1 April 1995.

*Stephen Parker*
*John Dewar*
*Brisbane, November 1995*

# Table of Cases

# Table of Statutes

* Family Homes and Domestic Violence Bill 1995 is tabled to clause number.

# Table of Statutory Instruments

# Chapter 1

# Introduction

## The scope of the book

This book sets out the substantive law concerning unmarried cohabitation in England and Wales. It appears to be concerned largely with heterosexual unmarried couples but this is because most statutory references to cohabitation require the parties to be a man and a woman. The common law and equitable remedies discussed here, however, are, in theory, equally available to homosexual and heterosexual couples. Whilst there are a number of cases that concern the ordering of custody or access to a homosexual parent, there has been very little case law concerning disputes between gay or lesbian people over property or other matters. No value judgment is intended by the emphasis on heterosexual couples.

## Definitions and terms

The three previous editions of this book used the term 'cohabitee'. This was, admittedly, slightly misleading as any two or more people living in the same household could be said to be cohabiting. It was also an irregular form of 'cohabitant' and in the third edition it was acknowledged that 'cohabitant', whilst hardly tripping off the tongue, may have gained the upper hand in official circles. In fact, just as 'cohabitee' began to appear in judgments, the legislature, following the Law Commission, has decided to use 'cohabitant' (*see* the Family Homes and Domestic Violence Bill discussed fully in Chapter 6). The timing of this development, combined with a reworking of the text following the addition of a second author, suggested that it was now right to concede defeat graciously and stake a claim to the new word in the title of this edition. The word 'mistress' is avoided except when it is the term used by others. Instead, those who have a sexual relationship but who are not living together are referred to as lovers.

Alternative terms have been put forward in the past, some more seriously than others. Examples include 'meaningful associate', 'special friend', 'significant other person', 'spouse equivalent', 'domestic associate', 'current companion' and 'lil' (short for live-in lover). One word that has not gained the currency it deserves is 'ummer', said to derive from the embarrassed resolution of the mother's dilemma when she introduces her daughter's cohabitant ' ... and this is Oliver, my daughter's um, er ... '.

The policy behind the Family Law Reform Act 1987 was to remove labels like legitimate and illegitimate from children so that, where distinctions are necessary at all, they are based on the marital relationship of the parents. Nevertheless, the concept of illegitimacy has not been removed from English law and so the term is used here when any alternative would simply blur the matter.

## The extent of cohabitation

Since the government's *General Household Survey* began collecting information on cohabitation in 1979, and particularly since it started asking questions in 1986 about men as well as women, it has become possible to begin building a picture of the prevalence of unmarried cohabitation in Great Britain as a whole.

The picture is not as clearly focused, however, as the picture that statistics on marriage can give us. There is, first, a definitional problem in deciding what it is one is trying to measure and then making that definition effective when collecting the data. Allied to this is a methodological problem of assessing the truth of the answers given to researchers. According to the 1984 *General Household Survey*, for example, 70 per cent of the women under 50 eventually found to be cohabiting had initially described themselves as married.

Recent figures (a summary of which by J Haskey and K Kiernan appears in (1990) Fam Law 442) show that in 1986–87 there were about 900,000 cohabiting couples in Great Britain as a whole, and about 444,000 dependent children living with them. About one-third of the cohabitants had been married at some time.

More recent figures are available in the 1992 *General Household Survey* and the 1995 edition of *Social Trends*. Expressed as a percentage of single people (ie not currently living with a spouse) in the age-band 16–59, about 15 per cent of men and 18 per cent of women were cohabiting. Of course, this is a wide age-group and it flattens the overall figure. If, for example, one takes the group 25–29, then 28 per cent of all unmarried men and women were cohabiting in 1992. If one narrows the gaze further, about one-third (36 per cent) of *divorced* men in that age-group were cohabiting, whereas just over one-quarter (26 per cent) of divorced women were doing so. Over 60 per cent of couples marrying for the first time have cohabited before getting married.

Taken together, these figures suggest that cohabitation is best viewed as an integral part of a cycle of family organisation (ie pre-marital cohabitation, marriage, divorce followed by post-divorce cohabitation with a new partner) rather than as a straight alternative to marriage, although some never-married cohabitants will undoubtedly have made a deliberate choice in favour of the unmarried state.

As for childbearing, married women are still more likely to have children than cohabiting women, but cohabiting women are more likely to have children than single non-cohabiting women. In 1986–87, in the age-group 25–29, 29 per cent of currently cohabiting women had a child compared with 70 per cent of married women. At the same time, 19 per cent of single *non*-cohabiting women in that age-group had a child. This particular age-group is where childbearing patterns are the most similar between single cohabiting and non-cohabiting women. If one takes all single women under 60, then 28 per cent of cohabiting women had a child compared with only 8 per cent of non-cohabiting women. Furthermore, if one takes the specific age-group 30–34, the figures were 42 per cent and 18 per cent respectively.

The most significant trend has been the growth of extra-marital births over the last 30 years. Between 1963 and 1993, the proportion of births outside marriage to all live births rose from one in 20 to one in three. In 1993, three-quarters of those births were registered jointly by both parents, and the parents were cohabiting in three-quarters of cases of joint registration. The practice of marrying after the conception of children has diminished. In 1979 23 per cent of births were to couples who married after conception. In 1988, the figure was down to 11 per cent (*see* (1991) Fam Law 246).

One in three cohabiting households contains dependent children. This is partly because cohabitation is especially prevalent among the divorced or separated (*see above*), who may have children from a previous relationship. Indeed, it has been suggested that 80 per cent of such cohabitants have children, mainly from former marriages. But there has also been an increase in the number of never-married cohabitants who are starting families.

## The general legal position today

Despite a certain amount of popular wisdom that there is no longer any difference between marriage and unmarried cohabitation today, this is far from the truth. It is true that references to unmarried couples are now scattered throughout statute law and there is now some evidence of the particular needs of cohabitants being recognised (*see*, for example, the Family Homes and Domestic Violence Bill discussed in Chapter 6). Often, however, statutes that are apparently even-handed do not operate that way as a result of the broader legal context in which they are situated. In the case of the Family Homes and Domestic Violence Bill, for example, the absence of any integrated set of rules regulating long-term occupation of the family home on the breakdown of the relationship means that the battered cohabitant, and particularly the cohabitant who has no beneficial interest in the property, may be in a considerably more difficult legal position than the battered spouse.

One cause of the markedly different treatment between married and unmarried couples in certain areas is the *absence* of legislation concerning money and property rights. For example, there is no duty on cohabiting couples to maintain each other and so there is no procedure whereby one partner can claim periodical payments from the other; a point made forcefully by Millett J in *Windeler v Whitehall* [1990] 2 FLR 505 at 506C. A recent, and very limited, exception to this is the power under s 12 of the Family Homes and Domestic Violence Bill to order that a cohabitant in occupation following an occupation order make periodical payments to the other cohabitant where the latter would have been entitled to occupy the property but for the order. Maintenance of children is a slightly different matter because the formula under the Child Support Act 1991 was devised with the needs of the custodial parent partly in mind. There are also now circumstances where a former cohabitant can be made to reimburse some of the income support being paid to his former partner if she is looking after their child (Social Security Act 1986, s 24A as amended by the Social Security Act 1990). This is by no means the same thing as a direct maintenance claim by the woman against the man, however, as she does not benefit from any money recouped by the state.

As for property claims, it will be possible for a court to order the transfer of a tenancy to a cohabitant under the Family Homes and Domestic Violence Bill, but most property disputes continue to be dealt with under equitable doctrines and, if anything, these may have become less generous to vulnerable cohabitants than in the days when Lord Denning was in the Court of Appeal. Of course, it need not be like this. It is possible to provide a regime for maintenance and property adjustment which nevertheless maintains a gap between marriage and cohabitation. A good model is to be found in the De Facto Relationships Act

1984 in New South Wales where discretion is conferred upon the state Supreme Court but it is a more restricted discretion than that available to the federal Family Court which deals with marriage breakdown. At the time of writing, the Law Commission has begun an inquiry into these matters.

This book does not attempt to chart systematically the various differences in treatment between marriage and cohabitation in English law. It seeks only to provide a succinct statement of the main areas of law that concern unmarried couples. As a general rule, however, it is safest to assume that the law on cohabitation starts from quite a different point than the law on marriage. Cohabitants are presumed to be legal strangers and their affairs are governed by the general law unless a rule to the contrary can be invoked. Spouses, on the other hand, are presumed to be in a relationship based on status. It is true that the direction of the modern law has been gradually to remove status consequences from marriage whilst at the same time attaching a kind of status to the fact of unmarried cohabitation. There is a long way to go, at least in England and Wales, before the two trends converge, if they ever do.

# Chapter 2

# Cohabitation and Matrimonial Proceedings

This chapter deals with the effect of cohabitation by one or both parties to a marriage on matrimonial proceedings in the family proceedings and divorce courts. Cohabitation may be relevant in matrimonial proceedings in various ways. First, parties to a divorce may have cohabited with each other before marrying or after divorcing. Second, one or both of the parties to a marriage may be cohabiting at the time of the proceedings. Third, one or both of the parties may cohabit after the proceedings. Each of these situations may affect the order that a court makes. We look at them in turn and consider also the practical problem of finding out the assets of a cohabitant.

## Pre-marital and post-divorce cohabitation between the parties

### Statutory rules

It is now quite common for couples to have lived together before marrying (*see* Chapter 1). If they subsequently separate or divorce, to what extent will their pre-marital cohabitation be taken into account by a court when deciding what financial provision and, in the case of the divorce court, property adjustment to make? In the light of a recent case, it is now necessary to ask a second question. If the parties live together after divorce, can this be taken into account in ancillary proceedings (perhaps ancillary proceedings re-opened after a successful application for leave to appeal out of time)?

Both the family proceedings court and the divorce court must consider specific statutory matters in arriving at a decision, and the list is largely similar for both courts. Under s 25 of the Matrimonial Causes Act 1973 (MCA 1973), as amended, the divorce court is directed to have regard to all the circumstances of the case, first consideration being given to the welfare while a minor of any child of the family who has not attained the age of 18. There then follows a list of particular matters, including (in shortened form) the resources of the parties, the pre-breakdown standard of living, the age of the parties and the duration of the marriage, any disability of the parties, contributions to the home and family, conduct (if that conduct is such that it would in the opinion of the court be inequitable to disregard) and loss of prospective benefit (such as a pension).

The family proceedings court is given a similar direction by s 3 of the Domestic Proceedings and Magistrates' Courts Act 1978 (DPMCA 1978), with the omission of a reference to loss of prospective benefit. In addition, MCA 1973, s 25A requires the divorce court to consider whether it would be appropriate to terminate the financial obligations of each party towards the other as soon after the grant of the decree as the court considers just and reasonable and specifically to consider whether periodical payments should be limited to the period necessary to allow the payee to adjust without undue hardship to the termination of her or his financial dependence on the other.

## Cases

The question has arisen whether the parties' conduct and contributions to the relationship *before* the marriage ceremony or after a decree absolute can be taken into account. A modern authoritative statement on this is still awaited. The cases over the last 20 years or so indicate a movement away from a strict position (that pre-marital cohabitation is to be ignored) to one where the courts might attach almost equal weight to behaviour in pre-marital cohabitation as in marriage. Nevertheless, the number of authorities is small. The strict position is exemplified by *Campbell v Campbell* [1977] 1 All ER 1. Here the parties had lived together for three years before marrying and for a further two years and four months afterwards. On appeal to the Family Division from the registrar's order in divorce proceedings, Sir George Baker P refused to listen to evidence of the parties' misconduct towards each other during the three years' pre-marital cohabitation and refused to treat the marriage as lasting for more than two years and four months. He said (at 6b):

> There is an increasing tendency I have found in cases in Chambers, to regard and, indeed, speak of the celebration of marriage as 'the paper work'. Well that is, to my mind, an entirely misconceived outlook. It is the ceremony of marriage and the sanctity of marriage that count; rights, duties and obligations begin on the marriage and not before. It is a complete

> cheapening of the marriage relationship, which I believe, and I am sure many share this belief, is essential to the well-being of our society as we understand it, to suggest that pre-marital periods, particularly in the circumstances of this case, should, as it were, by a doctrine of relation back of matrimony, be taken as part of the marriage to count in favour of the wife performing as it is put 'wifely duties before marriage'.

This case might have been decided on its own facts and the judge did say that he seemed to be faced with the profitless investigation of who fornicated first. A different approach, although also based on unusual circumstances, was taken by Wood J in *Kokosinski v Kokosinski* [1980] FLR 205. The parties had lived together for 24 years before marrying but they separated within a few months of the marriage. According to Wood J (at 218):

> This wife has given the best years of her life to this husband. She has been faithful, loving and hard-working. She has helped him to build what is in every sense a family business. She has managed his home and been a mother to and helped him to bring up a son of whom they are justly proud. I believe that she has earned for herself some part of the value of the family business.

In ancillary proceedings after obtaining a decree *nisi* of divorce on the basis of her husband's desertion, the wife applied for a lump sum. Counsel for the husband, citing *Campbell* in support, argued that MCA 1973, ss 21–25 were only intended to do justice between husband and wife and not between a 'common law husband' and 'common law wife'. Wood J noted, however, that the court was directed by s 25(1) to have regard to all the circumstances of the case. The factor of 'conduct' could be used to increase the share of one party, although it was generally used in the sense of misconduct to cut down financial relief. Furthermore, the words 'all the circumstances' were wide enough to cover events prior to the marriage.

The wife was granted a lump sum. *Campbell* was distinguished (at 215) because 'On the facts of that case it was abundantly clear that neither party was worthy of praise for his or her moral attitude, nor for his or her contribution to a home, nor the upbringing of a family.' Nevertheless, the policy considerations that motivated Sir George Baker were not ignored in *Kokosinski*. Wood J noted (at 220) that 'the occasions on which a court is likely to feel that justice requires such recognition of pre-marital relationships are likely to be few, possibly very few'.

Two subsequent cases seemed to confirm this speculation. In *Hayes v Hayes* (1981) 11 Fam Law 208 Balcombe J was considering what he described as 'on and off cohabitation' for six years prior to a marriage that lasted for seven weeks. He held that the cohabitation was of no significance because it lacked any semblance of permanence. In *Foley v Foley* [1981] FLR 215 the Court of Appeal said that the trial judge was entitled to distinguish between pre-marital cohabitation and marriage under s 25 and he could attach his own weight to the former. The trial judge's view that public opinion still generally recognised a stronger claim founded on years of marriage was upheld.

Recent cases appear to have moved away from this position, however, and there are instances when no distinction is drawn at all. In *Day v Day* [1988] 1 FLR 278 cohabitation of four years was followed by marriage which lasted only six weeks. On the wife's application for periodical payments the justices looked at the whole of the relationship and ordered the husband to pay £15 per week to the wife and £5 to each of her children (whom the husband had accepted as children of the family). Wood J in the Divisional Court found no ground to interfere with the justices' decision. *Hayes* was distinguished on the basis that the wife in this case was not working and there were two young children of the family.

In *Gojkovic v Gojkovic* [1990] 1 FLR 140 the parties had cohabited for nine years and then been married for a similar length of time. During their relationship they had amassed great wealth. The wife was awarded something over one-quarter of the £4m assets in view of her contributions to the whole of the relationship and this decision was upheld by the Court of Appeal. Whilst *Gojkovic* was obviously a 'big money' one (per Butler-Sloss LJ at 143C) in *Waterman v Waterman* [1989] 1 FLR 380, a case which involved much more modest circumstances, the Court of Appeal considered the whole of a relationship lasting 33 months, evenly divided between cohabitation and marriage, without drawing any distinction, in deciding that periodical payments for the wife should be made for five years with the possibility of an extension.

What was described as 'an unusal and exceptional case' was decided by Douglas Brown J in *S v S* [1994] 2 FLR 228 (at 230B). Here the parties lived under the same roof for 29 years, comprising six years' pre-marital cohabitation, eight years' marriage and 15 years of post-divorce cohabitation. The learned judge, referring only to *Campbell*, *Kokosinski*, and *Foley* (*above*) acknowledged that periods of marital and non-marital cohabitation have to be approached separately but he went on (at 246F):

> my duty, to be found in s 25(1), to have regard to all the circumstances of the case, requires that I give attention, and I do in fact give very considerable weight, to the part played by the wife in running the family home, being a mother to the chilren, working for a good part of the time and being a loyal 'wife' to a rising and successful businessman over the whole period …

He also expressed some doubts whether 'in 1993 public opinion would be exactly the same as that perceived' in *Campbell* and *Foley* (246E).

In the event, the wife was given leave to appeal out of time against the consent order made shortly after decree absolute and made a lump sum order and a transfer of property order in respect of a house acquired in joint names after the divorce and consent order.

Finally, it should be noted that the widely discussed 'wasted costs' case, *C v C* [1994] 2 FLR 34, probably did not hinge upon any finding as to the weight to be attached to pre-marital cohabitation. Here, the couple had lived together for seven years before marrying. The marriage lasted three years. The wife's solicitor held out for an unrealistically high order and later claimed to have regarded the pre-marital cohabitation as fundamental. The report in *Family Law* suggests that Ewbank J regarded as 'fanciful and unreasonable' the solicitor's view that the pre-marital cohabitation would result in an award of more than the wife's half-share in the joint assets ((1994) Fam Law 496). In the *Family Law Reports*, however, Ewbank J is reported as saying that 'the idea that the wife should have the *whole* equity in the houses seems to me to be fanciful and unreasonable' (at 44F, emphasis added). The learned judge seems therefore to have been addressing a different point.

## Cohabitation at the time of proceedings

This section deals with the situation where, at the time of the proceedings relating to a failed marriage, one or both of the parties are cohabiting. If it is relevant, the fact of cohabitation will be strong evidence from which adultery can be inferred for a divorce petition based on MCA 1973, s 1(2)(*a*) and will almost certainly be 'unreasonable behaviour' for the purposes of s 1(2)(*b*).

As we have seen, both the family proceedings court and the divorce court are given statutory guidance on how to determine financial relief. In practice, two of the statutory matters are of particular importance:

(a) the income, earning capacity, property and other financial resources that each of the parties to the marriage has or is likely to have in the foreseeable future; and

(b) the financial needs, obligations and responsibilities that each of the parties to the marriage has or is likely to have in the foreseeable future.

The fact that a party is cohabiting can be of relevance in determining her or his income, resources and needs, obligations and responsibilities. It is difficult to divide up the case law in a coherent way because we are dealing with complex permutations of circumstances. To ease exposition, however, we deal separately *below* with the relevance of cohabitation as a resource (ie a source of support) and as a liability (ie a source of obligations). We also deal separately with the position of the payer and payee under each subheading, treating the person against whom an application for periodical payments, a lump sum or transfer or settlement of property order is made as 'the payer' for these purposes. In theory, of course, it is irrelevant which spouse is making the claim. In so far as the situations discussed *below* concern the apportionment of resources between families with children, then what follows may need to be modified in the light of assessments made under the Child Support Act 1991. An absent parent's liability under the Act (discussed further in Chapter 10) will be an important financial obligation for this purpose.

**Cohabitation as a resource**

*Payer cohabiting*

In *Ette v Ette* [1965] 1 All ER 341, Mr Ette left Mrs Ette to live with another woman, Mrs J. Mrs Ette applied for maintenance as she was virtually without money. Her husband, by contrast, was living rent-free in Mrs J's 'comfortable and commodious country house', was Mrs J's business partner and was able in that capacity to draw whatever sums of money he required. He appeared reluctant to furnish the court with precise details of his financial position and Lloyd-Jones J held that 'the court in the absence of full and frank disclosure is entitled to draw inferences adverse to the husband as to his capacity or his faculties' (at 346d). The judge therefore took into account the sums that the husband received from the relationship with Mrs J in arriving at the sum to be paid to the wife. (*See also Re L* [1980] 1 FLR 39.)

The fact that the husband in *Ette* was unwilling to disclose the extent of his resources was a complicating factor in the case. Ordinarily, it seems, the courts will cease to treat the payer's cohabitation as a resource when it comes to the point of the new partner starting to subsidise the previous family. In *Macey v Macey* [1982] FLR 7 the Divisional Court held that a cohabitant's income 'frees' the payer's own income from which he or she can make financial provision to the former family but her income is not to be used directly. In *Brown v Brown* (1981) *The Times*, 14 July the husband was wholly maintained by his cohabitant. The Divisional Court held that only a nominal order for periodical payments should be made against him because a substantive one would entail the cohabitant discharging the husband's responsibilities, the husband having no income to be 'freed'.

This 'freeing' approach can also be applied to capital provision. In

*Martin v Martin* [1977] 3 All ER 762 the wife was living in the former matrimonial home, worth £11,000, whilst the husband and his cohabitant were living in a council house which (under the then legal position) would probably be put into his name by the council. If the former home were to be sold and the wife given half the proceeds of sale she would not have enough to buy another home. On appeal from the registrar's order for sale, Purchas J settled the property on the wife during her lifetime or until her remarriage or voluntary removal from the property, whichever occurred first, whereupon the proceeds of sale were to be divided equally. The wife's appeal was dismissed by the Court of Appeal where Stamp LJ said (at 765h): 'It is of primary concern in these cases that on the breakdown of the marriage the parties should, if possible, each have a roof over his or her head.' The application of this case is not confined to accommodation provided by a *cohabitant* but its relevance here is obvious. If a spouse is now living in a cohabitant's home in circumstances that indicate security of accommodation then the other spouse's need for somewhere to live is likely to be given priority over the cohabiting spouse's desire for a return of capital from the former matrimonial home (*see also Ibbetson v Ibbetson* [1984] FLR 545).

*Payee cohabiting*

The position of the cohabiting payee, usually the wife, has proved more troublesome for the courts to deal with. It seems clear that resources provided by a cohabitant do potentially reduce the claim. In *Suter v Suter* [1987] 2 FLR 232 the Court of Appeal went so far as to impute to the wife a rent that she ought to be seeking from her cohabitant, with the effect that the husband's maintenance liability was reduced. In a similar vein, if the payee has the benefit of accommodation from her cohabitant, this will affect the way that capital division is approached. In *W v W* [1975] 3 All ER 970 the former wife applied for a lump sum order under MCA 1973, s 23(1)(*c*). At the time, she was living with Mr S who had conveyed his house into their joint names. She argued that the reason for this was to give her security as she and Mr S did not intend to marry. She did not consider that she owned half the equity in the house. Sir George Baker P accepted that at the moment she did not have a half-share but that she might later obtain one by virtue of a resulting, implied or constructive trust (discussed in Chapter 8). At the very least she had an irrevocable licence to be in the house by virtue of her legal estate and this was something of value. Sir George Baker accordingly attempted to assess the value of the wife's 'interest' and treated this as part of her resources (thus potentially reducing her claim for a lump sum).

This case involved assessing a spouse's share in an asset owned jointly with a cohabitant and because it proceeded on an assumption about the *minimum* share the spouse might have it presents no difficulties. More difficult questions arise where one wants to determine the *exact* size of the share. Such a decision also inevitably involves a judgment about the entitlement of the cohabitant. One should note here the Court of Appeal decision in *Tebbutt v Haynes* [1981] 2 All ER 238 to the effect that a judge when making a property adjustment order in divorce has power to determine the interests of third parties, at least where they intervene in the cause. The need for the third party to intervene in the cause is not fully discussed in the case. One assumes that if the third party declines to intervene then the proceedings could be adjourned whilst separate proceedings for a declaration as to the beneficial interests are brought. Given the potential costs implications to the third party of these separate proceedings, it may encourage intervention in the cause. In the absence of an intervention it may be possible for the court, on the evidence available, to make a declaration sufficient for it to dispose of the matrimonial proceedings (*Harwood v Harwood* [1991] 2 FLR 274, CA).

The courts' approach of taking into account the resources actually or notionally received by the payee as a result of cohabitation cannot be applied if the new partner is wholly impecunious. In *Duxbury v Duxbury* [1987] 1 FLR 7, a case concerning very wealthy spouses, the Court of Appeal said that the judge below had been wholly justified in refusing to take into account the position of the wife's cohabitant (who was without means). Ackner LJ said (at 14D) that 'one is faced with essentially a financial and not a moral exercise'. The husband had argued that if the wife married her new partner then he would be under no liability to maintain her at all and any capital payment made by the husband to the wife now might result in considerable benefit to the cohabitant later. The Court of Appeal, in line with an apparent policy of not seeking to interfere with the choices that women make after the breakdown of their marriage (*see* the section on cohabitation after proceedings *below*), dismissed the argument. The trial judge's decision to award the wife a lump sum of £600,000 as part of a clean break was upheld.

## Cohabitation as a source of obligations

Although there are a considerable number of cases on the relevance of resources received from a cohabitant, in practice it is likely that the question of obligations *owed to* a cohabitant will more often come before the courts.

The standard early case is *Roberts v Roberts* [1968] 3 All ER 479. Here, the husband left the wife and child of the family to live with Mrs B and her three children. The wife applied to the magistrates' court for weekly maintenance but was awarded only £1 10s for herself and £1 for the child. She appealed, contending that the justices had not taken into account all the 'relevant circumstances of the case' as directed by s 2(1)(*b*) of the Matrimonial Proceedings (Magistrates' Courts) Act 1960 (now replaced by DPMCA 1978, s 3). Rees J, reading the judgment of the Divisional Court, found that 'a very substantial part of the weekly outgoings of the husband ... related to the upkeep of Mrs B and her children' (at 482C) and that the justices' decision could only have been arrived at by 'treating the husband's obligation to his mistress and her children as an allowable outgoing ranking in priority to his obligations to support the wife and the child of the marriage'(at 482G).

The Divisional Court found that maintenance in discharge of moral obligations was a relevant circumstance but remitted the case back to a fresh panel of justices for a rehearing because an 'innocent wife is generally entitled to be supported at a standard of living as near as possible to that which she enjoyed before the cohabitation was disrupted by the husband's wrongful conduct' (at 485D). Furthermore, it was said that it must be rare 'for it to be right that her claim to support should be postponed to the claim of a mistress, even though this must be taken into account for whatever weight it is held to bear' (at 486H).

References to 'innocent wife' and 'wrongful conduct' are out of date now owing to changes in family law designed to reduce the relevance of fault and the apportionment of blame. There is, however, no clear statement of the approach that should be taken under the new philosophy. In *Furniss v Furniss* [1982] FLR 46 the Court of Appeal implicitly gave equal consideration to the husband's liabilities arising out of each of his two marriages. In *Blower v Blower* [1986] 2 FLR 292 the Divisional Court reviewed the decision of a magistrates' court, which had declined to vary periodical payments made by a husband who was now living with another woman and her son. The justices appeared to have dismissed *Roberts* as irrelevant and the case was remitted for rehearing before a different bench. Heilbron J noted that the magistrates' court was obliged to consider the financial needs, obligations and responsibilities of each of the parties and said that there was nothing in this requirement that restricted the obligations or the responsibilities to those that were legally enforceable (ie obligations to a new spouse). This case does not, however, suggest the relative weights to be given to competing obligations to a former spouse and current cohabitant. Furthermore, *Blower* (and *Roberts*) involved obligations to 'step-children' of the new relationship and not the husband's own natural children by his new partner.

Apart from the practical argument that someone is more likely to support a present family in preference to a former one (and so the courts might as well recognise it), the operation of the income support (formerly supplementary benefit) legislation suggests another reason for attaching considerable weight to new commitments. The new family will be assessed as a single unit by the DSS. If the cohabiting spouse is in full-time work the whole family will be taken outside income support (*see* Chapter 3). If the periodical payments order to the former family brings the payer below the level at which he or she would have been entitled to income support then there can be no claim for benefit to top her or him up (being in full-time work) and the new family may therefore suffer a perilous drop in income. At the same time, the amount of maintenance will simply reduce, pound for pound, any income support being received by the old family. (This was, in fact, the effect of the decision in *Tovey v Tovey* (1978) 8 Fam Law 80.)

Finally a more recent decision of the Court of Appeal suggests an approach more favourable to the husband, although not one that is obviously in line with the policy behind the Child Support Act 1991. In *Delaney v Delaney* [1990] 2 FLR 457 the husband hoped to start a new family with his cohabitant. The wife sought periodical payments from him for herself and the three children. The Court of Appeal made a nominal order against him saying that a court should consider a husband's ability to meet the needs of his former family in the light of the realities of the world. A husband was entitled to balance his future aspirations against his reponsibilities to his former family. A court could take the wife's social security entitlement (in this case, to family credit) into account and avoid making orders that crippled the husband.

## Cohabitation after proceedings

In the cases discussed in the previous section, one of the parties was cohabiting at the time of the original proceedings. If the cohabitation commences later then either party to the marriage, or former marriage, may wish to have an existing order varied. By and large, the principles discussed above will apply. There are, however, some specific points that should be made concerning this situation.

### Effect of cohabitation on an earlier periodical payments order

Cohabitation by a payee will have no effect upon a lump sum order even though made for maintenance purposes. These orders are final. It may well be relevant, however, to a periodical payments order. Periodical payments orders do not, as a matter of law, terminate upon the payee beginning to cohabit. They only do so on the remarriage of the payee, death or the expiry of a fixed term order; *see* MCA 1973, s 28(1). It is possible, however, for the original order to be *expressed* as determinable on cohabitation because s 23(1) of the MCA 1973 and s 2(1)(*a*) of the DPMCA empower the courts to make orders for such term as may be specified.

In the absence of any express provision, it is always possible for the payer to return to the court for a downward variation or discharge of the order. Under s 20 of the DPMCA the family proceedings court can vary or revoke one of its orders. Revocation is, of course, permanent but the payee can return for a fresh order if circumstances change; presumably relying on the other spouse's failure to provide reasonable maintenance under DPMCA, s 1(*b*). The position in the divorce court is different because s 31 of the MCA 1973 (as amended) empowers the court, *inter alia*, to vary or discharge a periodical payments order or suspend any provision thereof. Cohabitation by the payee might therefore lead to downward variation (perhaps to a nominal level), suspension or discharge. If the latter, the payee will be unable to go back for a further order as she will no longer be the payer's spouse.

When considering an application for variation, the court is not confined to adjusting the order in proportion to the change in means of either or both of the parties, but can approach the matter *de novo* and look at the actual means of the parties at the time (see *Lewis v Lewis* [1977] 3 All ER 992). At this stage the decisions discussed in the section *above* become relevant because we are now dealing with a case of cohabitation at the time of the proceedings. Two cases in the Court of Appeal specifically on variation applications might, however, be taken as indicative of the current judicial approach.

In *Atkinson v Atkinson* [1988] 2 FLR 353 the former wife was in receipt of periodical payments amounting to £6,000 pa. She later began cohabiting with a man who, the trial judge found, might have been able to earn £8,000 in a managerial job (although, apparently through choice, he was only earning £3,900 pa). On the husband's application for a discharge or variation of the order, the periodical payments were reduced to £4,500 pa. The Court of Appeal dismissed the husband's appeal. The wife's cohabitation was not to be equated with remarriage or to be given decisive weight in the husband's application. The overall circumstances of the cohabitation were to be taken into account and here they were not such as to call for any reduction of periodical payments below £4,500 pa. Any further reduction would reduce the wife to virtual poverty. Following *Duxbury* (discussed *above*) the Court was anxious not to impose an unjustified fetter on the freedom of an ex-wife to lead her own life as she chooses following a divorce. For a similar decision *see Hepburn v Hepburn* [1989] 1 FLR 373.

**Effect of cohabitation on a property adjustment order**

A property adjustment order which provides for the outright transfer of property is final (*Minton v Minton* [1979] AC 593, HL and *Dinch v Dinch* [1987] 2 FLR 162, HL). Unless, therefore, there is a case for setting the order aside, perhaps by reason of a material non-disclosure (*Cook v Cook* [1987] 1 FLR 521, CA), cohabitation by either party will not affect the position. It is now quite common, however, for a *settlement* order to provide for specific consequences if, *inter alia*, the spouse who is given occupation of the home later cohabits (*MH v MH* [1982] FLR 429 at 437). Ordinarily it will lead to the immediate sale of the home and distribution of the proceeds in stipulated proportions. In *Chadwick v Chadwick* [1985] FLR 606 the registrar had ordered that the property should be held on trust for sale with the wife to have sole occupation and that the property should not be sold without her consent unless she remarried or cohabited. The wife appealed, contending that the conditions as to remarriage or cohabitation were unfair as she might decide to cohabit or marry an impecunious man who was unable to provide similar accommodation. The Court of Appeal said that the registrar could not be held to be wrong in restricting the wife by these contingencies. Cumming-Bruce LJ said that in order to do justice to the husband (who was being kept out of his capital in the house) it was necessary to impose some real inconvenience in the form of contingencies on the wife. Passing over the *non sequitur* in this argument, the wife was reminded of the necessity to select as her future consort a gentleman who was in a position to provide her with accommodation suitable to her needs. This is not the first time in this context that the Court of Appeal has expressed a view that women are expected to be dependent upon men. In *Harvey v Harvey* [1982] FLR 141 the Court of Appeal made an order similar to that in *Chadwick.* Purchas J, in the leading judgment, said (at 145): 'I have in mind that if she begins to cohabit with another man in the premises then obviously that man ought to take over the responsibility of providing accommodation for her.' It is not clear that such statements represent current thinking in the Court of Appeal. They sit oddly alongside *Atkinson* and *Hepburn* (*above*) and, in any event, settlement orders fell out of favour in the 1980s because of the exposed position in which they can leave the wife when sale has to take place. Not only might her share in the proceeds of sale be insufficient to enable her to buy a further property, she might also be regarded by the local authority as intentionally homeless (*R v Wimborne DC, ex p Curtis* [1985] FLR 486). There is, however, some indication that settlement orders are in a revival if the wife's housing position can be safeguarded (*Clutton v Clutton* [1991] 1 All ER 340, CA) and they have probably always been more popular with district judges than reported case law would suggest.

If a condition concerning cohabitation is to be included in a settlement of the former matrimonial home, then attempts should be made to define the duration of the cohabitation which will trigger sale. In this way the wife knows the amount of time she has in which to decide on the stability of the relationship. In any event, cohabitation should be dealt with as a condition in the order. A court should not accept an undertaking by the wife not to cohabit in the matrimonial home (*see Holtom v Holtom* (1981) *The Times*, 22 October).

## Discovering a cohabitant's means

In *Ette v Ette*, *above*, it was seen that the husband was reluctant to disclose the support he received from his cohabitant and so the Divisional Court considered itself entitled to draw inferences adverse to him. This raises the general question of how a cohabitant's resources can be discovered; a question that might arise in the context of investigating the cohabiting spouse's claim that he has to support his cohabitant, or in the context of investigating support received from a cohabitant. In *Wynne v Wynne and Jeffers* [1980] 3 All ER 659 Cumming-Bruce LJ said (at 664a):

> So where one of the parties, whether the applicant or the respondent to an application for financial provision or property adjustment, is in fact receiving support from a third party which increases his or her resources or reduces his or her needs or, alternatively, if the party is likely to be in that position in the foreseeable future, the facts relevant to such present or foreseeable support or reduction of needs are relevant to the inquiry that is imposed on the court under ss 23, 24 and 25 [of the Act].

The drafting of the Family Proceedings Rules 1991 (FPR 1991) has led to some uncertainty as to their scope. There are three provisions which are principally relevant. Under r 2.62(4) the district judge may at any stage of the proceedings, whether before or during the final hearing, order the attendance of any person for the purpose of being examined or cross-examined, and order the discovery and production of any document or require further affidavits.

It is clear that a cohabitant's attendance and examination can be compelled under the rule. This might be of limited use because the party seeking the cohabitant's attendance can examine, but not cross-examine her or him (*W v W* [1981] FLR 291). The district judge must presumably therefore be persuaded to take the lead if the cohabitant is reticent. Problems have arisen in connection with requiring the discovery and production of documents or the filing of affidavits. In *Wynne v Wynne, above*, which concerned the predecessor rule in the Matrimonial Causes Rules, Bridge LJ had no doubt that the power to order discovery was limited to orders against a party to the *lis* (*see* 662F), using discovery in the strict sense of disclosing to the other party the existence of all relevant documents which are or have been in the possession, custody or power of that person. Similarly, it was held that there was no power to order an affidavit from a third party, because (*inter alia*) the rule refers only to 'further' affidavits, and this implies that the person must already have sworn one. The Court of Appeal held that a cohabitant (who, incidentally had been the co-respondent in the main suit) could not be ordered to file an affidavit of means. It was said that clear words were required to make the rule applicable to a stranger to the *lis*.

The second and third provisions make the position even more complicated. Under r 2.62(7):

> Any party may apply to the court for an order that any person do attend an appointment (a 'production appointment') before the court and produce any documents to be specified or described in the order, the production of which appears to the court to be necessary for disposing fairly of the application for ancillary relief or for saving costs.

And r 2.62(8) adds:

> No person shall be compelled by an order under paragraph (7) to produce any document at a production appointment which he could not be compelled to produce at the hearing of the application for ancillary relief.

Speaking extra-judicially, Wilson J has referred to 'the great value of the newly created production appointment' and said that we 'should be proud of this carnivorous rule [ie r 2.62(7)], peculiar to the Division' (*see* (1994) Fam Law 504 at 506). He described a case that he had acted in whilst at the bar where his client, the husband, had alleged that the wife had bought her boyfriend a motor car. She denied this. By a production appointment against the garage, they had obtained the sale document. A second production appointment was taken against the manager of the branch of the bank which had drawn the draft for payment. They then applied for a third appointment against the English arm of the bank, at which point the wife admitted the existence of a substantial American bank account which had been drawn upon in the purchase of the car.

Perhaps in contrast, the Court of Appeal decision in *Frary v Frary*

[1993] 2 FLR 696 suggests that the production appointment should not be seen as a major innovation but as allowing an order in the nature of a *subpoena duces tecum* which operates before the hearing rather than at the hearing itself. The facts in this case were that the husband had been living with his cohabitant, Mrs R, for a year in Mrs R's house. It seems clear that Mrs R was a wealthy woman. The husband deposed that he hoped the relationship with Mrs R would be a lasting one. The wife applied by summons for an order that Mrs R attend the court and produce certain documents. The documents requested were of an extensive nature (copies of all statements of bank accounts, building society accounts, share certificates, tax returns and so on). The county court judge, on appeal from a decision of the district judge, granted the wife's application in part but also ordered that production was not required if Mrs R provided to the wife's solicitors a statement outlining her capital assets and income with sufficient detail to satisfy the solicitors. In other words, recognising that there was no power to order Mrs R to make full disclosure of her means, an order for extensive production was made which might induce her to agree to a less intrusive process.

Mrs R appealed successfully to the Court of Appeal. The crucial part of Ralph Gibson LJ's judgment seems to be as follows (at 703B):

> The [wife], however, had no intention of calling Mrs R. Mere production of the documents would be of little, if any, use without evidence as to what the documents were. If the [wife] had intended to call Mrs R to prove in full detail all her assets etc and if on the facts it was right to order the attendance ... at the production appointment, it might be made out that it was right so to do, but it seems to me to be most unlikely that such a course would appear right or convenient save in very rare cases. Before the application has been opened, it is difficult for the court to be satisfied of the need for such information.

He then went on to quote a passage from *Wynne v Wynne* where Bridge LJ had said ([1980] 3 All ER 659 at 662h) that it will only be in the rarest cases where it will be possible to say that full information about the property and income of, *inter alia*, a new lover will be relevant to issues under s 25 of the MCA.

The decision in *Frary* seems to be an invitation to a party to make clear that they intend to call the other party's cohabitant as a witness and then, under the cover of that statement, seek a production appointment for specific documents. Given the recognition, quoted earlier, by Cumming-Bruce LJ in *Wynne v Wynne* that present or foreseeable support, or reduction of needs, are relevant to the inquiry under ss 23–25 of the MCA, one would expect the application to be successful. It is respectfully suggested that the passage from Bridge LJ on which Ralph

Gibson LJ seemed to rely in *Frary* was addressing a different issue, namely *full* information. A properly limited application, tailored to the circumstances of the particular case, for documents which it is reasonable to suppose exist, might be viewed differently. It seems that Mrs R's apparent wealth turned out to be a weakness in the wife's case, seemingly because a judge could make some minimal assumptions about the husband's position, which would be sufficient to dispose of the wife's application and because the more wealthy the third party the more likely it is that production will be burdensome. Ralph Gibson LJ acknowledged (at 704B) that:

> [i]f there was a dispute as to what [Mrs R] was providing and what that was worth, it might well be right to order her to attend and to produce documents in order to demonstrate what she was providing. That, however, was not the point, nor is it now, and there was no attempt to get nor any need to seek for such information.

## Chapter 3

# Social Security

## Introduction

The concept of unmarried cohabitation is woven into the social security system in a number of contexts. In the past there were considerable differences in the way it was defined, depending on the benefit. The wording has now largely been standardised and the purpose of recognising cohabitants is fairly constant: to prevent them from obtaining an advantage in social security terms over a married couple who appear to be in similar circumstances. Cohabitation therefore normally reduces the total amount of benefit paid to the parties because benefit for a married couple, with whom cohabitants are equated, is usually less than the combined benefits of two single people. The 'cohabitation rule' is usually taken to mean a provision disentitling, or withdrawing benefit from, a woman because she cohabits but this is a generalisation and the so-called rule works differently according to the context.

The social security system underwent major changes in the late 1980s. The Social Security Act 1986 (SSA 1986) was brought into force in April 1988, abolishing supplementary benefit and family income supplement and replacing them with income support, the Social Fund and family credit. Social security legislation was then consolidated and amended in two major enactments; the Social Security Contributions and Benefits Act 1992 (SSCBA 1992) and the Social Security Administration Act 1992.

This chapter should only be used for assistance in a problem specifically concerning cohabitation and not for the wider purpose of working out entitlement to the benefit in question. To assist the reader, however, a general description of each benefit is given.

## Income support and the unmarried couple

### Income support

Like supplementary benefit before it, income support is a benefit designed to supplement existing resources and take the claimant up to a state-defined subsistence level. By virtue of s 124(1) of the SSCBA 1992, it is payable to someone over the age of 18 (or in narrowly prescribed circumstances, 16) if:

(a) his income does not exceed the applicable amount;
(b) he (and, if he is a member of a married or unmarried couple, the other member) is not engaged in remunerative work for at least 24 hours a week; and
(c) except in prescribed circumstances, he is available for and actively seeking employment and not receiving relevant education.

The family is treated as a unit of claim and for these purposes there are three types of family unit; couples, couples with children and single-parent families. The function of taking a family unit is so that the resources and (deemed) requirements of all the members can be aggregated and a single claim made (SSCBA 1992, s 136). It is assumed that the money paid to the claimant is then distributed equitably within the family unit although there is, of course, no enforceable support obligation between cohabitants.

Couples are divided into married and unmarried couples. An unmarried couple is defined by s 137(1) of the SSCBA 1992 as 'a man and woman who are not married to each other but are living together as husband and wife otherwise than in prescribed circumstances'. This is identical to the previous definitions in s 34(1) of the Supplementary Benefit Act 1976, as amended, and s 20(11) of the Social Security Act 1986.

A claim for income support can be made by whichever partner they agree should make the claim. In the absence of agreement, the Secretary of State has a discretion to determine which of them should claim (Social Security (Claims and Payments) Regulations 1987, reg 4(3)).

### The 'unmarried couple'

We have seen that the parties will be an unmarried couple if they are living together as husband and wife. The meaning of these words, and of similar prior formulations, has been a matter of controversy since 1948 when National Assistance was introduced, although initially a cohabiting woman's benefit was withdrawn under discretionary powers rather than specific regulations.

It is helpful to begin by identifying the possible sources of law that might assist in interpreting the definition. At one time, the appeal system for national insurance benefits was separate from that for supplementary benefit (ie income support). A pronouncement on cohabitation for the purpose, say, of suspending a widow's pension was therefore not directly relevant to a case concerning supplementary benefit. It certainly appeared that there was a different emphasis in practice, perhaps prompted by an acknowledgment that national insurance benefits were contributory and should only be stopped in clear cases. It then became apparent that decisions on national insurance and supplementary benefits were mutually applicable (R(SB)17/81 and R(G)3/81). One can therefore now look at all social security decisions, with a little caution being exercised about the older ones.

In addition to social security decisions, family law has long contained phrases like 'as husband and wife' and 'in the same household'. On the face of it cases on these words should be relevant in establishing cohabitation for social security purposes; an argument apparently accepted by Lord Widgery CJ in *R v SW London Appeals Tribunal, ex p Barnett* ((1973) unreported).

Thirdly, whilst obviously not a source of law, the old *Supplementary Benefits Handbook* (the *Handbook*) contained criteria which were said by Woolf J in *Crake v Supplementary Benefits Commission* [1981] FLR 264 at 270–71 to be 'admirable signposts'. For this reason, the discussion of authorities *below* is structured around the criteria in the most recent edition of the *Handbook*; criteria that are now reflected in the current edition of the *Adjudication Officers' Guide* (Vol 2, Pt 15, July 1992).

One important preliminary point was made at para 2.13 of the *Handbook* (1985 revision):

> What has to be decided, in each case in which the question arises, is whether the relationship between the man and the woman is such that they must be regarded as living together as husband and wife in the ordinary sense of the term. There is no single way by which the issue can be decided in every case. *See also* R(G)3/71.

A recent decision by Social Security Commissioner Rowland has emphasised the need to consider the parties' general relationship. In CIS/087/1993, Commissioner Rowland described the 'admirable signposts' as placing wholly inadequate emphasis on it. He held that the Social Security Appeal Tribunal below had erred in considering only the six criteria referred to.

*Membership of the same household*

According to the *Handbook*:

> The couple must be living in the same household and neither partner will

usually have another home where they normally live. This implies that the couple live together, apart from absences necessary for employment, visits to relatives etc.

The statutory definition of an unmarried couple does not refer to a 'household' but to 'living together'. The equation of the two is not apparently objectionable: it is hard to say that people in the same household are not living together and *vice versa*. Household and home are not, however, the same; R(SB)4/83. Family law cases may be relevant here. The concept of living in separate households under the same roof is well known to divorce practitioners and it often applies where the marriage has broken down but one of the parties is unable or unwilling to leave the home. For example, the provisions in s 2 of the Matrimonial Causes Act 1973 (MCA 1973) operate to discount a period or periods of reconciliation not exceeding six months, with the effect that they cannot prejudice the establishment of a basis for divorce in s 1(2). It is common where the parties have lived at the same address for more than six months after, say, one of them learned of the other's adultery to argue that they were actually living in separate households so that what is in effect a limitation period does not run. Another example is where a petitioner wishes to establish the *factum* of separation for a divorce based on two or five years' separation but where she has lived at the same address throughout or during more than six months of the relevant period.

Section 2(4) makes clear that it is co-residence in the same household that is relevant for the purposes of the six-month bar or the *factum* of separation and so the cases here might be of use in this context also. For example, reference might be made to the Court of Appeal decision in *Piper v Piper* (1978) 8 Fam Law 243 where the husband petitioned for divorce on the basis of five years' separation. There was evidence that he had visited the house frequently and that sometimes sexual intercourse took place. The Court of Appeal held that the husband was merely a visitor and the parties had not shared the same household.

Another source of potential relevance is the case law on s 1(2) of the Domestic Violence and Matrimonial Proceedings Act 1976 (DVA 1976). This subsection provides that the rules in the Act on ouster and non-molestation also apply to a man and a woman who are living with each other in the same household as husband and wife (*see* Chapter 6). In other words, the same houshold test helps to confer jurisdiction here whereas in divorce it tends to withdraw it (hence the need to argue separate households there). In *Butterworth v Supplementary Benefits Commission* [1981] FLR 264 Woolf J referred to a case on the DVA, *Adeoso v Adeoso* [1981] 1 All ER 107, but seemed to find it of little assistance because the facts there concerned a relationship on its last legs where the parties had little contact with each other. The case concerned the termination of the relationship whereas one is normally concerned in social security with its inception. Nevertheless, future cases on the Act could still be relevant.

Cases within the social security system on this aspect of cohabitation are relatively uncommon as most disputes concern the words 'as husband and wife'. Absences away from the alleged home can cause difficulties. In R(SB)30/83 the woman lived in a bed-sit near her university during term time but returned to live with the man during vacations. The Commissioner had to decide whether the couple lived together throughout the year or whether their separation during terms caused a break in the continuity of their alleged status as an unmarried couple. He held that there was cohabitation throughout the year so that the woman's resources during term time, principally her student grant, were aggregated with those of the man. This led to ineligibility on financial grounds. This decision probably marks the boundary of 'living together'.

It is not possible for someone to be a member of two separate couples, and therefore of two separate households, at the same time (R(SB) 8/85).

*Stability*

According to the *Handbook*:

> Living together as husband and wife clearly implies more than an occasional or very brief association … (I)n cases where at the outset the nature of the relationship is less clear it may be right not to regard the couple as living together as husband and wife until it is apparent that a stable relationship has been formed.

*Financial support*

According to the *Handbook*:

> In most husband and wife relationships one would expect to find financial support of one party by the other, or sharing of household expenses, but the absence of any such arrangement does not of itself prove that a couple are not living together.

The last part of this sentence was said in the Supplementary Benefit Commission Report *Living Together as Husband and Wife* (1976, para 55(3)) to be justified because otherwise there would be a strong incentive for the couple to arrange its affairs so as to safeguard the woman's claim to benefit. Given the scope for legitimate tax planning it is hard to see why such behaviour is self-evidently wrong, but the official view was upheld by the Commissioner in RI 3/71 (although *see* the Scottish case of *Patterson v Ritchie* [1934] SC (J) 42). Furthermore, in *Kaur v Secretary of State for Social Services* (1982) FLR 237 Sir Douglas Franks QC, sitting as a Deputy High Court judge, refused to interfere with a finding of cohabitation where the bills were divided equally between the parties. The *Adjudication Officers' Guide* (*above*) advises, however, that where couples keep their finances separate, this will be a factor leaning against a finding that the couple are living together as husband and wife (para 15035).

*Sexual relationship*

The DSS approaches this criterion in a similar way to that of financial support; its existence points towards a marriage-like relationship because, it is said in the *Handbook*, a sexual relationship is a normal part of marriage. On the other hand, its absence does not necessarily point away from it. This has been the most controversial of all the factors and the evidence is compelling that, at least in the past, some benefit officers have been too ready to infer cohabitation merely from co-residence and a sexual relationship.The *Adjudication Officers' Guide* provides that an Adjudication Officer should not initiate inquiries which would require answers to specific questions about 'the physical side of the relationship' but any information volunteered by the claimant will be relevant. In CIS/087/1993 (*above*) Commissioner Rowland took a different position and held that in an inquisitorial system questions may have to be asked by the Department and by tribunals where the information is not volunteered.

The absence of a sexual relationship is of course a feature of some marriages and so its absence from a relationship between unmarried people should clearly not *rule out* a finding of cohabitation. On the other hand, if the circumstances suggest a purely companionate relationship the absence of an *intention* to live together as husband and wife may well lean against a finding that the parties are an unmarried couple. In *Robson v Secretary of State for Social Services* [1982] FLR 232 the appellant was a seriously disabled widow aged 45 and the alleged cohabitant was in his late sixties. He was also disabled, having lost a leg. They shared a flat in order to share overheads but, although they were free to do so, they did not marry each other. Webster J said (at 236D) that often one had to decide on cohabitation for these purposes by considering the objective facts because usually the intention of the parties is either unascertainable, or, if ascertainable, is not to be regarded as reliable:

> But if it is established to the satisfaction of the tribunal that the two persons concerned did not intend to live together as husband and wife and still do not intend to do so, in my judgment it would be a very strong case

> indeed to justify a decision that they are, or ought to be treated as if they are, husband and wife.

In so far as the judge was talking about intention at large, these remarks would probably not command universal support. In the present context, however, it may be that intention will be an important factor in deciding a case where the parties do not have, and have not previously had, a sexual relationship. Support for this proposition can be found in R(SB) 35/85 and *Kingsley v Secretary of State for Social Security* [1983] FLR 143. In the latter case Comyn J said (at 149F):

> When members of the public, *prima facie* respectable, honest and decent people, are found to be living in such a relationship ie as an unmarried couple contrary to their own detailed evidence and in very unusual circumstances, I consider that they are absolutely entitled, and this court is absolutely entitled, to know exactly how the tribunal reached its decision.

The implication here is that, at the least, full reasons should be given for a finding of cohabitation in these circumstances so that a detailed review can be undertaken on appeal. Finally, in CIS/087/1993 (*above*) Commissioner Rowland held that where there has never been a sexual relationship between the parties, there must be strong alternative grounds for holding that the relationship is akin to that of husband and wife.

*Children*

According to the *Handbook*:

> When a couple are caring for a child or children of their union, there is a strong presumption that they are living as husband and wife.

In RI 2/64 the couple had lived in a caravan with a child of their union for two years and it was decided that 'no evidence of the financial arrangements between them could outweigh this'. Where one party *acts* as a parent to the other's child, this will be regarded as evidence in support of a conclusion that the parties are an unmarried couple.

*Public acknowledgement*

According to the *Handbook*:

> Whether the couple have represented themselves to other people as husband and wife is relevant. However, many couples living together do not wish to pretend that they are actually married. The fact that they retain their identity publicly as unmarried people does not mean that they cannot be regarded as living together as husband and wife.

Again, therefore, meeting this criterion is evidence of cohabitation but failing to do so is not necessarily evidence contradicting it. In CP 97/49 the adoption of a common surname was held to be 'compelling evidence' and in RI 5/68 it was regarded as 'very significant'. 'Holding out' need not, however, take the form of adopting a common surname. In *Campbell v Secretary of State for Social Services* [1983] FLR 138 the appellant maintained that the relationship was one of housekeeper and employer, although she had sold the majority of her furniture when moving into the man's house and intended to apply for a joint tenancy of the property. Whilst accepting that it was a borderline case, Woolf J refused to interfere with the tribunal's finding of cohabitation. The intention of applying for a joint tenancy was not the sort of step that one would expect a lodger or housekeeper to take with a person with whom she is lodging or for whom she is housekeeping (at 141F).

*Subjective criteria*

Whilst the above criteria used by the DSS are useful, as far as they go, they relate largely to manifest or objective circumstances. It may be proper in many cases that they do. On the other hand, there are cases where the circumstances appear to satisfy most of the criteria and yet one still has reservations about finding that the parties are an unmarried couple because of the quality of the relationship, its context or the subjective meaning with which the parties have endowed the arrangement. We have seen that in *Robson v Secretary of State* [1982] FLR 232 Webster J referred to the intention of the parties and in *Crake v SBC*; *Butterworth SBC* (reported together and cited frequently as principal authorities), Woolf J also referred to intention. He said (at 267A):

> If there is the fact that they are living together in the same household, that may raise the question whether they are living together as man and wife, and, indeed, in many circumstances may be strong evidence to show that they are living together as man and wife; but in each case it is necessary to go on and ascertain in so far as this is possible, *the manner in which and why they are living together in the same household* [emphasis supplied].

And (at 269D):

> If the only reason that Mr Jones went to that house temporarily was to look after Mrs Butterworth in her state of illness and, albeit, while doing so, acted in the same way as an attentive husband would behave towards his wife who suffered an illness, this does not amount to living together as husband and wife because it was not the intention of the parties that there should be such a relationship.

It may be that the approaches in these cases are treated as confined to companionate relationships and to ones where there is a strong element of caretaking. The Commissioner's decision in R(SB) 17/81 indicates a preference for reliance on objective criteria. Here the claimant and Miss G were both students when they moved into a one-bedroom flat. The claimant continued to live there when his course finished. They shared expenses but Miss G lent him about £10 a week. They spent most of their social life together but in the vacations they went back to their respective families. They said that they had not regarded themselves as intending to marry and there was nothing permanent about the relationship. Dr Rice rejected the approach of Webster J in *Robson* and seemed to suggest (incorrectly) that that was an isolated one. He preferred to confine himself to the conduct of the parties and found that the parties were an unmarried couple. It is not clear that this method can be reconciled with a later decision of his in CSB258/1983 where the tribunal had found cohabitation between the claimant, who was 63 and suffering from osteo-arthritis and Parkinson's disease, and an old family friend aged 73 who had lived in the household for two years and looked after her. Dr Rice held, with some apparent hesitation, that the tribunal had made an error of law in concentrating on the services provided rather than the capacity of the person providing them.

## Other benefits

### Family credit

This is the second income-related benefit within s 123 of the SSCBA 1992 and is the successor to family income supplement. Whereas income support is not available where one member of the family is in remunerative work (as defined), family credit is designed for this situation. There must, however, be a child or person of a prescribed description in the same household (SSCBA 1992, s 128(1)(*c*)). Broadly, family credit is a benefit intended to supplement the earnings of someone with children in cases where income supplement is unavailable.

The concept of an unmarried couple is relevant to family credit in three ways. First, income and assets of the couple are aggregated to determine financial eligibility. Second, either party can be engaged in remunerative work for the family to satisfy this requirement. Third, either party can be responsible for the child or person of a prescribed description.

In a slight difference from income support (where the couple may agree as to who should make the claim), the claimant for family credit shall be the woman, unless the Secretary of State is satisfied that it would be reasonable to accept a claim by the man.

The definition of unmarried couple is, of course, the same for income support and housing benefit.

### Housing benefit

Section 130 of the SSCBA 1992 provides basically that a person is entitled to housing benefit (which, since the introduction of the now defunct community charge benefit, gives assistance with rent only) if:

(a) he is liable to make payments in respect of a dwelling in Great Britain which he occupies as his home;
(b) there is an appropriate maximum housing benefit in his case; and
(c) he is financially eligible.

As with the other income-related benefits (income support, family credit and council tax) the family is treated as a single unit so that entitlement by one member of a family to a benefit excludes entitlement to that benefit for any other member for the same period (SSCBA 1992, s 134(2)).

As with income support and family credit, therefore, the concept of an unmarried couple is relevant. The definition and its interpretation are the same as given *above*.

### Council tax benefit

This benefit replaced community charge benefit when the community charge was replaced by the council tax. It came into force on 1 April 1993.

Council tax benefit is a means-tested benefit which reduces or extinguishes liability to the tax. It is paid by the local authority, even if the claimant is on income support and it must be claimed separately from income support. If a claimant is a member of an unmarried couple (*see above*) then the income and capital of each partner is aggregated. If one partner is an exempt person, for example a full-time student, then the other partner may be eligible for a 25 per cent reduction in council tax, provided there is no other liable adult living in the property. See generally SSCBA 1992, s 31 and the Council Tax Benefit (General) Regulations 1992.

### Child benefit

By virtue of s 142 of the SSCBA 1992 a person who is responsible for one or more children in any week is entitled to child benefit in respect of the child or each of the children for whom he is responsible. The meaning of 'child' is defined in s 142 and is basically a person who is under the age of 16 or under the age of 19 and receiving full-time education. Responsibility, which is a key concept, is dealt with in s 143(1):

a person shall be treated as responsible for a child in any week if:
(a) he has the child living with him in that week; or
(b) he is contributing to the cost of providing for the child at a weekly rate which is not less than the weekly rate of child benefit payable in respect of the child for that week.

Rules of priority between claimants are found in Sched 10 to the Act. Briefly, the effect is that someone within s 143(1)(*a*) has priority over someone in s 3(1)(*b*). If, say, both cohabitants are within s 3(1)(*a*) then para 4(2) of the Schedule provides that 'as between two persons residing together who are parents of the child but not husband and wife, the mother shall be entitled'. Mere co-residence and unmarried parenthood therefore brings this paragraph into operation.

The weekly rate of child benefit in 1994–95 is £10.20 for the only or eldest child and £8.25 for others, and it is tax free. The fact of cohabitation is primarily relevant as disentitling a claimant from so-called 'one-parent benefit' (ie child benefit increase) which is an addition for one child only (in 1994–95 at a rate of £6.15 per week). Under reg 2(2) of the Child Benefit (Fixing and Adjustment of Rates) Regulations 1976 the increase is not available to a claimant living with someone 'as his spouse'. Although this does not follow the now common formulation used to describe an unmarried couple the test is presumably the same.

Cohabitation for these purposes continues throughout temporary absences. Regulation 11(3) of the Child Benefit (General) Regulations 1976 provides that:

> Where two persons are parents of a child but not husband and wife they shall be treated as residing together for the purposes of the Act during any period of temporary absence the one from the other where they would be so treated but for such temporary absence.

### Widow's benefits

Prior to the SSA 1986, the three major widow's benefits were:
(a) widow's allowance, payable for a period of 26 weeks from the date of death;
(b) widowed mother's allowance; and
(c) widow's pension.

The last two commenced six months after the death.

Widow's allowance was replaced on 11 April 1988 by widow's payment, which is a single tax-free lump sum payable immediately on bereavement in order to offset financial problems. It is based on the widow's late husband's contribution record. It is not, however, available if at the time of her husband's death she and a man to whom she is not married are living together as husband and wife (SSCBA 1992, s 36(2)). The payment is a single lump sum of £1,000 and no increases are payable for dependent children (unlike the former widow's allowance which it replaces) or for a dependent adult or female childminder.

Widowed mother's allowance remains payable to a widow who at the time of her husband's death has a child or children to look after, provided her husband's contribution record satisfies the contribution conditions (SSCBA 1992, s 37). It is payable immediately on bereavement and can continue until the youngest child reaches the age of 16, or up to 19, if continuing in education. Cohabitation by the widowed mother suspends the right to the allowance (s 37(4)(*a*)), and the same wording is used as for widow's payment, whereas remarriage by the widow extinguishes it. This provides a relatively rare advantage for cohabitation over marriage in so far as social security is concerned. By cohabiting rather than marrying she leaves open the possibility of a resumption of allowance if the relationship fails before the children reach the maximum age. It seems that the test for cohabitation will be the same as in income support; *see* RI 3/81.

Widow's pension is also payable immediately on bereavement. It is paid to a claimant aged 45 or over, with the full rate of pension becoming payable at 55 (SSCBA 1992, s 38). It ceases at 65 (although it might be replaced by retirement pension at 60 if the widow retires). Again, cohabitation suspends the right to benefit whereas remarriage extinguishes it (s 38(3)(*c*)).

## Industrial injuries benefits

The industrial injuries scheme was substantially altered by s 39 of, and Sched 3 to, the SSA 1986 in an effort to integrate it within the national insurance scheme and there are now no provisions of particular relevance to cohabitants; *see* now SSCBA 1992, Pt V. The Pneumoconiosis etc (Workers' Compensation) Act 1979 remains relevant, however. The Act provides for lump sum payments to claimants disabled by industrial lung diseases (such as pneumoconiosis, byssinosis and mesothelioma) caused by noxious dust at work. If the disease causes death then the dependants listed in s 3 are entitled to the payments. One of these dependants is a 'reputed spouse who was residing with the deceased' but only if the deceased left neither a *de jure* spouse who was residing with him or who had been entitled to receive maintenance payments from him nor a child within the meaning of s 3(2). Strangely, reputed spouse is not defined and this may cause problems where the parties either did not hold themselves out as married or when it was known generally that they were not married even though they held themselves out to be. In either of those cases it may be difficult to argue that they were 'reputed' to be married to each other.

## Retirement pension

A cohabitant cannot rely upon her former partner's contributions for the purposes of retirement pension whereas a widow or divorcee may; *see* SSCBA 1992, s 48.

## War pensions

Under Art 12 of the 1964 Royal Warrant, in the case of the army, and the equivalent provisions of the Order in Council (Royal Navy) and Order by Her Majesty (Royal Air Force), a general allowance is paid to a war pensioner for dependants. This category can include an unmarried woman living with him as his wife who has care of a child for whom an allowance may be made. On death a pension may be awarded to an 'unmarried widow' so long as she has in her charge his child and is in receipt of a child allowance. Whilst these provisions have an interesting historical background (discussed fully in the first edition of this book), their relatively minor practical importance makes further discussion here unwarranted.

Chapter 4

# Taxation

Prior to the Finance Act 1988 (FA 1988), and in particular prior to the introduction of separate taxation for husbands and wives, cohabitants were often able to enjoy significant tax advantages over married couples. The effect of recent changes is to reduce markedly the differences in treatment between married and unmarried couples. The balance of advantage now favours married couples, although much depends on the circumstances. Changes to the additional personal allowance, covenants of income, the treatment of maintenance payments and mortgage interest relief have certainly reduced the planning opportunities for cohabitants.

This chapter gives only a very brief introduction to the taxes in question and it should be used specifically for determining how cohabitation might affect the tax position. It should not be used for deciding tax liability at large.

One last preliminary point concerns the recent decision of *Rignall v Andrews* [1991] 1 FLR 332. The taxpayer claimed that his cohabitant fell within the meaning of 'wife' in the Income and Corporation Taxes Act 1970 and that he should therefore be entitled to the former married man's allowance. Surprisingly, the General Commissioners upheld the argument but it was overturned by Ferris J in the Chancery Division. As far as one can tell, there is no possibility in any taxation legislation of arguing that words like 'marriage', 'spouse', 'husband' and 'wife' can embrace marriage-like relationships.

## Income tax during cohabitation

### General

Leaving aside problems of residence, domicile and income from abroad, the basic formula for computing income tax liability is quite simple.

Statutory income is computed according to rules in Schedules and Cases in the Income and Corporation Taxes Act 1988 (ICTA). From this are deducted charges on income (in effect, income that is not taxed in that taxpayer's hands) to produce 'total income'. From total income an individual deducts personal reliefs (in effect, tax-free slices of income) to arrive at taxable income. The personal reliefs relevant to this chapter for 1994–95 are as follows:

| | |
|---|---|
| Personal allowance (under 65) | £3,445 |
| Personal allowance (65–74) | £4,200 |
| Personal allowance (over 75) | £4,370 |

That taxable income is then taxed at three rates. In 1994–95, the first £3,000 is taxed at the 'lower rate' of 20 per cent, the next £20,700 is taxed at the 'basic rate' of 25 per cent and the remainder at the 'higher rate' of 40 per cent; FA 1994, s 95.

For 1994–95 and subsequent years certain reliefs are given by way of reduction in the tax liability rather than by deduction from total income. These include the Married Couple's Allowance and the Additional Personal Allowance (*see below*). In 1994–95 these allowances are calculated as 20 per cent of £1,720 or, if less, the amount which reduces the person's income tax liability (as defined) to nil. For 1995–96 the relief is restricted to 15 per cent. Higher deductions are available where the elder spouse is aged 65–74 and 75 or over. The rules for the allocation of the married couple's allowance since 1993–94 have permitted considerable flexibility in the transfer of the allowance between the spouses.

### Additional personal allowance in respect of children

Under s 259(1) of ICTA 1988, so far as is relevant for our purposes, a woman who is not throughout the year of assessment married and living with her husband; and a man who is neither married and living with his wife for the whole or part of the year nor entitled to transitional relief for a separated couple (not discussed here), may claim an additional personal allowance if she or he can prove that a 'qualifying child' is resident with her or him for the whole or part of the year of assessment.

A qualifying child, under s 259(5), is one who is under 16 or, if over that age, is receiving full-time instruction at an educational establishment. Furthermore the child must either be a child of the claimant or be under the age of 18 at the start of the year and be maintained by the claimant for at least part of the year. 'Child of the claimant' is defined for these purposes by s 259(8) of ICTA 1988 to 'include' the claimant's step-child, illegitimate child *if he has married the other parent after the child's birth* and an adopted child if the child was under the age of 18 when adopted. The formulation of the words emphasised in the previous sentence has its origins in the old child tax allowances. Contrary to the general policy of the modern law, it treats an illegitimate child differently from a legitimate one. The illegitimate child of the unmarried couple is excluded from the definition. To be a qualifying child for the purposes of the additional personal allowance, therefore, eligibility must be established by the claimant through the other method: that is, by showing that she or he has been maintaining the child. It further follows that the allowance cannot be claimed for such a child who is over the age of 18, even where he or she is in full-time education. One imagines that the Inland Revenue will take a liberal view as to what amounts to maintenance for part of the year. It is quite arguable that anyone who has income and lives with his or her child must be maintaining the child to some extent, even if much of the child's maintenance comes from another source, and if the parent has no total income at all then he or she would not be claiming the relief in the first place.

The purpose of this allowance is to give the same relief to a sole or cohabiting parent as would be given to a married couple. Hence the additional personal allowance and the married couple's allowance are the same amount. Before the FA 1988 it was possible for an unmarried couple with two qualifying children, each to claim the additional personal allowance. Each therefore enjoyed the same personal reliefs as a married man and so they were better off than a married couple on the same income. This possibility was closed off by s 259(4A) of ICTA 1988 with effect from the tax year 1989–90. The subsection now provides:

> Where:
> (a) a man and a woman who are not married to each other live together as husband and wife for the whole or any part of a year of assessment; and
> (b) apart from this subsection each of them would on making a claim be entitled to an income tax deduction,
>
> neither of them shall be entitled to such a reduction except in respect of the youngest of the children concerned (that is to say, the children in respect of whom either would otherwise be entitled to an income tax reduction).

If each parent is *prima facie* entitled to the additional personal allowance in respect of the *same* child, they can agree under s 260 of ICTA 1988 on the allocation or apportionment of it. Obviously, this decision will be informed by the particular financial circumstances of the parties. To be clear, however, even if each brings a child into the relationship from a former family, only one additional personal allowance can be claimed in this family unit and it will be in respect of the youngest qualifying child.

## Income-splitting within the cohabiting family

Income-splitting is not a term of art. By it is simply meant a procedure whereby a slice of income is shifted away from the initial recipient and taxed in the hands of another. Two kinds of income-splitting have been particularly useful for cohabitants in the past: a covenant by one to the other or to the other's child (ie a child by a different partner); and payments to a child under a court order. Both of these were radically affected by changes to the law since the FA 1988.

*Covenants by one cohabitant to the other or to the other's child*
A covenant by one cohabitant to make 'annual payments' to the other or the other's child was effective to transfer the tax liability on those sums from the payer to the payee. Annual payments must possess the quality of recurrence, although the amount can be variable and the payments contingent on some event occurring or not occurring. For the scheme to work for cohabitants, the payments had to be capable of lasting for at least six years and most covenants were drafted to last for seven years from the date of the first payment.

The purpose of the scheme was, of course, to transfer the income to the cohabitant or cohabitant's child with unused personal reliefs, or with a lower marginal rate of tax, and so achieve an overall tax saving. An agreement for annual payments was, however, only effective to shift basic rate liability. The payments were therefore added back to the payer's income for the purpose of computing his higher-rate liability. It was possible to draft a covenant whereby one paid to the other an annual sum until the expiration of seven years or the cessation of the cohabitation, whichever was the earlier. Because the payments could last for more than six years they did not fall foul of the anti-settlement provisions in ICTA 1988. Such a scheme would have no tax advantages for *spouses* because annual payments were treated under Schedule D, Case III as unearned income of the payee. Under the old tax treatment of spouses, a wife's unearned income was always treated as that of her husband whilst she was living with him, so the tax burden was not shifted.

In 1988, s 36 of the FA inserted a new s 347A into ICTA 1988 which stated that, as a general rule, a payment shall not be a charge on income unless, *inter alia*, it was a payment of interest, a covenanted payment to charity or made for *bona fide* commercial reasons in connection with the individual's trade, profession or vocation. It follows that other covenanted payments remain the income of the payer and are taxed in her or his hands. The new rule applies to covenants made on or after 15 March 1988. Old covenants continue to be tax effective provided that particulars were received by an inspector of taxes by 30 June 1988. No relief is now available, however, in respect of a payment becoming due after 5 April 1994 where the payment is for the benefit, maintenance or education of a person who attained the age of 21 after that date and on or before the day on which the payment became due (FA 1994, s 79(2)). There will presumably be some of these covenants still on foot and it is important that they are not varied without careful consideration. Variation will amount to a new covenant and come under the new rules. Note: At the time of writing, the settlement anti-avoidance provisions are to be replaced by Sched 17 to the Finance Bill 1995. Apparently, tax relief on covenants made before 15 March 1988 will be abolished. Further details are not known, but *see* (1995) Fam Law 115.

*Payments by a cohabitant to her or his child under a court order*

Prior to the changes effected by the FA 1988, maintenance payments by a cohabitant to her or his own unmarried minor child were tax deductible by the payer if they were made under a court order. Although the payments were then taxed in the hands of the child, in most cases the child would have an unused personal allowance against which to set them. Cohabiting couples could make use of this procedure to considerable advantage. In particular, a mother could seek a maintenance order against the father with the father's consent and the tax benefits would follow.

Since 15 March 1988, however, new rules have been in effect and they are now to be found in ss 347A and 347B of ICTA 1988. Now, the payments are made out of the payer's taxed income and are not taxed in the hands of the recipient; ie they are no longer effective to transfer tax liability. There is currently a new form of limited relief in the case of payments by a spouse or former spouse under a legal obligation, calculated in a similar way to the calculation of the married couple's allowance.

Transitional arrangements apply to maintenance under a court order made before 15 March 1988 (or before 1 July 1988 if the application for the order was made before 15 March). The order can still be varied without losing the benefit of the transitional arrangements provided, *inter alia*, the maintenance is to a child under the age of 21 (*see* FA 1988, s 36(4)). The effect of the transitional arrangements is that the payments still attract tax relief under the old rules but it is retricted to the total maintenance payments for which the payer was entitled to relief in 1988–89 (FA, s 38(3)). The relief has been further restricted in the case of payments becoming due after 5 April 1994. Tax relief on the first £1,720 will be restricted to 20 per cent in 1994–95 and to 15 per cent in 1995–6. Payments in excess of this qualify for tax relief at the taxpayer's top marginal rate.

Finally on the question of income-splitting, circumstances may permit the employment of one cohabitant by the other or the formation of a business partnership. Employment can have significant advantages where the partners have different marginal tax rates or one has unused personal allowances. Partnership has a range of possible tax advantages. Specialist advice should be sought. The fact of cohabitation has no particular bearing on the matter. Similarly, consideration can be given to the transfer of income-producing assets by one cohabitant to another, although capital gains tax and inheritance tax implications may follow (*see below*).

## Mortgage interest relief

Before 1 August 1988, cohabitants enjoyed a major tax advantage over married couples in that loans made to them for the purpose of buying their home were not aggregated. Each cohabitant could claim tax relief on the interest paid on loans of up to £30,000 so that the family enjoyed a maximum of £60,000.

The Finance (No 2) Act 1988 amended the rules so that the £30,000 loan limit is a limit *per residence* and is not related to the person. The new rules are to be found in ss 356A–357 of ICTA 1988. The Finance Act 1994 introduced a new structure for interest relief and new methods of giving the relief. Reference should be made to a specialist work. The relief in 1994–95 is limited to 20 per cent and in 1995–96 to 15 per cent.

Loans taken out before 1 August 1988 are protected from these changes, but care must be exercised to ensure that the protection is not lost. If there is any time during which the house is occupied by only one person entitled to the relief then the new 'per residence' rules come into effect. Specialist advice should be taken about the possibility of a third person 'buying in' to the property before one of the cohabitants moves out. The original occupier may then be able to continue under the old rules (ie a personal maximum of £30,000) and the new occupier will come under the new rules (ie, in a case where there are two occupiers, £15,000, *see below*).

If the loan is protected then that protection is limited by the situation as at 31 July 1988. Under the old rules a joint loan was apportioned between the couple in the proportions in which they actually paid the interest (although there was, in practice, little or no scrutiny of the claimed apportionment). It appears, however, that the apportionment as at 31 July 1988 will affect the protection. For example, if the couple undertook liability for a £60,000 mortgage and at the end of July 1988 the woman was paying two-thirds of the interest, then she is assumed to have had responsibility for two-thirds of the loan. The man's protected relief is therefore only on £20,000 (ie one-third of the debt). The snag is that the woman is only entitled to relief on £30,000 (because that was and is the personal maximum) rather than the £40,000 balance. In effect, mortgage interest relief on £10,000 has been lost.

If the loan was taken out on or after 1 August 1988 then cohabitants may be at a disadvantage when compared with spouses. The rules are complex but essentially the maximum loan limit (currently £30,000) is divided by the number of people eligible for relief ('sharers'). In the ordinary case of cohabitation, each will therefore be attributed a maximum of £15,000. This can only be used by each of them if each does actually pay half the interest. Spouses, on the other hand, can allocate their 'sharer's limit' between themselves so that the whole of the £30,000 is covered, regardless of who actually pays the interest. Cohabitants have no such facility. It is important therefore for one to put the other in funds, if need be, so that each can claim up to the sharer's limit. Although the position is not entirely clear, it seems that the Inland Revenue is mainly concerned with the formal question of who is actually handing over the interest to the lender.

Finally, it is possible that an unmarried couple have separate residences (and therefore separate mortgages), perhaps because they work at a distance from each other and are together mainly at weekends. Separate mortgage interest relief on £30,000 of each loan will therefore be possible. Married couples are restricted to relief on one residence only (the house first purchased, *see* s 356B(5)).

## Income tax on separation

Because the fact of cohabitation has little bearing on the tax position of the parties the fact of their separation is equally immaterial. Because of the removal of tax relief on maintenance payments to children, there are no tax considerations to bear in mind when seeking an order in respect of the children. (The new form of limited relief on maintenance is available only to a spouse or former spouse on payments to, or for the benefit of, the other spouse.)

One should remember the possibility of arranging a substitute sharer before one of them moves out of the home so that any protected mortgage interest relief under the old rules is not lost to the remaining occupier (*see above*).

If the couple fall under the new rules, when one cohabitant leaves the house it is understood that the Inland Revenue will allow the remaining partner the full limit of £30,000 without the need for formal alteration of the mortgage liability.

For the purposes of timing any sale of the property, the rules discussed in the following section concerning exemption from capital gains tax should be considered. Some periods of absence are allowed without affecting the principal private residence exemption.

## Capital gains tax

### General

Because of indexation relief for inflation, the exemption of gains on specified assets such as the principal private residence, the annual exemption of gains (in 1994–95, £5,800) and the relief on gifts and death, capital gains tax (CGT) is of little concern to many people. In so far as it is, then there can be advantages in cohabitation over marriage, although much depends on the individual circumstances.

Leaving aside questions of residence and domicile, CGT is levied on the total amount of chargeable gains that accrue to a person on the disposal of assets in a year of assessment after deducting allowable losses—s 2 of the Taxation of Chargeable Gains Act 1992 (TCGA 1992). For 1994–95 the first £5,800 chargeable gains, less allowable losses, are exempt. Net gains over that amount are charged to tax at the taxpayer's marginal income tax rate (although there can be circumstances where the gains will take the person into a higher rate).

Spouses are treated differently from other people in respect of disposals between themselves. The transferee spouse is treated as acquiring the asset for whatever was the base cost of the asset in the hands of the transferor so that there is deemed to be no chargeable gain on this occasion (TCGA 1992, s 58). When the transferee in turn disposes of the asset the gain will be the difference between the base cost to the original transferor, or its value at 31 March 1982 if the asset was acquired before then, and the value of the asset at the time of disposal to the third party.

Whilst this sounds like an advantage for spouses, it is not always so. If the parties are cohabiting then the disposal by one to the other can take advantage of the transferor's annual exemption in the year of disposal. When the transferee disposes of the assets then the transferee's annual exemption can also be used. If the parties were married to each other then the whole gain is rolled up and treated as the transferee's when he or she comes to dispose of the asset. Only one annual exemption has therefore been available.

### Principal private residence exemption

The principal private residence exemption can be of more benefit to cohabitants than spouses. Section 222 of the TCGA 1992 gives relief in respect of, *inter alia*, a gain accruing to an individual so far as it is attributable to the disposal of, or of an interest in, a dwellinghouse or part of a dwellinghouse which is, or has at any time in his period of ownership been, his only or main residence. Section 102 defines the extent of the relief given. By virtue of subs (1) if the house has been the individual's only or main residence throughout the period of ownership, or throughout the period of ownership except for all or any part of the last 36 months, then there is complete relief. If subs (1) does not apply, a fraction of the gain attributable to the period of non-occupation is chargeable, subject to indexation relief. Even so, certain cumulative periods can be treated as periods of residence provided that the house was the sole or main residence both before and after such periods. These are listed in s 223(3):

(i) three years for any purpose,
(ii) unlimited absence due to an employment or office performed wholly abroad,
(iii) four years, where residence elsewhere is required by an employer.

The principal private residence provisions can be more advantageous to cohabitants than spouses because s 222(6) provides that in the case of a husband and wife living together there can only be one sole or main residence. Cohabitants can, however, each have a main residence (eg as with mortgage interest relief discussed *above*, because they work in separate places and are together mainly at weekends). In circumstances short of this, careful use of the exemptions may still lead to considerable relief. For example if the woman decides to move into the man's house she can be absent from her own house for three years, then move back to re-establish residence and sell it at any time within the next 36 months without losing any principal private residence relief. Whilst this might sound a little far-fetched, it is not uncommon for one partner to want to retain her or his own property whilst assessing the relationship. Property inflation in the years of absence could give rise to chargeable gains considerably in excess of the annual exemption, even after indexation relief.

## Inheritance tax

### General

Inheritance tax (IT) is charged on the value transferred by a chargeable transfer—s 1 of the Inheritance Tax Act 1984 (IHTA 1984). A chargeable transfer is defined in s 2(1) as a transfer of value made by an individual which is not an exempt transfer. As a general rule a transfer is for value if as a result the value of the transferor's estate immediately after the transfer is less than it would be but for the transfer (s 3(1)). The main difference between IT and its predecessor, capital transfer tax, is that an outright lifetime transfer between individuals is potentially exempt (and is therefore known as a potentially exempt transfer or PET), rather than potentially chargeable (s 3A). If the donor survives for seven years it becomes actually exempt. The same also applies to transfers into an accumulation and maintenance trust and a trust for the disabled.

Inheritance tax works on a similar cumulative basis to capital transfer tax. Most transfers now fall out of accumulation after seven years (rather than ten as under capital transfer tax) although if a potentially exempt transfer becomes actually chargeable through the death of the transferor within seven years, it can have a so-called knock-on effect entailing cumulation adjustments over a period of up to 14 years.

The rate of tax on any transfer depends on the cumulative total of transfers (other than exempt transfers) in the previous seven years. The accumulation principle applies to transfers made on death as well as to lifetime transfers which are immediately chargeable (eg transfers into trust) or which become chargeable because the transferor dies within seven years of making them. No tax is payable on the first part of the cumulative total (in 1994–95, £150,000). Above this limit the tax is charged at 40 per cent.

Lifetime transfers that are chargeable when made (ie those not exempt or potentially exempt), such as a transfer into a discretionary trust, are charged at half the rates of tax applicable for transfers made on or within seven years of death. Where such a transfer is made within seven years of death, tax will become due at the full rate but it will be tapered for transfers more than three years before death.

Most cohabitants were probably rarely affected by capital transfer tax during their lifetimes and it is even less likely that they will be affected by IT. Nevertheless property prices are now so high that on death a cohabitant's estate might well attract IT and there is considerable scope for lifetime planning. In addition, if the couple separate it would be wise to keep one eye on IT when arriving at any settlement. For these reasons we concentrate here on what might loosely be called exemptions although there are, in fact, two categories: dispositions that are not treated as transfers of value in the first place and those that are but are exempted.

Under the capital transfer tax legislation, spouses potentially had a clear advantage over cohabitants because transfers between them were generally exempt from tax during their joint lives and on death. Cohabitants, as in most other tax legislation, are treated as separate individuals. The distinction still remains in IT (ITA 1984, s 18) but may matter less because of the potentially exempt nature of lifetime transfers between cohabitants. Any *inter vivos* transfer of value between cohabitants will therefore be, at worst, a potentially exempt transfer, if the conditions in s 3A of ITA 1984 are satisfied. In such a case it might be wise to consider term assurance. Two policies may be desirable. The first should be taken out by the donee on the life of the donor for seven years at a reducing rate reflecting the tapering relief. The second should be taken out by the donor's presumptive residuary beneficiaries who might be prejudiced by adjustments to the cumulative total.

### Dispositions without gratuitous intent

By virtue of s 10(1):

> A disposition is not a transfer for value if it is shown that it was not intended, and was not made in a transaction intended, to confer any gratuitous benefit on any person and either—
> (a) that it was made in a transaction at arm's length between persons not connected with each other, or
> (b) that it was such as might be expected to be made in a transaction at arm's length between persons not connected with each other.

Because cohabitants, as such, do not fall within the definition of 'connected persons' in s 270 (which incorporates, with amendments, the definition in s 286 of the TCGA 1992) then a transfer without gratuitous intent between them would not be a transfer for value. The most likely occasion when this would arise would be on separation where a transfer was being made as part of a settlement. For example, if one party has made contributions to the purchase of the home such as give rise to a beneficial interest under the rules discussed in Chapter 8 *below* but it is not clear how large that interest is, it would presumably be proper to arrive at an apportionment which cuts through the Gordian knot in order to settle the matter. (The courts themselves have not been conspicuously successful in arriving at a clear method of quantifying beneficial interests arising under resulting, implied or constructive trusts and so there is no reason why the parties' genuine attempt at settlement should be impugned.)

Another example would be a transfer in order to buy out a liability to maintain. There is no common law support obligation between cohabitants as such and so this should not be the focus of a settlement. On the other hand, if the parties accept that a maintenance obligation arose because of an express or implied contract made, say, before they began living together or when they bought a house or when a child was planned, then the transfer can be in settlement of any claim arising under that contract.

### Annual exemption

Outright lifetime gifts are exempt up to a total of £3,000 per donor in an income tax year (ITA 1984, s 19(1)). If a person's gifts in one year are below the exemption limit, the unused balance of the exemption can be carried forward to the next following year only; but in calculating the unused balance of the exemption for any year, gifts in that year are set against the exemption for the year in priority to any unused balance brought forward (s 19(2) and (3) of the ITA 1984). Thus, subject to the provisions concerning small gifts (*below*), annual gifts can be made of up to £3,000 by one cohabitant to another which will not go into the accumulation even if the transferor does not survive for seven years, assuming that no other lifetime transfers are made in those years.

### Small gifts

Lifetime gifts are exempt from IT up to a total of £250 per recipient in any tax year (s 20 of the ITA 1984). The annual and small gifts exemptions together mean that in the example in the preceding paragraph, the annual gifts can be £3,250. There is no provision for carrying forward an unused portion of the £250 to the following year.

### Normal expenditure out of income

By virtue of s 21(1) of the ITA 1984:

> A transfer of value is an exempt transfer if, or to the extent that, it is shown—
> (a) that it was made as part of the normal expenditure of the transferor, and
> (b) that (taking one year with another) it was made out of his income, and
> (c) that, after allowing for all transfers of value forming part of his normal expenditure,

the transferor was left with sufficient income to maintain his usual standard of living.

This relief may be less significant in the future because a standard occasion for it, the seven-year covenant, no longer enjoys income tax advantages described in the first section of this chapter. With old covenants and court orders, however, to the extent that they are not exempted by other provisions and the potentially exempt transfer rules, the payments may be exempted as normal expenditure out of income. This will of course also be the case with new annual payments, but there will be no income tax consequences.

### Maintenance of an illegitimate child

By virtue of s 11(4) of the ITA 1984:

> A disposition is not a transfer of value if it is made in favour of an illegitimate child of the person making the disposition and is for the maintenance, education or training of the child for a period ending not later than the year in which he attains the age of eighteen or, after attaining that age, ceases to undergo full-time education or training.

This relief is available as an alternative to normal expenditure out of income relief and might be particularly important if the maintenance left the transferor with insufficient income to maintain his usual standard of living (so that the normal expenditure relief is unavailable).

### Death

Whilst many cohabitants will not need to be concerned about IT in respect of transfers made during their joint lives, either because of the potentially exempt transfer rules or because of the other exemptions mentioned *above*, the position might well be different on death. There is no 'common law spouse' exemption for transfers between cohabitants, although one was suggested during parliamentary debates in 1975 over capital transfer tax. For this reason it may be wise to make strategic *inter vivos* transfers, coupled perhaps with term life assurance.

## Conclusion: cohabitation versus marriage

It may be helpful to conclude this chapter with a summary of the possible advantages and disadvantages of cohabitation compared with marriage.

(1) Cohabitants may have separate residences—it being a matter of linguistic judgment only whether they should still be called cohabitants—and they may each then have separate mortgage interest relief up to £30,000 and separate principal private residence exemptions for CGT. In each tax, spouses are limited to one residence.

(2) With old 'protected' mortgages, cohabitants continue to enjoy mortgage interest relief on loans of up to £60,000, whereas spouses are restricted to £30,000. Under the new rules, however, cohabitants cannot allocate unused relief between themselves, whereas spouses can.

(3) Old income-splitting schemes for cohabitants are largely preserved and they may still be more advantageous than the current tax position of spouses.

(4) The married couple's allowance is available to childless married couples. Childless cohabitants, however, are restricted to their personal allowances. If cohabitants have a child or children, one additional personal allowance can be claimed and the gap with spouses is closed.

(5) In CGT and IT there is no exemption for transfers between cohabitants, whereas there is between spouses. In CGT this can work to the advantage of cohabitants by enabling the transferor's annual exemption to be used in the year of transfer.

# Chapter 5

# Homelessness

The principal duties on a local authority to house the homeless are contained in Pt III of the Housing Act 1985 (formerly the Housing (Homeless Persons) Act 1977). This chapter looks first at the main provisions of the Act. It then discusses their application to cohabitants when the family as a whole is homeless. Finally it considers homelessness on the dissolution of the family. Particular emphasis will be placed in the final section on breakdown of the relationship caused by, or accompanied by, domestic violence. This conveniently leads into Chapter 6 which deals with domestic violence specifically.

## Housing Act 1985, Pt III

### Introduction

Part III of the Housing Act 1985 (HA 1985) does not provide a comprehensive safety net for families with acute accommodation problems or for individuals on the breakdown of a relationship. A chapter in a book of this nature cannot cover all the detailed circumstances that may arise. Furthermore, as with much law, there may be a considerable gap between the rule book and the practices of officials.

When originally enacted in the Housing (Homeless Persons) Act 1977, the provisions were described as appallingly drafted, frequently vindictive and extravagantly complex. Since then there have been some amendments but the basic structure has remained intact. At the time of the first edition of this book in 1981 it was possible to attempt a reasonably comprehensive coverage of the main cases on the Act but the volume of case law since then makes that unrealistic now. The reader is therefore referred to specialist texts, in particular to the annotated copies of the HA 1985 now available.

In addition to a knowledge of the provisions of the Act and the main cases, the practitioner should be familiar with the *Code of Guidance* issued by the Department of the Environment and Welsh Office. Section 71(1) provides that 'in relation to homeless persons and persons threatened with homelessness, a relevant authority shall have regard in the exercise of their functions to such guidance as may from time to time be given by the Secretary of State'. The current edition was issued in 1991. As its name suggests, the *Code* is only guidance and, provided that the authority does have regard to it, there is no obligation to follow it (*see*, eg, *de Falco v Crawley BC* [1980] 1 All ER 913 at 921g). It has been suggested that, in practice, if an authority deviates from the *Code* there is a *prima facie* case that it has not been taken into account and so the authority may then have to justify the departure.

The Department of the Environment issued a White Paper in 1995 which foreshadowed a number of changes to the homelessness provisions.

### Challenging a local authority's decision: judicial review and breach of statutory duty

Challenging a local authority decision under the Act has become progressively more difficult since 1977. Initially there was thought to be a choice between proceedings for judicial review in the Divisional Court on the one hand or proceedings in the county court or High Court for damages and an injunction for breach of statutory duty on the other. It was then held by the House of Lords in *Cocks v Thanet DC* [1982] 3 All ER 1135 that an applicant wishing to challenge the local authority's decision must normally seek the public law remedy of judicial review. The consequences of this decision are that the aggrieved person must comply with the 'safeguards' in Ord 53 of the Rules of the Supreme Court. Leave to apply is required on the basis of sworn evidence which makes frank disclosure of all relevant facts known to the applicant, the court has discretionary control of both discovery and cross-examination and the normal decision in a successful application is to make an order of *certiorari* quashing the authority's decision and referring it back rather than substituting the court's own decision. Furthermore, the applicant must act with considerable speed; normally within three months from the authority's decision. These consequences were intended by the House of Lords to protect from harassment public authorities on whom Parliament has imposed a duty to make public law decisions (*see* Lord Bridge at 1139e).

Proceedings for breach of statutory duty may still be possible where the basic decision of the authority is not being challenged; in other words where the issue is not whether there is a duty. For example, if the applicant is content with the nature of the decision concerning the duty but challenges the way that the duty is being discharged then an action for damages for breach of duty could be brought.

The impression given by a glance at the law reports is that the flow of cases to the courts was not staunched as a result of *Cocks*, although the worsening housing position in England and Wales might simply have meant that there was a larger number of applications for leave and consequently a larger number of cases going to hearing. The House of Lords returned to the issue in *Pulhofer v Hillingdon LBC* [1986] 2 FLR 5. The precise decision in that case has been reversed by statute, as we will see, but the remarks of Lord Brightman will no doubt be borne in mind by the Legal Aid Board and judges hearing applications for leave. He said that he was troubled by the prolific use of judicial review for the purpose of challenging the performance by local authorities of their functions under the Act. Furthermore (at 29H):

> Although the action or inaction of a local authority is clearly susceptible to judicial review where they have misconstrued the Act, or abused their powers or otherwise acted perversely, I think that great restraint should be exercised in giving leave to proceed by way of judicial review ... The ground on which the courts will review the exercise of an administrative discretion is abuse of power, eg bad faith, a mistake in construing the limits of the power, a procedural irregularity or unreasonableness ... verging on an absurdity.

As a consequence of this limitation on the extent to which a local authority's decision can be challenged it is important for a practitioner to try to find out as much as possible about what the authority was told by the applicant and what decision the authority arrived at on the basis of that information. It may then be possible to bring oneself within one of the accepted grounds in administrative law for quashing a decision; in particular that the authority has failed to take into account all the relevant factors or has taken into account irrelevant ones. Particularly useful may be s 106(5) of the HA 1985:

> At the request of a person who has applied to it for housing accommodation, a landlord authority shall make available to him, at all reasonable times and without charge, details of the particulars which he has given to the authority about himself and his family and which the authority has recorded as being relevant to his application for accommodation.

It will be seen that there is no duty to provide all the information with which the authority was supplied, although in practice some authorities will do so on request, but further information may be disclosed at discovery once proceedings have been issued. Section 106 is not confined to applications for accommodation on the grounds of homelessness. A more specific set of duties is set out in Pt III of the Act for homelessness cases. Under s 62 if the authority has reason to believe the applicant may be homeless it must make such inquiries as are necessary to determine that question and, depending on its conclusion, further duties may then arise. Section 64 provides for the contents and form of the notification to the applicant of the results of those inquiries. A practitioner should check that the notification complies with the requirements of that section because it may reveal, *inter alia*, an erroneous approach to the Act.

### The scheme of the Housing Act 1985, Pt III

In practice, there are four conditions to be satisfied before the authority is under the full duty to ensure that permanent accommodation becomes available for the applicant's occupation:

(1) The applicant must be homeless or threatened with homelessness.
(2) The applicant must have a priority need.
(3) The applicant must not be intentionally homeless or intentionally threatened with homelessness.
(4) The applicant, or a person who might reasonably be expected to live with him, must have a local connection with the housing authority's area (although an authority can only evade the responsibility to rehouse if it is satisfied that there is another authority, to which Pt III of the Act applies, with whom there is a local connection).

If one or more of the above conditions is not satisfied, there are still various duties on the housing authority to make appropriate enquiries, to furnish advice and appropriate assistance or to provide temporary accommodation.

We examine the four conditions in detail when considering homelessness of the family as a whole and then deal separately with special considerations that apply when the family is breaking up.

## Homelessness of the family as a whole

### Is the applicant homeless (or threatened with homelessness)?

A person is homeless if he or she has no accommodation in England, Wales or Scotland (s 58(1)). The Act gives the circumstances when the applicant is to be treated as having no accommodation. This occurs if there is no accommodation that he, together with any other person who normally resides with him as a member of his family or in circumstances in which it is reasonable for that person to reside with him:

(a) is entitled to occupy by virtue of an interest in it or of an order of a court, or
(b) has an express or implied licence to occupy ... , or
(c) occupies as a residence by virtue of any enactment or rule of law giving him the right to remain in occupation or restricting the right of another to recover possession.

*The meaning of 'accommodation'*

As originally drafted the Act contained no definition of the central concept of accommodation and this led to the House of Lords deciding in *Pulhofer v Hillingdon LBC*, *above*, that there were no rules. The sole question was whether the applicant had what could properly be described as accommodation within the ordinary meaning of that word in the English language. Section 14(1) of the Housing and Planning Act 1986 has now inserted s 58(2A) into the HA 1985 to give further guidance. The accommodation must be such as is reasonable for the applicant to occupy. In determining this, regard may be had to the general circumstances prevailing in relation to housing in the district of the local housing authority. Even if the applicant does have accommodation within (a), (b) or (c) *above*, he is still treated as homeless if he cannot secure entry to that accommodation, or if occupation of it will lead to violence or threats which are likely to be carried out by a person residing in it (s 58(3)(*a*) and (*b*)). The final basic provision is that a person is threatened with homelessness if it is likely that he will become homeless within 28 days (s 58(4)).

It is essential that the practitioner proceeds methodically through the Act and asks this question about homelessness (or threatened homelessness) before going further. In particular, this first question must be distinguished from the question whether the homelessness is intentional (*see below*), although the distinction is sometimes hard to see clearly.

*Accommodation for members of the applicant's family*

The wording in s 58 that requires special consideration for present purposes is that which brings in the housing needs of persons other than the applicant (eg a cohabitant or children) because it may be that the applicant taken alone is not homeless but the accommodation he has is not reasonably adequate for his family. The applicant is considered 'together with any person who normally resides with him as a member of his family or in circumstances in which it is reasonable for that person to reside with him'. This is a rather complicated formulation but it is suggested that there are two separate questions to be answered:

(1) Does the other person normally reside with the applicant?
(2) If so, is that other person either a member of the applicant's family or is it reasonable for them to live together?

It will be seen therefore that in this interpretation normal residence is a constant requirement but it may be coupled with either 'membership of a family' or 'reasonableness of cohabitation'. An alternative interpretation of these words is that normal residence is only connected with membership of the family so that there are two alternative groups; normally resident members of the family and others with whom it is reasonable for the applicant to live.

The different interpretations produce different results if the applicant wishes to claim that it is reasonable for him to live with someone whom he has not yet lived with (or does not normally live with). In the first interpretation there is no possibility of adding such a person to the applicant's accommodation requirements. It is suggested that the first interpretation is better because it is difficult to make the statutory words read properly if one tries to sever normal residence from the second group of those with whom it is reasonable for the applicant to live. For our purposes this distinction may not matter because, after all, cohabitation is essential for cohabitants. More important for us is the way that the courts may interpret the words setting out the two groups.

Dealing first with 'member of his family', para 5.3 of the *Code of Guidance* says that the phrase should be taken to cover 'established households where there is a blood or marriage relationship'. The *Code* goes on to define the phrase 'any other person ... in circumstances in which it is reasonable for that person to reside with him' as including ('insofar as they do not form a family') 'any cohabiting couples'. This seems to suggest, although not very clearly, that cohabitants could qualify either under the first limb as 'members of the applicant's family', but only if they 'form a family' (a phrase which is not defined), or under the second limb. This is not entirely helpful because it is not clear whether all cohabiting couples are to be taken as members of the same family (so as to qualify under the first limb) or only some of them. If only some of them then how does one decide? The phrase may be construed in the same way as similar words in Sched 1 to the Rent Act 1977 which deals with succession to a statutory tenancy by a member of the deceased's family. The relevant cases are discussed fully in Chapter 7 but it suffices here to say that the courts have required a considerable degree of permanence in the relationship or approximation to marriage before a bereaved cohabitee will qualify. However, the specific inclusion of cohabitants in the second group rather than the first may imply a stricter test of membership of the same family.

Whatever interpretation is adopted by the courts, some cohabitants will have to qualify in the second group; namely those with whom it is reasonable for the applicant to reside. 'Reasonableness' is now clearly tested objectively because of the words 'it is reasonable', whereas under the 1977 Act the wording was 'the authority consider reasonable' which gave less scope for challenging an authority's *bona fide* finding. The *Code of Guidance* indicates that this group includes, in addition to cohabiting couples, those who are housekeepers or companions of elderly or disabled people.

### If so, is there priority need?

By virtue of s 59 the following have priority need:

(a) a pregnant woman or a person with whom a pregnant woman resides or might reasonably be expected to reside;

(b) a person with whom dependent children reside or might reasonably be expected to reside;

(c) a person who is vulnerable as a result of old age, mental illness or handicap or physical disability or other special reason, or with whom such a person resides or might reasonably be expected to reside;

(d) a person who is homeless or threatened with homelessness as a result of an emergency such as flood, fire or other disaster;

(e) someone within a group of persons described as having a priority need by the Secretary of State.

Priority need is a prerequisite to substantive rights under Pt III of the Act, although by s 65(4) authorities are still bound to provide advice and assistance to those who are not in priority need. Cohabitants with dependent children clearly have a priority need. The *Code of Guidance* states that authorities should treat as dependent all those under the age of 16 and others under the age of 19 who are receiving full-time education or are otherwise unable to support themselves. The child need not be a child of either of them and a residence order should not be required by the authority *(R v Ealing LBC, ex p Sidhu* (1982) FLR 438 and para 6.4 of the *Code of Guidance*). The *Code* also recognises that children may be dependent on more than one parent, for example, where they spend equal time with both parents but in different households (reflecting the Court of Appeal's decision in *R v London Borough of Lambeth, ex p Vagliviello* [1990] 22 HLR 392); but such cases are likely to be unusual (*see R v Port Talbot BC, ex p McCarthy* [1991] 23 HLR 207 where Butler-Sloss LJ said that a local authority was 'entitled to take into account that the children reside with one parent and visit the other parent. There may be exceptional circumstances where children visit both parents, but it would certainly be unlikely to be the normal arrangement', at 210).

Those childless cohabitants who do not seem to fit into other groups of priority need should not be deterred from applying. It may be that they are vulnerable for a special reason (group (iii)) and a local authority cannot make a general policy that childless couples should never fall within this group (*AG, ex rel Tilley v London Borough of Wandsworth* [1981] FLR 373, CA).

### If so, is the homelessness intentional?

If the answers to the two questions dealt with in the preceding sections are affirmative then the authority comes under a duty by virtue of s 65(3) to secure that accommodation is made available for the applicant's occupation for such period as it considers will give him a reasonable opportunity of securing accommodation for his occupation and to furnish him with advice and such assistance as it considers appropriate in the circumstances in any attempts he may make to secure that accommodation becomes available for his occupation. In effect there has now arisen a duty to provide temporary accommodation and advice and assistance. If the applicant is only threatened with homelessness then the duty to provide advice and assistance alone arises.

In order for the full duty under the Act to arise (subject to questions of local connection, *below*) the authority must not be satisfied that the applicant became homeless intentionally. The full duty in s 65(2) is to secure that accommodation becomes available for the applicant's occupation and by virtue of s 75 the accommodation must also be available for occupation by any other person who might reasonably be expected to reside with him. Section 69(1) as inserted by s 14(3) of the Housing and Planning Act 1986 gives guidance on the suitability of accommodation to be provided in discharge of the full duty.

Intentional homelessness has been the most controversial issue under the Act and its predecessor. Section 60(1) provides that:

> A person becomes homeless intentionally if he deliberately does or fails to do anything in consequence of which he ceases to occupy accommodation which is available for his occupation and which it would have been reasonable for him to continue to occupy.

A similar formulation is provided in subs (2) for intentionally bringing about a threat of homelessness. Some guidance on *mens rea* is provided in subs (3) which says that an act or omission in good faith on the part of a person who was unaware of any relevant fact shall not be treated as deliberate. The section also provides that regard may be had, in determining whether it would have been reasonable for a person to continue to occupy accommodation, to the general circumstances prevailing in relation to housing in the authority's district.

All the elements of the definition must be satisfied before the homelessness is intentional. These elements are:

(1) The applicant must deliberately have done something or failed to do something.
(2) The accommodation must have been lost in consequence of the act or omission.
(3) There must have been occupation as opposed to a failure to take up accommodation.
(4) The lost accommodation must have been available for his occupation.
(5) It must have been reasonable for the homeless person to continue to occupy the accommodation.

Because the amount of case law on intentional homelessness is now so large we shall only pick out here those aspects of particular relevance to a homeless cohabiting family and we will turn later to other aspects relevant on the dissolution of the family.

*Cohabitation itself leading to homelessness*

The first matter of concern is where the *cohabitation itself* leads to homelessness. In *R v Wimborne DC, ex p Curtis* [1986] 1 FLR 486 the cohabitation triggered a sale provision in an order that had been made on the woman's divorce. She applied for accommodation and the council regarded her as intentionally homeless because she had deliberately done something in consequence of which she had lost accommodation—namely cohabited. Mann J quashed the local authority's decision because there was no evidence that it had directed itself to the prior matter (element (4) *above*) of whether the applicant had been occupying accommodation 'available for her occupation'. This expression is clarified in what is now s 75, which says that accommodation is available for a person's occupation only if it is available for occupation both by him and by any other person who might reasonably be expected to live with him. The failure of the authority to consider whether it was reasonable to expect the applicant to live with her new partner meant that its decision had to be quashed. This case shows that if the council had gone through the correct reasoning its decision might have been upheld. (*See also R v Peterborough City Council, ex p Carr* (1990) 22 HLR 206.)

*Imputation of conduct to other cohabitant*

Another important aspect is the extent to which one cohabitant's conduct will be imputed to the other thereby defeating an application from that other. The local authority may be tempted so to impute because otherwise there may be a duty to rehouse not only the 'innocent' party but also the alleged 'guilty' party. This is because the duty is to rehouse the applicant and anyone who might reasonably be expected to reside with him. Whilst the issue is not confined to cases concerning cohabitants it does seem to have arisen frequently in such cases. In *Lewis v North Devon DC* [1981] 1 All ER 27, Woolf J held that a woman who lived with a man who became homeless intentionally was not necessarily barred by his conduct or by the fact that he might benefit undeservingly if she were given accommodation from being entitled to housing under the Act. On the other hand, the policy of the Act was that the authority should consider the family unit as a whole and the authority was entitled to take into account the conduct of the other members of the family. It could assume, in the absence of evidence to the contrary, that the applicant was a party to that conduct.

A further case of acquiescence by a cohabitant was *R v Cardiff City Council, ex p Thomas* (1983) 9 HLR 64. The judge was again Woolf J and, although he restated the principle in essence, he found acquiescence by the man in the woman's conduct which resulted in the loss of the council tenancy of which they were tenants. This was so even though the man was in prison at the time of the conduct and of the proceedings. The man had been offered the opportunity to attend the hearing and there was no evidence of attempts by him to persuade her to desist in the conduct that had persisted up to the hearing.

One final case on this point perhaps indicates the stricter approach that the courts might take since the House of Lords' observations in the *Pulhofer* case. In *R v East Hertfordshire DC, ex p Bannon* (1986) 18 HLR 515, possession proceedings were instituted against the male tenant for arrears of rent, nuisance and annoyance. In effect the complaints were being made against the family as a whole. The parties had lived together for about 13 years and had seven children. The relationship broke down and the woman applied for rehousing. The authority found that she had acquiesced in the man's conduct although she was only directly responsible for one act of nuisance. It accordingly decided that she was intentionally homeless. Webster J dismissed the application holding that the authority was entitled to consider acquiescence in the conduct of the family as a whole, either in the sense of being a party to it or in the sense of doing nothing to prevent it, and on the basis of the material before it one could not say that the decision was unreasonable.

### If not, is there a local connection with another housing authority?

Having come this far we have determined that the full duty to secure accommodation has arisen but s 65(2) states that duty is subject to s 67. Under s 67(2) the application can be referred to another local housing authority if the initial authority is satisfied that the following conditions are met:

(a) neither the applicant nor any person who might reasonably be expected to reside with him has a local connection with the district of the authority to whom his application was made; and
(b) the applicant or a person who might reasonably be expected to reside with him has a local connection with the district of that other authority; and
(c) neither the applicant nor any person who might reasonably be expected to reside with him will run the risk of domestic violence in that other district.

The third condition is more likely to arise where the family has split up and the applicant is afraid to return to her original district. It is discussed below in the context of dissolution of the family.

'Local connection' is defined in s 61 which refers, basically, to past and present residence, employment, family associations and special circumstances. There is no duty on the local authority to inquire into local connection and it can decide not to refer the application to another authority even if it considers that all the conditions in s 67(2) are satisfied.

One decision relevant here is that of the Court of Appeal in *R v Hillingdon LBC, ex p Streeting* [1980] 3 All ER 413. The applicant was a refugee from Ethiopia. She lived with the deceased, an Englishman, in various countries. The deceased died in Libya and the applicant and child came over for the burial in Yorkshire. She was granted a limited permission to remain and was later given refugee status because of the political situation in Ethiopia. The defendant authority argued that there was no local connection with its area when she applied for housing and that the Act must be read as limited to 'our own homeless' (*sic*). This argument was rejected in the Divisional Court and on appeal and the decision to refuse her application was quashed. The case underlines the need for all of the conditions in s 67(2) to be satisfied. Here there was no other authority to whom responsibility could be passed.

Finally it should be noted that if the full duty to secure that accommodation becomes available for the applicant's occupation is established, there is no requirement that the authority must discharge it by housing the applicant *in its area*; *see R v Bristol City Council* [1979] 3 All ER 344, discussed further *below*. It must, however, ensure that the applicant is provided with accommodation for indefinite occupation (*R v Camden LBC, ex p Wait* [1987] 1 FLR 155).

## Homelessness on the dissolution of the family

This section concentrates on those aspects of HA 1985, Pt III that are specifically relevant on the breakdown of the relationship; in particular where there has been domestic violence. The same subheadings are used as in the preceding section.

### Is the applicant homeless (or threatened with homelessness)?

As we have seen, s 58(3) of the Act provides that even if the applicant is deemed to have accommodation by falling within one of the three categories of s 58(2) she is still treated as homeless if she cannot secure entry to it or if it is probable that occupation of it will lead to violence from some other person residing in it or to threats of violence from some other person residing in it and likely to carry out the threats. In addition, the applicant is not to be treated as having accommodation unless it is accommodation that it would be reasonable for her to occupy (s 58(2A)). Fear of violence may mean that it would not be reasonable for her to occupy the premises. In this connection, the local authority is bound to take into consideration the particular physical or mental needs or requirements of the particular applicant (*R v Broxbourne BC, ex p Willmoth* (1990) 22 HLR 118). The violence that is feared may be violence that is likely to take place outside the home (*Hammell v Royal Borough of Kensington and Chelsea* [1989] 2 FLR 223, CA).

Problems may well arise in proving the violence, or threats of it, although these have not featured prominently in case law; probably because attention has been concentrated on 'intentionality' and whether the victim should have used the courts to obtain a remedy (*see below*). The *Code of Guidance* at para 5.9 advises authorities to 'respond sympathetically to applications from women who are in fear of violence; the fact that violence has not yet occurred does not, on its own, suggest that it is not likely to occur'. The *Code* also makes clear that an authority cannot assume that a civil injunction will be effective, and states that an applicant is under no obligation to seek one before being treated as homeless. Nevertheless, the applicant is well advised to produce what evidence she can that if she entered the home violence would result (*R v Purbeck DC, ex p Cadney* [1985] 2 FLR 158).

In the early years of the 1977 Act's operation there were frequent suggestions that local authorities regarded women who were staying in battered wives' refuges as not being homeless in that they had a licence to occupy as a residence. The courts have firmly dismissed such an argument saying that there is no necessary inconsistency between being homeless and having some temporary accommodation or shelter (*see Williams v Cynon Valley DC* [1980] LAG 16 and *R v London Borough of Ealing, ex p Sidhu* [1982] FLR 438).

**If so, is there priority need?**

On the breakdown of a relationship a woman who qualifies as homeless within s 58 will have a priority need if she is pregnant or if there are dependent children residing with her or who might reasonably be expected to reside with her. Despite the seeming practices of some authorities, it is not justifiable to have a general rule that residence orders are required before the applicant can show that a child is one who might reasonably be expected to reside with her (*R v Ealing LBC, ex p Sidhu, above*). As the *Code* puts it, authorities must be alert to the fact that 'the immediate needs of the child might overrule the formal care position'. However, a court order may be useful evidence that children might 'reasonably be expected to reside with the applicant' where they are not doing so at the date of the application.

A battered woman who neither has dependent children nor is pregnant may qualify as in priority need under the category of those who are vulnerable as a result of a special reason (s 59(1)(*c*)). Paragraph 6.17 of the *Code of Guidance* says that authorities should secure wherever possible that accommodation is available for battered women without children who are have suffered violence at home or are at risk of further violence if they return home. One wonders why battered women within this description are not expressly referred to in s 59 or have not been designated as a specified group by the Secretary of State under s 59(2).

**If so, is the homelessness intentional?**

This question was discussed *above* when homelessness of the family as a whole was considered. The likely circumstances particular to separation where an authority might consider the homelessness to be intentional are where the applicant is considered responsible for the breakdown of the relationship or has not done enough to assert domestic rights to return to the home. The first of these situations could probably only legitimately be claimed in the case of a violent man who has been excluded from the home. It will be rare, however, for the local authority to be required to consider this because he is unlikely to be in priority need.

It is the second of these situations, failure to obtain a domestic remedy, which is more likely to be an alleged omission within s 60(1). The *Code of Guidance* at para 7.11(*b*) says that 'it would not normally be reasonable for someone to continue to occupy accommodation if she was a victim of domestic violence, or threats of violence from inside or outside the home'. It goes on to add that 'authorities should not automatically treat an applicant as intentionally homeless because she has failed to use legal remedies'. In the light of this, it is not possible to say that a reasonable authority could never require a woman to use domestic remedies; for example to have the man excluded from the home under the Family Homes and Domestic Violence Bill (discussed in the following chapter); *see R v Eastleigh Borough Council, ex p Evans* [1986] 2 FLR 195, but no general policy of an authority to that effect could presumably be upheld. The chances of a finding of intentional homelessness must be greater if the woman has not previously tried to obtain a remedy than if she has obtained one which has proved ineffective.

At one time, it could have been argued (as indeed it was in the previous edition of this book) that a cohabiting woman was in a better position here than a married woman because the legal redress potentially open to her was less adequate. After all, the cohabiting woman has no automatic statutory right to occupy the home analogous to the 'matrimonial home rights' conferred on spouses by the Family Homes and Domestic Violence Bill; and, if she has no contractual licence or right to occupy by virtue of a property interest, it is quite possible that any exclusion order she obtained would be of limited duration. It could therefore be argued that, since her legal position is weaker than her married sister's, she is less likely to be treated as having omitted to do something that would materially have improved her housing position.

However, this view must be reassessed in the light of the powers now available to the courts to transfer tenancies under Sched 1 to the Children Act 1989 (for the benefit of children), to transfer tenancies between cohabitants under Sched 4 to the FHDVB (both discussed more fully in Chapter 7) and in view of the fact that an order under cl 9 of the FHDVB will confer some of the 'matrimonial home rights' on a successful applicant for the duration of the order (cl 9(10)). A failure by a cohabitant to take action under this legislation where appropriate may now constitute an omission and lead to a finding of intentional homelessness.

Finally, however, it should be said that the family courts do not like to be used simply to satisfy the local authority's administrative requirements (*see* the ridiculous proceedings the applicant was told to initiate in *Warwick v Warwick* [1982] FLR 393) and this point should be made forcibly to an authority that is suggesting that an injunction be sought.

### If not, is there a local connection with another housing authority?

The most likely circumstance where this might be an issue is where the woman wishes to move out of the district of the former home, perhaps for fear that the man will be violent to her even if she lives in other accommodation locally, and so applies for housing in a different district. Section 67(2)(*c*) provides that one of the conditions for referral of the application to another authority cannot be satisfied if the applicant will run the risk of domestic violence in the area of that other authority (and not just at the former home). A local authority cannot rely on the local connection provisions without first making *specific* inquiries about the possibility of domestic violence if the applicant were referred to another authority (*Patterson v LB Greenwich* (1994) 24 HLR 159). The meaning of 'domestic' for these purposes is clarified in s 67(3) with the effect that if the woman runs the risk of violence from a person with whom, but for the risk of violence, she might reasonably be expected to reside, or from a person with whom she formerly resided or if she runs the risk of threats of violence from such a person which are likely to be carried out then her application cannot be referred to the other authority.

The case of *R v Bristol CC, ex p Browne* [1979] 3 All ER 344 suggests a disturbing way in which this safeguard might be ineffective. Here the applicant and her seven children left the matrimonial home in Tralee, the Republic of Ireland, on medical advice because of her husband's violence. She went to a refuge but the husband discovered her there so the refuge arranged for her and the children to go to a refuge in Bristol. When she sought accommodation from the respondents, Bristol City Council, the housing officer contacted the welfare officer in Tralee. He said that he was aware of the husband's violence and assured Bristol that he would arrange secure accommodation for her and the children. Bristol thereupon offered to pay the fare for the applicant and the children. To be clear, Bristol were not here relying on the local connection conditions because Tralee was not a local housing authority in England, Scotland or Wales to which the application could be referred. In fact, Bristol was *discharging* the full duty to rehouse by securing accommodation from some other person. Understandably, in view of the fact that Mr Browne had already found her at the original refuge in Tralee, Mrs Browne did not wish to return there and applied for judicial review. The Divisional Court dismissed her application and Lloyd J said (at 351a):

> Obviously she will not go back to the same house, but there is other accommodation in the same area. The risk involved in her going back was, in my judgment, a matter for the council to consider together with the community welfare officer in Tralee. The passage from the affidavits which I have read shows that the risk was considered very carefully by the council. The view which they formed is quite clear, namely that accommodation can be provided in Tralee without risk to the applicant and her children.

> There is no material on which this court can possibly interfere with that conclusion or say that it was not justified.

These remarks underline the way in which the principles of administrative law operate in housing cases with the courts reluctant to interfere with *bona fide* decisions of local authorities; a reluctance that has increased since the *Browne* case. In essence the Divisional Court was relying on the uncorroborated and unsworn views of the Tralee welfare officer. Although the case is unusual in that it involved a return to a district out of the jurisdiction, nevertheless it presumably means that an authority can still arrange for the rehousing of an applicant in another district *within* the jurisdiction even if it could not refer the application itself back to that district because s 67(2)(*c*) was not satisfied. In other words, duties under the Act can be discharged by sending *her* back but not by sending her application back.

## Duties to children under the Children Act 1989

The Children Act 1989 (CA 1989) imposes a number of duties on local authority social services to safeguard and promote the welfare of children in their area who are 'in need' (s 17 of the CA 1989). A homeless child would be a child 'in need' for these purposes and there is a specific duty resting on a local authority to provide accommodation for such children (s 20(1)). A social services authority is empowered to request the assistance of another authority (including a local housing authority) in discharging its functions under the 1989 Act, and the requested authority is obliged to comply with the request if it is compatible with its own statutory duties and does not unduly prejudice the discharge of its other functions (s 27 of the CA 1989).

At one time, it was thought that these provisions might impose duties on housing authorities at least to consider providing accommodation for families with children even where the family in question did not qualify under the homelessness provisions (for example because they were intentionally homeless). In *R v Northavon DC, ex p Smith* [1993] 2 FLR 897, the Court of Appeal quashed the decision of a local housing authority to refuse the request of a social services authority for assistance in the discharge of its functions towards an intentionally homeless family. The housing authority had simply relied on its finding that the family were intentionally homeless as grounds for refusing to assist social services, and the Court of Appeal held that this was an inadequate basis for its decision: the housing authority should have reconsidered its decision afresh in the light of the social services department's request.

However, even this shred of procedural protection was removed on appeal to the House of Lords ([1994] 2 FLR 671), who held that the provisions of the CA 1989 did not alter the duties of a housing authority under the HA 1985 and that the duty of co-operation imposed by s 27 CA 1989 was not enforceable by judicial review. The housing authority was therefore entitled to rely on its finding of intentional homelessness as sufficient reason for refusing to comply with the request from social services. There was, though, no doubt in the *Northavon* case that the family were entitled to some assistance, even if that assistance fell short of permanent accommodation: the question was from which authority. There was certainly an element of the social services department in *Northavon* seeking to place the financial burden of assisting the family entirely on the housing authority. The tenor of the House of Lords' judgments was that authorities should co-operate with each other, and that judges will not intervene in that process through judicial review.

It has also been held that the power in s 27 to request help from another authority does not apply where the authority is a unitary one with responsibility for both social services *and* housing (as most London authorities are). As Hoffmann LJ put it in *R v London Borough of Tower Hamlets, ex p Byas* (1993) 25 HLR 105, 'you cannot ask yourself for help'. The unsatisfactory consequence of this decision is that the impact of s 27 (which, as we have seen, may be minimal in any event) depends on the structure of local government in any given area.

# Chapter 6

# Domestic Violence

## Introduction

This chapter has been almost entirely rewritten following the introduction of the Family Homes and Domestic Violence Bill (the FHDVB). The Bill will replace the Domestic Violence and Matrimonial Proceedings Act 1976 (the DVA). The DVA was the main source of injunctive protection open to cohabitants but it was limited in its scope. For example, owing to some unclear wording it was thought to be available only to those who were actually living together at the time of the application or who had been living together at the time of the last incident of violence. In the latter case, that incident needed to have been fairly recent. This tended to exclude a former cohabitant who was seeking protection from violence arising after the separation.

Another limitation of the DVA was the requirement, imposed by case law and Practice Note, that any ouster under the Act had to be for a limited period only, usually three months (*see Davis v Johnson* [1978] 1 All ER 1132 and Practice Note [1978] 2 All ER 1056). This contrasted with exclusion of a spouse under the Matrimonial Homes Act 1983, where there was no such requirement.

In the light of these limitations, and others not mentioned here, previous editions of this book contained extensive discussion of other forms of injunction that might be available. The FHDVB renders much of that discussion unnecessary. There are nevertheless occasions when injunctive protection might be sought in proceedings concerning children. A separate clause has been included dealing with this, and it includes new material following the implementation of the Children Act 1989 (CA 1989).

The discussion in this chapter is largely confined to matters that are relevant to cohabitants or former cohabitants, although some reference has been made to provisions concerning spouses and other 'associated persons' where this is necessary to a fuller understanding.

## The Family Homes and Domestic Violence Bill 1995

### General

The Bill is the product of a Law Commission Report (No 207, *Domestic Violence and Occupation of the Family Home*, 1992). A draft Bill was attached to the Report, most of which was adopted in the Bill introduced to Parliament. A court may certainly make reference to a Law Commission report for the purpose of ascertaining the mischief which the statute is intended to cure, but not for the purpose of discovering the meaning of the words used by Parliament to effect such cure (Lord Browne-Wilkinson in *Pepper v Hart* [1992] 3 WLR 1032 at 1052G). In *R v Secretary of State for Transport, ex p Factortame Ltd* [1990] 2 AC 85, the House of Lords also referred to a Law Commission report for the purpose of drawing an inference as to Parliamentary intention from the fact that Parliament had not expressly implemented one of the Law Commission's recommendations.

The principal changes introduced by the FHDVB, relevant to our concerns, are these:

(1) Some uniformity of jurisdiction has been introduced so that the three levels of courts have similar powers (subject to some restrictions on the powers of magistrates). Previously, the DVA was expressed only to be relevant to the county court, although there was a suggestion that the powers in the Act were also available to the High Court (see the third edition of this book, p 81).

(2) Many of the limitations of the the DVA have been overcome, in particular the limited nature of relevant applicants and respondents.

(3) There has been some standardisation of remedies between spouses and cohabitants.

(4) The relevance of the interests of children to the exercise of the court's discretion to oust the non-custodial parent has become somewhat clearer.

(5) An attempt has been made to balance the competing policies of protecting property rights and protecting victims of violence.

(6) Express provision has been made to regulate the position of a non-entitled cohabitant who is living in the property under an occupation order in relation to third parties, such as landlords and mortgagees.

(7) There is more clarity about the duration of occupation orders.

(8) Powers have been given to the court to order the transfer of a tenancy, either into the sole name of one of the joint tenants or into a non-tenant's name.

In so far as cohabitants are concerned, the Bill makes provision for 'occupation orders', 'non-molestation orders' and the transfer of tenancies. The first two are the primary concern of this chapter, with a particular emphasis on protection from violence. In Chapter 7, which deals with occupation of the home, we look further at the property-related consequences of an occupation order and we discuss fully the new provisions on transfer of tenancies. Inevitably there is a degree of overlap but we have tried to provide clear cross-references.

## Important terminology

The Bill contains a number of important terms and the following are those of most relevance to unmarried cohabitation.

*Cohabitants and former cohabitants*
According to cl 1:

> For the purposes of this Bill—
> (a) 'cohabitants' are a man and a woman who, although not married to each other, are living together as husband and wife; and
> (b) 'former cohabitants' shall be construed accordingly, but does not include cohabitants who have subsequently married each other.

This definition of cohabitant is very similar to that used in the definition of an unmarried couple in social security legislation (*see* Chapter 3) but differs from that in the DVA, where there was a requirement that the parties live in the same *household*. It is not clear whether there is any significance to the omission of a household test, first because in deciding whether the parties were living together as husband and wife attention will obviously be given to whether they were in the same household, and secondly because the Bill also has a concept of 'associated persons' which picks up those household members who are not spouses and cohabitants (*see below*).

*Associated persons*
According to cl 2:

> For the purposes of this Bill a person is associated with another person if—
> (a) they are or have been married to each other,
> (b) they are cohabitants or former cohabitants,
> (c) they live or have lived in the same household, otherwise than merely by reason of one of them being the other's employee, tenant, lodger or boarder,
> (d) they are relatives,
> (e) in relation to any child, they are both persons falling within subclause

(2) [which states that a person falls within this subclause in relation to a child if (a) he is a parent of the child or (b) he has or has had parental responsibility for the child], or

(f) they are parties to the same family proceedings (other than proceedings under this Bill).

A body corporate cannot be associated with another person under (e) or (f).

The category of 'relatives', in para (d), is defined in cl 30. This definition ensures, amongst other things, that parents and their children will be 'associated persons' for the purposes of the Bill. As we shall see, this means that children can apply for both occupation and non-molestation orders.

Where a child has been adopted or freed for adoption, two persons are associated with each other if (a) one is a natural parent or grandparent of the child and (b) the other is the child or any person who has adopted the child or with whom the child has been placed for adoption (cl 2(3)).

The concept of 'parental responsibility', in the context of unmarried parents, is fully discussed in Chapter 10.

*Relevant child*

A 'relevant child' for the purposes of the FHDVB is, under cl 3:

(a) any child who is living with or might reasonably be expected to live with either party to the proceedings,

(b) any child in relation to whom an order under the Adoption Act 1976 or the Children Act 1989 is in question in the proceedings, and

(c) any other child whose interests the court considers relevant.

*Occupation orders*

An occupation order means an order under cll 7, 9 or 10 of the Bill (*see* cl 11(1)). These are discussed under separate sub-headings below. Briefly, an order under cl 7 is one granted to an applicant who has an entitlement to occupy the home by virtue of a beneficial estate or interest or contract, irrespective of whether the respondent has such an entitlement. The parties must be, or have been, associated persons and have used the dwellinghouse, or have intended to use it, as their home. By contrast, an order under cl 9 is one made in favour of a *non*-entitled applicant against a respondent who *is* entitled. Under this section, the parties must be, or have been, spouses or cohabitants: the powers available under this clause do not extend to 'associated persons'. Clause 9, then, can enable the exclusion of a property owner by a non-property owner. An occupation order under cl 10 is also available only to spouses and cohabitants (rather than the wider category of 'associated persons') and is made where neither party has an entitlement to occupy. For example, the parties might be living in a parent's house without charge. An order under cll 9 or 10 cannot exceed six months but it is renewable.

As will be seen below, an occupation order confirms or confers the applicant's right to occupy the property and may go further by excluding the respondent from the dwellinghouse or a defined area in which it is included. Further rights accompany different kinds of occupation order, for example the right of a non-entitled occupant to make mortgage and rent payments, the details of which are discussed *below*.

It is open to a child to apply for an occupation order under cl 7 because a child and its parents will be 'associated persons' either as a consequence of co-residence in the same household (cl 2(*c*)), or because they are 'relatives' (cl 2(*d*)). However, a child will be able to apply only under cl 7 (because he or she will not qualify as a spouse or cohabitant under cll 9 or 10), and then only if (a) she is an entitled applicant under cl 7 and (b) in the case of a child under 16, the leave of court has been obtained (cl 14(1)). Before granting leave, the court must be satisfied that the child has sufficient understanding to make the application (cl 14(2)). This requirement of leave also applies to applications by children for non-molestation orders. It seems strange that a child's ability to invoke cl 7 should turn on the child's property entitlements, but this seems to be an inevitable consequence of the Bill's distinction of treatment between those who are entitled and those who are non-entitled.

*Non-molestation orders*

A non-molestation order, under cl 13, means an order containing either or both of the provisions below:

(a) a provision prohibiting a person ("the respondent") from molesting another person who is associated with the respondent, and
(b) a provision prohibiting the respondent from molesting a relevant child.

It may be expressed to refer to molestation in general or to particular acts of molestation (cl 13(5)).

These provisions are similar to those in the DVA except that an application can be made by one associated person (for example a relative, including a child) against another, whereas the DVA was limited to spouses and cohabitants. The meaning of 'molestation' itself is discussed *below*.

*Harm*

'Harm', in relation to a child, has the same meaning as in s 31 of CA

1989; that is, 'ill-treatment or the impairment of health or development' (s 30(1)). 'Ill-treatment' is then further defined as including 'sexual abuse and forms of ill-treatment which are not physical'; 'health' includes physical or mental health; and 'development' means 'physical, intellectual, emotional, social or behavioural development'.

In relation to any other person, 'harm' means 'ill-treatment or the impairment of health' (FHDVB, cl 30(1)). 'Health' has the same meaning as for children, while 'ill-treatment' in relation to adults is left undefined.

The concept of harm is important because the presence or likelihood of *significant* harm creates a rebuttable presumption that a restriction or exclusion provision should be included in an occupation order. Where it is not demonstrated, however, a more discretionary balancing exercise is carried out by the court. 'Significant harm' is also a concept used in the Children Act, although 'significant' is not defined in either Act: but cl 30(2) reproduces s 31(1) of the CA 1989 which states that where the question of whether harm suffered by a child is significant turns on the child's health or development, his health or development shall be compared with that which could reasonably be expected of a similar child.

## Non-molestation orders

### *Clause 13 of the FHDVB*

We have seen above the definition of a non-molestation order. Clause 13(2) provides that a court may make such an order:

> (a) if an application for the order has been made (whether in other family proceedings or without any other family proceedings being instituted) by a person who is associated with the respondent, or
> (b) if in any family proceedings to which the respondent is a party the court considers that the order should be made for the benefit of any other party to the proceedings or any relevant child even though no such application has been made.

For these purposes, the definition of 'family proceedings' is extended to include proceedings in which a court has made an emergency protection order which includes an 'exclusion requirement' (*see* the following clause on orders in proceedings concerning children).

The order can be made for a specified period or until further order (cl 13(6)). It may be varied or discharged on the application of either the applicant or respondent (cl 19(1)). Where the order was made by a court acting of its own motion under cl 13(2)(*b*), the court may also vary or discharge the order of its own motion (cl 19(1)). A non-molestation order made in other family proceedings shall cease to have effect if those proceedings are withdrawn or dismissed.

As we will see *below*, the order can be made *ex parte* (cl 15) and can have a power of arrest attached to it (cl 17).

The High Court, county courts and magistrates' courts are all given jurisdiction to make non-molestation orders (see the definition of 'court' in cl 25). However a magistrates' court may decline jurisdiction if it considers that the case can more conveniently be dealt with by another court (cl 27(2)).

*The meaning of molestation*

No definition of 'molestation' is given in the FHDVB. There is, however, some authority under earlier legislation and on the court's inherent jurisdiction to restrain molestation during the course of litigation.

'Molestation' has been given a wide meaning. It includes pestering (*Vaughan v Vaughan* [1973] 3 All ER 499) and 'any conduct which can properly be regarded as such a degree of harassment as to call for the intervention of the court' (Ormrod LJ in *Horner v Horner* [1982] 2 All ER 495 at 497g). It is certainly broader than 'violence', which was the concept relevant to a spouse's application for a protection order under the to be repealed s 16 of the Domestic Proceedings and Magistrates' Courts Act 1978. In *F v F* [1989] 2 FLR 451, Judge Fricker QC in the York County Court said that molestation is deliberate conduct which substantially interferes with the applicant or a child, whether by violence or by intimidation, harassment, pestering or interference that is sufficiently serious to warrant the intervention of the court. The element of intent has been emphasised by the Court of Appeal (*see Johnston v Walton* [1990] 1 FLR 350).

*When a non-molestation order is likely to be granted*

In deciding whether to make an order, the court must have regard to all the circumstances including the need to secure the health, safety and well-being—

> (a) of the applicant or ... the person for whose benefit the order would be made, and
> (b) of any relevant child. (cl 13(4))

Although this subsection provides new guidance on the making of non-molestation orders, it does not say, in terms, that evidence of past molestation is a prerequisite to the making of the order. This contrasts with the assumed position under the DVA. In *Spindlow v Spindlow* [1979] 1 All ER 1132, Lawton LJ said that molestation must be proved before a non-molestation order could be made as it was 'clear from the wording' of the section (although there were no actual words on the subject in the section). Some other case law under the DVA may continue to be relevant. It was held by the Court of Appeal that it is inappropriate to grant a non-molestation order against someone who is mentally ill to the extent that he is incapable of understanding what he is doing or that what he is doing is wrong (*Wookey v Wookey* [1991] 2 FLR 319). It was also held by Judge Fricker in *F v F* [1989] 2 FLR 451 that a non-molestation order could not be granted to an applicant who was still in full cohabitation with the respondent and who intended to continue in full cohabitation with him. The purpose of an injunction under s 1 of the DVA, he said, was to enable someone to free herself from cohabitation with the respondent and to keep free from it. Apart from some *obiter dicta* in *Davis v Johnson* [1978] 1 All ER 1132, however, no authority was adduced for the proposition and it is unclear that the decision can stand following *E v E* (1995) Fam Law 183, where the Court of Appeal upheld a non-molestation order that had been made when parties were still living together. Nevertheless, it might not be said that the parties were in 'full' cohabitation because the wife was given sole use of a particular room in the house and the parties' work patterns were such that they were in the house together for only a short time.

## Occupation orders

When defining 'occupation orders' earlier some general description was given of the three different kinds of order. It is necessary now to explore the distinction in some detail because each order has its own particular rules and consequences. The account which follows is largely confined to a description and analysis of the legislation. As family lawyers will know, however, there is a large body of case law concerning when an ouster order under the DVA should be granted (see pp 73–75 of the third edition of this book). After a period of uncertainty, it became established in the mid-1980s that the criteria in the Matrimonial Homes Act 1983, whereby a court could make an order between spouses regulating the occupancy of a matrimonial home, were also to be applied in cases under the DVA (*Richards v Richards* [1984] FLR 11, *Lee v Lee* [1984] FLR 243 and *Thurley v Smith* [1984] FLR 875). It also became clear that ouster orders were to be regarded as 'extreme', 'drastic' and 'draconian' measures, and only to be granted in situations of urgency (*see* eg *Summers v Summers* [1986] 1 FLR 343, *Wiseman v Simpson* [1988] 1 FLR 490 and *Tuck v Nicholls* [1988] 1 FLR 283). They were not to be granted as readily as non-molestation orders and, ordinarily, they should not be granted on the basis of affidavit evidence alone. The extreme nature of the order required a proper investigation by examination and cross-examination of the parties (*Shipp v Shipp* [1988] 1 FLR 345 and *Whitlock v Whitlock* [1989] 1 FLR 208).

The extent to which these authorities will continue to be relevant is yet to be established. Both the DVA and the Matrimonial Homes Act 1983 will be completely repealed by the FHDVB and there will be a self-contained statutory code. Arguably, Parliament has had the opportunity to include provisions to the effect that restriction or exclusion provisions are only to be granted in urgent circumstances, and it has declined to take up that opportunity. One could say, therefore, that the courts should refrain from adding any further limitation. Furthermore, the new legislation treats separately those cases where property owners are to be excluded. The application of the DVA was conditioned to a certain extent by an undercurrent of concern about property owners being dispossessed. The legislature has now addressed that issue and this may lead to a different attitude amongst judges.

The High Court, county courts and magistrates' courts are all given jurisdiction to make occupation orders (*see* the definition of 'court' in cl 25). However a magistrates' court cannot entertain any application or make any order involving a disputed question of entitlement to occupy unless it is unnecessary to determine the question in order to deal with the application or make the order (cl 27(1)). As a separate matter, a magistrates' court may decline jurisdiction if it considers that the case can more conveniently be dealt with by another court.

*Where the applicant, or both the applicant and the respondent, are entitled occupants—cl 7 orders*

Clause 7(1) provides, so far as is relevant to cohabitants, that a person entitled to occupy a dwellinghouse by virtue of a beneficial estate or interest or contract or by virtue of an enactment giving him the right to remain in occupation may apply to the court for an order under the clause if the dwellinghouse is or has at any time been the home of the person entitled and of another person with whom he is associated (thus including cohabitants and former cohabitants—see the definition of 'associated persons' *above*) or was intended by the person entitled and any such other person to be their home.

In determining whether a person is entitled to occupy a dwellinghouse by virtue of an estate or interest, the court must disregard any right to possession of the dwellinghouse conferred on a mortgagee under the mortgage, whether or not the mortgagee is actually in possession (cl 23(1)).

Although the applicant must have an entitlement to occupy by virtue of a beneficial estate or interest, contract or enactment, there is a special provision for an applicant who has an equitable interest but who does not hold or share the legal estate. In a curiously worded subclause, the Bill seems to provide that such a person has a choice (cl 9(9)). He or she can apply either under cl 7 as an entitled applicant or under cl 9 as a non-entitled applicant. We discuss this further when dealing with cl 9 orders as there may be some tactical considerations to be borne in mind.

Nothing in cl 7 refers to whether the *respondent* (ie the associated person against whom the order is being sought) must have an entitlement to occupy, thus indicating that an order is available either way.

The orders that the court can make, insofar as cohabitants are concerned, are set out in subcll (2) and (3). Subclause (2) contains the main ones. Where the respondent is a *non*-entitled occupant (so that it is a 'property owner' versus a 'non-property owner') then the court may (using the paragraph letters of subcl (2), but without quoting *verbatim*):

(a) enforce the applicant's entitlement to remain in occupation as against the respondent (ie prevent the respondent from evicting her or him);
(b) require the respondent to permit the applicant to enter and remain in the dwellinghouse, or part of it (ie make the respondent allow the applicant back in);
(c) regulate the occupation of the dwellinghouse by either or both parties (presumably, for example, by allocating different parts of the dwellinghouse to the parties or providing for time-sharing);
(f) require the respondent to leave the dwellinghouse or part of it (ie an exclusion order); or
(g) exclude the respondent from a defined area in which the dwellinghouse is included.

Where the respondent is also an entitled occupant (for example, they share the legal and beneficial interests, or the tenancy, jointly), there is a further order available:

(d) prohibit, suspend or restrict the exercise by the respondent of the right to occupy the home.

It seems to follow, therefore, that to exclude a *non*-entitled respondent the appropriate order is made under para (f) whereas to exclude an entitled respondent one should rely upon para (d).

The court is also given power in subcl (3) to declare that the applicant is an entitled occupant. This would mean that if there is likely to be any dispute, entitlement can be established without separate proceedings and at the outset.

The criteria to be considered when making an order are contained in subcll (5) and (6). It might be helpful to consider them in reverse order because subcl (6) contains circumstances where a court normally *must* make an order, whereas subcl (5) is more open ended.

Subclause (6) provides for what might be called the 'significant harm' test and is quoted almost in full:

> If it appears to the court that the applicant or any relevant child is likely to suffer significant harm if an order under this clause containing one or more of the provisions in subclause (2) ... is not made, the court shall make the order unless it appears to the court that—
> (a) the respondent or any relevant child is likely to suffer significant harm if the order is made, and
> (b) the harm likely to be suffered by the respondent or child in that event is greater than the harm likely to be suffered by the applicant or child if the order is not made.

This subclause basically means that an order must be made if there is a likelihood of significant harm to the applicant or a relevant child unless the making of the order is itself likely to cause even more harm to the respondent or the child than the applicant or child would suffer if it is not made.

The matters contained in subcl (5) become relevant where there is no likelihood of significant harm. They are also relevant even when the significant harm test in subcl (6) applies because they guide the court in deciding *what kind* of order to make. In deciding whether to exercise its powers and, if so, in what manner, the court must have regard to all the circumstances including:

(a) the respective housing needs and housing resources of the parties and of any relevant child;
(b) the respective financial resources of the parties; and
(c) the likely effect of any order, or of any decision by the court not to exercise its powers under subcl (2) *above*, on the health, safety or well-being of the parties and of any relevant child.

It is important to note that violence or molestation are not said in the Bill to be prerequisites to the making of an occupation order. This was also the case with the DVA (*see Spindlow, above*) but the general policy of restricting ouster orders against cohabitants to urgent situations tended to limit them to instances of personal danger. Now that the legislature expressly requires the court to consider all the circumstances, whilst referring, *inter alia*, to health, safety or well-being, and bearing in mind that if significant harm exists then subcl (6) is likely to cut in anyway, there is presumably no warrant for attaching any greater significance to violence as a factor than is provided for in the legislation.

An order under cl 7 may be made for a specified period, or until the occurrence of a specified event or until further order (cl 7(9)). It may be varied or discharged by a court on the application of either the applicant or the respondent (cl 19(1)). It will be seen therefore that the Bill does not stipulate a time limit for an occupation order under cl 7, presumably because it is an *entitled* occupant whose safety or well-being is being protected.

Once an order is made, attention turns to the consequences. We deal *below* with some issues which are common to different forms of occupation order or to occupation and non-molestation orders alike, but it is important to focus briefly on the possible peculiar consequences, or non-consequences, of a cl 7 order. The FHDVB makes no provision for the acquisition by a cohabitant with a cl 7 order of what might be called rights against third parties. The rights we refer to are the rights which have long been available to a non-entitled *spouse* under the Matrimonial Homes Act and which are now contained in FHDVB, cl 4(2) to (5). The rights are explored in more detail in Chapter 7, but briefly they are the right to:

(a) have any payment or tender of rent, mortgage instalments or other outgoings treated as being as good as if made by the other spouse (cl 4(2));
(b) have her or his occupation treated as occupation by the other spouse for the purposes of the Rent Acts and Housing Acts (cl 4(3));
(c) have any payment made in respect of a mortgage recognised for the purposes of acquiring a beneficial interest, irrespective of how the mortgagee treats it (cl 4(4));
(d) be joined as a party to any proceedings brought by the mortgagee to enforce the security (cl 23(3)); and
(e) have the above rights bind trustees where the home is held under a trust (cl 4(5)).

The new legislation will provide that these rights are accorded to a cohabitant with a cl 9 order for so long as the order is in force (*see below*). The reason why they are not accorded to a cohabitant with a cl 7 order is presumably because they are thought to be unnecessary. The cohabitant already has an entitlement to occupy and seemingly enjoys these rights against third parties already. This might not always be the case, however, because of the way that an entitled occupant is defined. Entitlement for these purposes is having a 'beneficial estate or interest or contract' or statutory right to occupy. At least one case arises where a cohabitant seems to be entitled to occupy within the meaning of these words (and therefore must use cl 7: cl 9(1)(*c*)) but where the third party rights do not subsist. This is where, say, the man beneficially owns the fee simple or lease but grants the woman a contractual licence to occupy the property, whether expressly or impliedly (*see* Chapter 7). Here, her entitlement to occupy arises from a contract and so she must apply for an occupation order under cl 7 (because she is 'entitled' and thereby excluded by cl 9(1)(*c*), from invoking cl 9, but falls outside cl 9(9)—the clause conferring choice—which applies only to 'equitable interests' in the house or interests 'in the proceeds of sale', neither of which would apply to a licensee). If she obtains an exclusion order against the man, but then tenders payment to the mortgagee or lessor, the latter are not obliged to accept it from her. Similarly, her occupation is not treated as occupation by the man for the purposes of security of tenure under the Rent Acts or Housing Acts. She is not a spouse and therefore cannot rely on the rights in cl 4(2) to (5); nor does she have an occupation order under cl 9 which, as we will shortly see, *does* carry with it these rights as against third parties.

Finally on cl7 orders, it should be noted that a cohabitant who has only an equitable interest in an unregistered dwelling is not given the right to enter a class F land charge under what is now cl 5 of the FHDVB. This contrasts with a spouse in the same position. Because there does not appear to be any land charges entry available to such a cohabitant (although there would be an appropriate entry on the register in the case of registered land), it remains important to take the steps referred to in Chapter 8 to protect her beneficial interest against third parties and in the meantime not to move out of the property. Otherwise, the respondent can make an effective disposition to a third party and jeopardise her beneficial interest, leaving a personal action only for breach of trust.

*Where the respondent is entitled to occupy but the applicant is not—cl 9 orders*

We are dealing here with the situation where a non-property owner seeks an occupation order against a property owner, whilst bearing in mind that cl 9(9) permits a cohabitant with only an equitable interest to be treated as a non-entitled applicant for these purposes.

Unlike cl 7, this clause is not available to all 'associated persons' but only to cohabitants, former cohabitants and former spouses. Clause 9(1) provides, so far as is material to this discussion:

> Where—
> (a) one cohabitant, former cohabitant or former spouse is entitled to occupy a dwellinghouse by virtue of a beneficial estate or interest or contract or by virtue of any enactment giving him the right to remain in occupation, and
> (b) that dwellinghouse—
> (i) in the case of cohabitants or former cohabitants, is the home in which they live together as husband and wife or a home in which at any time they so lived together or intended so to live together, ... [and]

> (c) the other cohabitant, former cohabitant or former spouse is not so entitled
>
> the cohabitant, former cohabitant or former spouse not so entitled may apply to the court for an order under this clause against the other ...

As with cl 7 orders, in determining whether a person is entitled to occupy a dwellinghouse by virtue of an estate or interest, the court must disregard any right to possession of the dwellinghouse conferred on a mortgagee under the mortgage, whether or not the mortgagee is actually in possession (cl 23(1)).

Clause 9 stipulates a mandatory provision to be contained in any order and a set of optional provisions. If the applicant is already in occupation, the order *must* contain a provision giving her the right not to be evicted or excluded from the dwellinghouse or any part of it by the respondent for the period specified in the order and prohibiting the respondent from evicting or excluding her during that period. If the applicant is not in occupation at the time of the order, the order *must* contain a provision giving her the right to enter into and occupy the dwellinghouse for the period specified in the order and requiring the respondent to permit the exercise of the right (see cl 9(2)(*a*) and (*b*)).

Subclause (3) then lists the optional provisions by cross-referring to four of the possible cl 7 orders. These are later described in subcl (6) as 'restriction or exclusion' provisions. Keeping the paragraph letters in cl 7(2), these are orders which:

> (c) regulate the occupation of the dwelling-house by either or both parties,
>
> (d) prohibit, suspend or restrict the exercise by the respondent of his right to occupy the dwellinghouse,
>
> (f) require the respondent to leave the dwellinghouse or part of the dwellinghouse, or
>
> (g) exclude the respondent from a defined area in which the dwellinghouse is included.

Clause 9 then lists separately the criteria to be considered in deciding whether an occupation order should be made at all and whether the optional restriction or exclusion provisions should be included.

In deciding whether the occupation order should be made at all, and if so in what manner, subcl (4) requires the court to have regard to all the circumstances, including the matters referred to in cl 7(5)(*a*) to (*c*). (These were described *above* and are basically: respective housing needs and housing resources; respective financial resources; and likely effect on health, safety or well-being.) Clause 9(4) then lists the following further matters which are, in paraphrased form:

(a) the nature of the relationship, the length of time during which the cohabitants have lived together as husband and wife and whether there are or have been children of both of them or for whom they have or have had parental responsibility;

(b) the length of time that has elapsed since they ceased living together; and

(c) the existence of any pending proceedings between the parties under Sched 1, para 1(2)(*d*) or (*e*) to the Children Act 1989 (*see* Chapters 7, 8 and 10) or relating to the legal or beneficial ownership of the dwellinghouse.

It will be noted that the Bill does not say what bearing these matters have on whether any order should be made. Furthermore, it is not entirely clear what some of them mean. It is not clear, for example, how one usefully analyses 'the nature of the relationship' so as to decide whether the non-entitled applicant should be allowed to occupy the property.

Once it has been decided that an occupation order should be made, the question arises whether a restriction or exclusion provision should be included. Clause 9(6) invokes the same balance of harm test as applies to cl 7 orders; namely, that if it appears to the court that the applicant or a relevant child is likely to suffer significant harm if a restriction or exclusion order is not made then the order *must* be made unless the respondent or relevant child will suffer significant harm if the order is made and that harm is greater than will be suffered by the applicant or child if it is not made.

Assuming that the significant harm test is not triggered, the court must have regard to all the circumstances, and have fresh regard to the matters in cl 7(5)(*a*) to (*c*) (respective housing needs and housing resources; respective financial resources; and likely effect on health, safety or well-being).

The reasoning paths for the occupation order itself and the restriction or exclusion provisions which might also be included have some common considerations but they are not identical. They have in common that all the circumstances must be considered, including the matters in cl 7(5)(*a*) to (*c*). They differ, however, in that the matters in cl 9(4) (nature of relationship, length of time since separation and pending proceedings) are only explicitly relevant to the making of the basic occupation order, and the balance of harm test is only explicitly relevant to the inclusion of a restriction or exclusion provision.

There then follow some particular rules governing cl 9 orders or consequences attaching thereto. In particular, the effect of a cl 9 order must be limited to a specified period not exceeding six months, although it may be renewed for one or more periods not exceeding six months (cl

9(8)). It may be varied or discharged at any time on the application of either the applicant or the respondent (cl 19(1). This subclause therefore continues, in part, the practice under the DVA of making exclusion orders in favour of cohabitants for short periods only, but it stipulates six months rather than the old three months and it makes clear that fixed term orders are only essential where they are made in favour of non-entitled applicants.

Clause 9(9) then provides, as we have seen, that a cohabitant who has an equitable interest in the dwellinghouse but not a legal estate can choose whether to apply under cl 7 or cl 9. In order to unravel this, one needs to be reminded of the different consequences of the orders. A cl 7 order can be for a period exceeding six months, and this therefore offers an advantage over a cl 9 order. However, as we saw above, a cl 7 order does not give the applicant the rights mentioned earlier against third parties. Thus, for example, a mortgagee or landlord is not obliged by virtue of the order to accept a tender of instalments or rent. Of course, one can argue to them that the order would not have been granted without some proof or admission as to the tenderer's equitable interest but, in practical terms, this might not win the day.

Moving on to a broader point, the rights against third parties which accompany a cl 9 order do not provide the applicant with complete security. For example, in the case of premises occupied under a tenancy, they do not in themselves guard against the respondent giving notice to quit and thus terminating the tenancy. The matter is explored fully in Chapter 7 but at this stage it should be noted that the application for the occupation order might be accompanied by an application for an injunction restraining the respondent from giving a notice to quit. An application for the transfer of the tenancy into the name of the applicant should also be considered.

Finally under cl 9, there are some specific provisions to do with mortgagees. A cohabitant with a cl 9 order (ie a non-entitled occupant) does not acquire any larger right against the mortgagee to occupy the dwellinghouse than the entitled cohabitant has by virtue of his estate or interest and of any contract with the mortgagee (cl 23(2)). If the mortgagee takes proceedings to enforce the security, the cohabitant with a cl 9 order is entitled to be made a party to the action if the court does not see a special reason against it, and if it is satisfied that the applicant may be expected to meet the mortgagor's (ie the entitled cohabitant's) liabilities or obligations in a way which might affect the outcome of the proceedings (cl 23(3)).

*Where neither the applicant nor the respondent is an entitled occupant —cl 10 orders*

Where neither party is entitled to remain in occupation of the dwellinghouse in which they live or lived together as husband and wife, either of them can apply for an order against the other under cl 10. An example of this situation would be where the parties live as bare licensees in a home provided by a relative.

In this situation, the court can make a 'restriction or exclusion' order (*see* the preceding section). The matters in cll 7(5) and (6) apply to the exercise of the court's powers (ie, the balance of harm test and then all the circumstances, including respective housing needs and resources, respective financial resources and likely effect on health, safety or well-being).

An order under cl 10 is, like a cl 9 order, to be made for renewable periods of up to six months.

*Matters applicable to all three occupation orders*

An application for an occupation order can be made in other family proceedings or without any other family proceedings being instituted (cl 11(2)). This addresses the long-standing concerns about injunctions in family cases that they are often desired where the applicant is unable to show a legal right or equitable interest in need of protection. It also overcomes the jurisdictional difficulty in the county court that injunctions can ordinarily only be granted in other proceedings.

If an order is sought under one clause but the court considers it has no power to make an order, it may do so under another clause if it has power according to that clause; ie it can treat the application as being under the correct clause (cl 11(3)).

*Matters applicable to cl 7 and cl 9 orders*

Where one at least of the parties is an entitled occupant, so that the order must be either under cl 7 or cl 9, cl 12 confers upon the court powers to make additional orders at the time or any time thereafter concerning repair and maintenance of the dwellinghouse, payment of rent, mortgage or other outgoings, the making of periodical payments to the party not in occupation, and the possession or use of furniture or other contents. These powers, and the matters to be taken into account in exercising them, are discussed in Chapter 7.

## *Ex parte* non-molestation and occupation orders

Clause 15(1) enables the court to make *ex parte* orders, and orders on shorter notice than provided by rules of court, where it is just and convenient to do so.

By virtue of subcl (2), the court must have regard to all the circumstances, including:

(a) any risk of significant harm to the applicant or a relevant child if the order is not made immediately,
(b) whether it is likely that the applicant will be deterred or prevented from pursuing the application if an order is not made immediately, and
(c) whether there is reason to believe that the respondent is aware of the proceedings but is deliberately evading service and that the applicant or relevant child will be seriously prejudiced by the delay involved—
  (i) where the court is a magistrates' court, in effecting service of proceedings, or
  (ii) in any other case, in effecting substituted service.

Where a court makes an *ex parte* order, it must give the respondent the opportunity to make representations relating to the order at an *inter partes* hearing 'as soon as just and convenient' (cl 15(3)).

Clause 15 introduces some legislative guidance on the making of *ex parte* orders that was clearly necessary, in view of the apparently diverging practices among county courts applying the DVA. The demand for *ex parte* injunctions increased greatly after the DVA came into force and the courts became concerned that some applications were unnecessary—*see Masich v Masich* (1977) 7 Fam Law 245 and *Ansah v Ansah* [1977] 2 All ER 919. A Practice Note was issued officially discouraging them ([1980] 2 All ER 919). In *G v G* [1990] 1 FLR 395 the Court of Appeal held that a court should only act *ex parte* in an emergency where there was real immediate danger of serious injury or irreparable harm. The new legislation will presumably make it unnecessary to return to these cases. It was also decided that it is undesirable for there to be a long period between the granting of an *ex parte* exclusion order and the return date (Sir John Donaldson MR in *Benesch v Newman* [1987] 1 FLR 262 at 264). This decision presumably continues to have effect and is underlined by cl 15(3), *above*.

## Undertakings

Clause 16 makes clear that a court may accept an undertaking from a respondent in any case where the court has the power to make an occupation or molestation order. Although a power of arrest cannot be attached to an undertaking, the courts are now prevented from accepting an undertaking in any case where a power of arrest (*see below*) would be attached to the order (cl 16(2)). This is a welcome change to the law and should ensure that undertakings are not used where a power of arrest is justified.

## Powers of arrest

*The power*

Under the DVA, a judge could attach a power of arrest to an order restraining violence and an order excluding the respondent from the home or an area within which the home was included. The judge could only do so, however, if the respondent had caused actual bodily harm to the applicant or a child living with the applicant and the judge considered that he was likely to do so again. These provisions were entirely new to family law when they were introduced. An injunction is an order of a civil court and, hitherto, only civil law enforcement agencies could take any action. Perhaps due to this novelty, the provisions were expressed restrictively by the legislature and interpreted restrictively by the judiciary (*see* pp 75–77 of the third edition of this book for further discussion). Concerns were then expressed by commentators about the need for actual bodily harm to have been caused before a power of arrest could be included in the order and about the reluctance of the courts, in some regions at least, to attach a power at all.

Clause 17(1) of the FHDVB now *requires,* and not merely allows, a court to attach a power of arrest to specified provisions in any occupation or non-molestation order unless it is satisfied that in all the circumstances of the case the applicant or relevant child will be adequately protected without such a power of arrest. If, however, the occupation or non-molestation order is made *ex parte* or on short notice there is no actual requirement, but the court *may* attach a power of arrest to specified provisions if it appears:

(a) that the respondent has used or threatened violence against the applicant or a relevant child, and
(b) that there is a risk of significant harm to the applicant or child if the power of arrest is not attached to those provisions immediately.

Where this power is used, the court may provide that the power of arrest is to have effect for a shorter period of time than the other provisions of the order (cl 17(4)).

*Powers of arrest not limited in time*

With the exception just discussed, nothing in the FHDVB limits the duration of a power of arrest, although the power obviously terminates on the expiry or revocation of the order itself. Under the DVA, as a result of the seeming burden on the police imposed by the need to retain indefinitely orders containing a power of arrest, a Practice Note was issued ([1981] 1 All ER 224). This recommended that powers of arrest should normally not last for more than three months in the first instance. That advice can presumably no longer be sustained, given that the legislation will now impose a duty to include a power of arrest unless the court is satisfied there is no need (*see above*).

*Effect of a power of arrest*

Clause 17(6) provides that where a power of arrest is attached to an order, including an *ex parte* order, a constable may arrest without warrant a person whom he has reasonable cause for suspecting to be in breach of any such provision. We saw *above* that the power must be attached to specified provisions of the order, rather than generally, and so care is necessary to ensure that there is reasonable cause to suspect breach of those provisions. It is interesting to note that although the court is now given little discretion about attaching a power of arrest when the relevant circumstances are made out, the decision whether to arrest nevertheless remains a discretionary one.

*The consequences of arrest*

The person arrested must be brought before a 'relevant judicial authority' within the period of 24 hours beginning at the time of arrest, and the relevant judicial authority may then remand him. No account is taken of Christmas Day, Good Friday or any Sunday in calculating the 24-hour period (cl 17(7)). A relevant judicial authority means a High Court judge, county court judge or justice of the peace, as the case may be, depending on which court made the order (cl 30(1)). The person arrested does not have to be brought back to the same county court or magistrates' court that made the order.

Further provisions are given in Sched 2 concerning remands in custody and on bail (cl 17(11)). The position is somewhat complicated but basically the remand is for periods of up to eight clear days at a time, renewable.

The FHDVB also contains new powers to remand for the purpose of enabling a medical examination and report to be made. If this power is exercised, the adjournment must not be for more than four weeks at a time, and if the respondent is remanded in custody the adjournment must not be for more than three weeks at a time (cl 18(1)). Furthermore, where there is reason to suspect that the respondent is suffering from mental illness or severe mental impairment, the judge or magistrate is given the same power as the Crown Court has under s 35 of the Mental Health Act 1983 to remand the accused to hospital for a report on his mental condition (cl 20).

### Where no power of arrest attached to the relevant provision

Where there is no power of arrest to the relevant provision and the applicant considers that the respondent has failed to comply with an occupation order or a non-molestation order, including one made *ex parte*, the applicant may apply to the relevant judicial authority for the issue of a warrant for the arrest of the respondent (cl 17(8)). The application must be substantiated on oath and the judge or magistrate must not issue the warrant unless there are reasonable grounds for failing to comply with the order (cl 17(9)). Once the respondent is brought before the court under the warrant, the court may remand the respondent on bail or in custody (*see above*). The judge or magistrate may also remand for a medical examination and report under cl 18(1) and (2).

The power of a High Court or county court judge to issue a warrant for arrest in respect of a breach of an injunction is a new and welcome one. Previously, tipstaffs and bailiffs were the officers used in committal proceedings.

## Orders in proceedings concerning children

There may be some circumstances in which, from the point of view of any children involved, the protection from violence or abuse offered by occupation orders will be inadequate. This is most likely to be the case where the parents' relationship is satisfactory, or at least neither wants to exclude the other from the home, but where the children are still at risk from one parent; or where the threat to the children comes from someone who is not an 'associated person' under the FHDVB, and who is therefore outside the scope of the orders available under that Bill. In such cases, there are other powers available to exclude an abusing parent or individual. These derive from CA 1989 and the High Court's inherent jurisdiction to protect children.

These powers interact with the duties of local authorities to protect children in their area, a full discussion of which is beyond the scope of this book. Nevertheless, some reference to these duties, and to the associated powers, is unavoidable, since they may affect a parent's continued occupation of the family home.

### Exclusion requirements in interim care orders and emergency protection orders

In its Report No 207, on *Domestic Violence and Occupation of the Family Home* (1992), the Law Commission thought that there were cases of child abuse in which a child would suffer more harm than good through being removed from the home, and where any threat to the child could be dealt with by removing the abuser. As the law stood at the time, there was no obvious legal means of achieving this. The Commission therefore recommended that a new power should be introduced to enable a court to make an order excluding an abuser from the child's home in certain circumstances. These powers will be introduced by the FHDVB as amendments to the CA 1989.

Under the new provisions, the power arises only where a local authority has applied for, and a court has decided to make, an interim care order or an emergency protection order (under ss 38 and 44 of the CA 1989 respectively). In such a case, the court may include an 'exclusion requirement' in the order, which is defined as any one or more of the following provisions:

(a) requiring the relevant person to leave a dwellinghouse in which he is living with the child;
(b) prohibiting the relevant person from entering a dwellinghouse in which the child lives; and
(c) excluding the relevant person from a defined area in which a dwellinghouse in which the child lives is situated (ss 38A(3) and 44A(3) of the CA 1989).

Before imposing such a requirement, the court (in addition to making an interim care or emergency protection order) must be satisfied that the following conditions exist:

(a) that if the relevant person is excluded, the child will cease to suffer, or cease to be likely to suffer, significant harm; and
(b) that another person living in the house (whether a parent or some other person) is able and willing to give the child the care which it would be reasonable to expect a parent to give and consents to the order being made (ss 38A(2) and 44A (2)).

The conditions are slightly more complex where emergency protection orders are concerned, for reasons that need not concern us here. A power of arrest can be attached to an exclusion requirement. A court may accept an undertaking from the relevant person in any case where it would have the power to include an exclusion requirement (ss 38B and 44B). A power of arrest cannot be attached to such an undertaking; but, presumably, the general provision in cl 16(2) of the FHDVB (which prevents a court accepting an undertaking in any case where a power of arrest would be attached to the order) applies in this context.

If this power is used, it will result in a situation in which the abusing parent is excluded from the home and the child is at home but may be removed at any time by the authority, under the aegis of the interim care or emergency protection order. In order to avoid the possibility of the child being removed *and* the abuser being excluded simultaneously, there is a rule that the exclusion requirement lapses if the authority exercises its powers to remove the child from the home (ss 38A(10) and 44A(10)).

**Section 8 orders**

It may be possible to frame an order under s 8 of the CA 1989 so as to have the effect of excluding an individual from the family home. The possibilities are discussed *below*. In each case, the court's paramount consideration in making the order will be the welfare of the child (s 1 of the CA 1989). Possible applicants for such an order include the parent or other primary carer of a child, or a local authority. A parent, however, will usually have the alternative of an occupation order under the FHDVB, assuming that the person to be excluded is 'associated' with the applicant in the required way. Indeed, if a case can be dealt with under the FHDVB, the courts may be reluctant to hear applications brought under the CA 1989 (in accordance with the general principle established in *Richards v Richards* [1984] 1 AC 174, that where Parliament has spelt out what must be done in a particular type of case, litigants cannot bypass the legislation so provided: per Lord Hailsham at pp 199–200). Section 8 orders, therefore, are probably best seen as a last resort, to be used only in those cases to which the FHDVB has no application.

There seem to be three ways in which s 8 orders might be used. First, a contact order could be framed as an order for 'no contact' (*see Nottinghamshire CC v P* [1993] 2 FLR 134) and made against either the custodial parent or the person whom it is sought to exclude from the home. There are, however, problems of enforcement associated with these orders, especially when made against a custodial parent who does not see the need for it. Second, a 'prohibited steps' order could be worded to have the effect of prohibiting entry by a named person into the home *(Re H* [1995] 1 FLR 638). Problems arise here too, from the rule that prohibited steps orders cannot be used to achieve the same result as a contact order (s 9(5)), the effect of which is to confine the use of prohibited steps orders to those cases where a contact order is not available (for an example, *see Re H above*). Third, a specific issue order could be used to determine where a child should live and with whom (*Pearson v Franklin* [1994] 1 FLR 246). However, this can only be done when no right of occupation would be interfered with (eg where the custodial parent is sole tenant or owner of the property in question: *see Pearson v Franklin, above*).

There is an air of contrivance surrounding the use of s 8 orders in this context, and the case law may have been driven by a desire to make good the shortcomings of the old law on ouster orders. Since the law is to be improved by the FHDVB, s 8 orders should now be seen as a last resort.

### Orders under the inherent jurisdiction

It may also be possible to exclude a parent or other individual from the home by means of an injunction granted under the High Court's inherent jurisdiction. However, in accordance with the general principle that enacted legislation should be used first (*see Richards*, *above*), there will be little need to invoke the jurisdiction. Nevertheless, there are reported cases in which local authorities (who require leave before invoking the jurisdiction: s 100(3) of the CA 1989)—but not, so far, individuals—have been granted injunctions under this head excluding an individual from a home, in spite of their extensive statutory powers to act to protect children (*see Devon CC v S* [1994] 1 FLR 355 and *Re S (Minors) (Inherent Jurisdiction: Ouster)* [1994] 1 FLR 623).

## Orders in other proceedings

In previous editions of this book there was extensive discussion of injunctions in actions for assault and battery, nuisance, trespass and possession. There was also discussion of binding over orders in the magistrates' court. In the light of the extended categories of parties that can obtain occupation and non-molestation orders, and the new circumstances and courts in which they can be obtained, it has not been thought necessary to continue with that material (*see*, however, pp 82–94 of the third edition of this book).

## Compensation for criminal injuries

Compensation for criminal injuries suffered in a domestic context can be sought if the perpetrator is convicted; *see* s 35 of the Powers of the Criminal Courts Act 1973. There may also be compensation available under the Criminal Injuries Compensation Scheme. At the time of writing, the status of the Scheme is in some doubt. Although the Scheme was put on a statutory footing by ss 108–117 of the Criminal Justice Act 1988, those provisions were not brought into force. Instead a revised Scheme was issued under the Royal Prerogative. The validity of the exercise of the prerogative has been challenged and a decision is awaited from the House of Lords.

## Chapter 7

# Occupation of the Home

This chapter deals with the methods by which disputes over occupation of the home may be decided. Whilst it assumes that the relationship has broken down, a cohabitant who is interested in her legal position during the continuance of the relationship can still be advised about the remedies discussed here and also the methods of protecting a beneficial interest in the home discussed in Chapter 8.

The Family Homes and Domestic Violence Bill (FHDVB) will introduce some coherence into a previously chaotic area of law, in that it has created the beginnings of a statutory code regulating occupation of the family home. Nevertheless, the FHDVB is by no means exhaustive: there remain a patchwork of other remedies available to protect occupation and there are undoubtedly situations where a cohabitant is in a very much less secure position than a spouse.

The five principal ways in which a cohabitant who is not solely and beneficially entitled to the property might remain in occupation are:

(a) by obtaining an occupation order under the FHDVB;
(b) by seeking an order transferring the tenancy;
(c) by making use of landlord and tenant law;
(d) by establishing a licence to occupy; or
(e) by establishing a beneficial interest in the proceeds of sale.

## Occupation orders

A cohabitant may be able to remain in occupation if she obtains an occupation order under the FHDVB. The Bill was discussed fully in Chapter 6. Proof of violence is not strictly a condition precedent to the grant of such an order but it is, of course, potent evidence. The court should decide the matter by taking into account the circumstances referred to in cll 7 and 9 of the FHDVB. Such an order may, but need not, exclude the other partner from the home (cl 7(2); cl 9(3)).

An occupation order under cl 7 (ie in favour of a cohabitant who already has an entitlement to occupy) may be made for a specified period or last until a specified event or further order. An occupation order under cl 9 (ie in favour of a cohabitant who has no entitlement to occupy) can only be made for periods of up to six months at a time (cl 9(8)). A cohabitant who has a beneficial interest but no legal estate may choose to apply under either section (cl 9(9)).

**Tenancy in the respondent's sole name**

It is assumed under this subheading that the home to which the occupation order relates is held on a periodic tenancy, or a fixed term tenancy with no material sale value, vested in the sole name of the respondent. A major potential problem for the applicant here is agreement between the respondent and the landlord. The respondent can give notice to quit or surrender the tenancy and the landlord can then obtain possession against the woman and grant a new tenancy to the respondent (*see* further, *below*).

*Respondent giving notice to quit or surrendering tenancy*

If the applicant obtains an occupation order against the tenant under cl 9 of the FHDVB permitting her to enter and remain in the home, then it is possible that a notice to quit or surrender by the tenant would be a breach of the order because it would interfere with the right of occupation conferred by the order. This is particularly so if the order is one under cl 9(2)(*b*) (ie where the applicant is not in occupation on the date of the order), because such an order requires the tenant to permit the applicant to exercise her right to occupy. It is less obviously the case where the applicant is already in occupation and the order is therefore made under cl 9(2)(*a*), since such an order merely restrains the tenant from 'evicting or excluding' the applicant during the period of the order. Any cl 9 order *must* contain one of the orders in cl 9(2).

The argument that the respondent's notice to quit is a breach of an occupation order was strengthened by a recent decision of the Court of Appeal in *London Borough of Harrow v Johnstone* [1995] *New Property Cases* 47. The majority of the court seems to have held that a notice by a non-occupying joint tenant was a breach of an order against her which prohibited her (whether by herself or by instructing or encouraging any other person) from excluding the other joint tenant. It does not appear to have been material in this case that the parties were joint tenants.

If there is only a non-molestation order, it is possible that a notice to quit or a surrender by the respondent would also be a breach of that order. This is more likely to be the case where the respondent has already found a permanent place to live and appears only to be interested in causing as much distress to the applicant as possible. It is quite possible, however, that the respondent is motivated more by a concern to terminate his liability under the lease or tenancy agreement.

Even if, in the circumstances, the respondent is in breach of the order by determining the tenancy, this may not help the applicant unless perhaps the landlord knew the full facts. The applicant might be advised to produce the court order to the landlord so as to try to fix him with sufficient notice to put him in contempt of court if he co-operates with the respondent. This may only have advantage if the tenancy is for a fixed term and therefore requiring the landlord's agreement to a surrender. At the same time, however, by informing the landlord one is also alerting him to the possibility of obtaining possession of the property (on the grounds that the tenant has gone out of possession) without the help of the respondent: although, as we shall see under the next heading, there are limits to the landlord's ability to obtain possession on this ground where an occupation order is in force. The Court of Appeal's decision in *London Borough of Harrow v Johnstone* (*above*), where the parties were joint tenants, suggests that a landlord (in that case a local authority) may be abusing the process of the court by seeking possession where the occupier was protected by an occupation order. However, the injunction in that case was worded specifically to prevent the departing tenant from serving a notice to quit whereas, as we have seen, an occupation order is not always so worded.

*Landlord taking possession proceedings*

Where an occupation order has been made under cl 9 of the FHDVB (ie in favour of an applicant who is not the tenant), the occupation of the applicant shall be treated, for the purposes of the Rent Act 1977, as occupation by the tenant as the tenant's residence; and, for the purposes of the Housing Act 1985 and Pt 1 of the Housing Act 1988, occupation of the house by the applicant as her only or principal home is treated as occupation by the tenant as his only or principal home (cl 4(3) and cl 9(10)). In other words, a cl 9 order protects the successful applicant from possession proceedings brought by the landlord on the ground that the tenant has gone out of possession.

### Tenancy in joint names

Where both parties are tenants, then an application for an occupation order may be made only under cl 7. Thereafter, much depends on whether the tenancy is a public or private sector tenancy and, in turn, whether a private sector tenancy falls within the Rent Act 1977 or the Housing Act 1988. The efficacy of a notice to quit by one of them is particularly relevant. These matters are all discussed in more detail *below*. The implications of *LB of Harrow v Johnstone* (discussed *above*) should also be noted.

**Respondent is sole beneficial owner**

If the home is freehold or long leasehold and vested solely and beneficially in the respondent, then the applicant will have difficulty in preventing a disposition of the property, such as a sale. Although a cl 9 occupation order may confer some of the the 'matrimonial home rights' on a successful applicant (cl 9(10)), these will not include the power to protect the statutory rights by a Class F land charge or a notice under the Land Registration Act 1925.

Again, it may be possible to argue that the disposition of the property amounts to a breach of the occupation order. In view of the importance attached to property rights under the old DVA 1976 (eg by the two Court of Appeal benches in *B v B* [1978] 1 All ER 821 and *Cantliff v Jenkins* [1978] 1 All ER 836) there is less likelihood that the argument would succeed when the respondent has invested purchase money in the property than in the case of periodic tenancies discussed *above*.

A practical obstacle to the sale of the property during the life of the order will, of course, be the actual presence of the applicant in the property. The respondent might not be able to convince a prospective purchaser that he can give vacant possession on completion. If the disposition is a mortgage, however, then her presence might not be such a deterrent. Lenders are now wary of taking security when third parties are known to be occupying but banks do sometimes lend on a second charge after making only perfunctory inquiries. If the woman has no rights in the land, and we are assuming here that she does not, then she has nothing to attract the protection of s 70(1)(*g*) of the Land Registration Act 1925 (giving an overriding interest) or the doctrine of constructive notice (where the title is not registered) (*see*, further, Chapter 8).

However, an occupation order under cl 9 (but not cl 7) may confer some protection in these circumstances because, for so long as the order is in force, any mortgage payments made by the applicant shall be as good as if made by the respondent (cl 4(2) and cl 9(10), discussed further *below*). Although the mortgagee is not obliged to accept such payments, the mortgagee cannot complain if a payment or tender is properly made by the applicant. Further, an applicant in these circumstances will be able to apply to be made a party to any action brought by the mortgagee to enforce the security, provided that the court does not see any special reason against it and is satisfied that the applicant's chances of making the payments are sufficiently good to affect the outcome of the proceedings or at least ought to be considered under s 36 of the AJA 1970, (s 23(3)). This means that the applicant is not vulnerable to a mortgagee where the man defaults on the loan repayments, provided of course that the applicant has the means to meet mortgage repayments herself. In this respect, an occupation order confers protection not just from another partner, but from a third party lender. This further underlines the importance of seeking the protection conferred by an occupation order as quickly as possible.

When an order expires, the respondent is free to sue for possession and he will be successful unless the applicant can show she has a right to remain there by virtue of a licence (*see below*).

## Beneficial ownership held jointly

Where beneficial ownership is held jointly the woman is in a stronger position. The respondent will presumably not be able to obtain an order for sale under s 30 of the Law of Property Act 1925 (LPA 1925) while the occupation order is in force as this would be tantamount to one court defeating the order of another. The principles on which applications under s 30 should be decided are discussed *below*. If the applicant shares the beneficial ownership in the home but is not a joint tenant of the legal estate, then she should consider whether it is necessary to protect her beneficial interest in the manner described in Chapter 8. Such an applicant would have the choice of seeking an occupation order under cl 7 or cl 9 (cl 9(9)).

## Payment of outgoings

The FHDVB confers a comprehensive jurisdiction on the courts to regulate payment of outgoings while an occupation order is in force. Under cl 12, a court may, on making an occupation order under cll 7 or 9, or at any time thereafter, impose on either party obligations as to the repair and maintenance of the house or as to the discharge of rent, mortgage or other payments or outgoings. A court may also order a party occupying the house to make payments to the other party in respect of the accommodation, but only where the other party would (but for the order) be entitled to occupy the house by virtue of a beneficial estate or interest, a contract or statutory right of occupation. A court may also grant either party possession or use of furniture or other house contents and may order either party to take reasonable care of furniture or other house contents and to take reasonable steps to keep them secure. In exercising its powers, the court must have regard to all the circumstances of the case, including the parties' financial needs and financial resources and their existing or foreseeable financial obligations to each other and to any relevant child.

While these powers regulate obligations with respect to outgoings as between the parties, they do not by themselves deal with the position *vis-à-vis* a third party, such as a landlord or mortgagee. This is dealt with, in a roundabout way, by cl 9(10) which states that so long as a cl 9 order is in force, any person granted the right to occupy (or not to be evicted) by virtue of the order shall be entitled to the protection conferred on spouses by cl 4(2)–(5) of the Bill. In effect, for these purposes only, a person in whose favour a cl 9 order has been made is treated as if he or she were a spouse entitled to the rights against third parties conferred by cl 4(2)–(5), and their partner shall be treated as if he or she were the other spouse. The effect of cl 4(3) has already been considered.

Under cl 4(2), any payments of rent, mortgage instalments or other outgoings (whether or not made in pursuance of a cl 12 order) made by the applicant shall 'be as good as if made by' the other party. The effect of this is presumably to prevent a landlord or mortgagee from seeking possession where payments of rent or mortgage instalments are made by the applicant rather than the tenant or borrower, thereby enhancing the applicant's occupational protection (assuming the means to pay).

In the case of mortgage repayments, cl 4(4) states that a lender may treat payments made by the applicant as having been made by the other partner (ie the original borrower). A lender who elects not to do so would not be able to take possession proceedings against an applicant who was able and willing to pay (cl 4(2)). Either way, the subsection makes it clear that, whatever the lender decides, the decision shall not affect the parties' entitlements under the law of trusts (discussed in Chapter 8).

## Transfer of tenancies

An occupation order offers a degree of immediate occupational protection. We have seen, however, that there are limits to the protection it provides, especially where the respondent is a sole tenant of the property in question; and even where the parties are joint tenants, we shall see later that recent case law developments have increased the vulnerability of one joint tenant to the other's notice to quit (eg *Hammersmith and Fulham LBC v Monk* [1991] 3 WLR 1144, discussed *below*). In such cases, a successful applicant for an occupation order would be well advised to make an immediate application for a transfer of the tenancy into her (sole) name. There are now two statutory routes open to cohabitants for this purpose: under the FHDVB and Sched 1 to the CA 1989.

## Transfers of tenancies between cohabitants under the FHDVB 1995

As we shall see in the next section, the position of cohabitants with respect to rented property at the end of a relationship depends on a variety of factors, such as the willingness of a departing partner to co-operate in maintaining the applicant's occupancy of the premises, or (in the case of the public sector) the ability of a joint periodic tenant to collude with a housing authority in bringing the tenancy to an end and securing a new grant of accommodation elsewhere. Further, the powers available under Sched 1 to the CA 1989 (discussed later) offer only a contrived solution to the problem of tenancies: they are, in theory at least, available only to ensure proper provision by parents for children and not to ensure justice between parents themselves.

It was this unsatisfactory state of affairs that prompted the Law Commission (in Report No 207, *Domestic Violence and Occupation of the Family Home*) to recommend the extension of the court's powers to transfer tenancies between spouses (under Sched 1 to the MHA 1983) to include transfers between former cohabitants. This is now enshrined in Sched 4 to the FHDVB. There is no comparable power to transfer *freehold or long* leasehold property between cohabitants, save for those available under Sched 1 to the CA 1989, discussed later in this chapter and in more detail in Chapter 10. Some may question why tenant cohabitants should be singled out for special treatment in this way.

We shall see from what follows that the power to transfer tenancies arises quite independently of any issue of domestic violence. Instead, the court is given a wide discretion to transfer tenancies, triggered only by cessation of the parties' cohabitation.

The power applies to any 'relevant tenancy', that is, a protected or statutory tenancy under the Rent Act 1977, a secure tenancy within the meaning of s 79 of the HA 1985 or an assured tenancy within Pt 1 of the HA 1988. It also applies to certain agricultural tenancies (para 1). Subject to conditions to be discussed, the power is exercisable at any time after the cohabitants have ceased to live together (para 3). The conditions are that:

(a) one cohabitant is entitled, either in his own right or jointly with the other, to occupy a house under a relevant tenancy; and

(b) the house in question is a home in which they lived together as husband and wife (paras 3 and 4).

The effect of an order is to transfer the tenancy to the other cohabitant subject to all covenants, obligations, liabilities and incumbrances and to any covenant of indemnity executed on an earlier assignment of the tenancy (para 7).

If the transferor is a successor under the relevant provisions of the Housing Acts 1985 and 1988, then the transferee will be deemed also to be a successor (para 7(3) and (4)). In the case of a Rent Act statutory tenancy, the effect of an order will be to substitute the transferee for the transferor as the statutory tenant (para 8(1)).

In deciding whether to exercise this power, the court must have regard to 'all the circumstances of the case', including:

(a) the circumstances in which the tenancy was granted or, as the case may be, the circumstances under which either or both cohabitants became tenants (intended by the Law Commission to mirror the 'underlying purpose' reasoning found in cases arising under s 30 of the LPA 1925: *see below*);
(b) the respective suitability of the parties as tenants; and
(c) the factors contained in cl 7(5)(*a*),(*b*) and (*c*), that is: the housing needs and resources of the parties and of any relevant child; the parties' financial resources; and the likely effect of any order, or of any decision not to make an order, on the health, safety and well-being of the parties and of any relevant child.

In addition, where the applicant is 'non-entitled' (ie is not a co-tenant of the property), the court must also consider the criteria in cl 9(4)(*a*) and (*b*) FHDVB (ie some, but not all, of the criteria that apply to an application by a non-entitled applicant for an occupation order under cl 9 of the FHDVB, also discussed in the previous chapter): that is, the nature and length of the parties' relationship, whether there are children of the parties or for whom both have parental responsibility and the length of time that has elapsed since they ceased to live together.

If, at the end of this rather cumbersome process of reasoning, the court decides to order a transfer of the tenancy, it may direct that the transferee make payments to the transferor (para 10). The purpose of these payments is to compensate the transferor for loss of the tenancy, and the court is directed to have regard to all the circumstances, including:

(a) the financial loss that would otherwise be suffered by the transferor as a result of the order;
(b) the parties' needs and financial resources; and
(c) the parties' financial obligations (including obligations to each other and to any relevant child).

If immediate payment of the sum ordered would cause the transferee financial hardship, then the court has power to direct that the sum ordered shall be paid at a later date or in instalments, but only if the hardship to the transferee arising from making immediate payment in full would be greater than the hardship flowing to the transferor from making such a direction (paras 10(2) and (5)).

As noted *above*, the purpose is to compensate the transferor for the loss of the tenancy, but it is unclear how this loss might be calculated, especially where the tenancy has no market value. The Law Commission suggested that compensation might be appropriate for loss of an accrued 'right to buy', or for removal expenses and the payment of a deposit for new accommodation in the private sector (Report No 207, paras 6.10–11).

The effect of a transfer is to terminate the transferor's liabilities and obligations under the lease or tenancy from the date of the order (para 7(2)). This means that the landlord cannot look to the original tenant for rent (but the landlord will have the right to be heard by the court before an order is made: para 14(1); and we have seen that the court is specifically directed to consider the transferee's suitability as tenant). There is also a power to make orders apportioning liabilities between the parties in respect of the house that have accrued before the date of the order (para 11).

### Orders under Sched 1 to the Children Act 1989

Another route is to seek a transfer of the tenancy under Sched 1 to the CA 1989. The Sched 1 powers are discussed in more detail in Chapter 10. Provided there are children, the parent with care of them may seek to have a tenancy transferred by the court into her name, in exercise of its power to make orders against a parent transferring property to or 'for the benefit of' children (para 1(2)(*e*)). This would give the caring parent an exclusive right to occupy the home. The need to rely on Sched 1 for these purposes will be much reduced in view of Sched 4 to the FHDVB, but there may be some cases where Sched 4 may not be available—for example, where the parties are still cohabiting.

It has been held that an order transferring a tenancy from joint names into the woman's sole name is a proper exercise of this power, since it is no objection that the property is not transferred directly to the children, nor that someone else (ie the caring parent) benefits from the transfer (*K v K (Minors: Property Transfer)* [1992] 2 FLR 220). If the purpose of the transfer is to provide a home for the children, that will be for their 'benefit'. Indeed, it has been suggested that 'the right to apply [under

Sched 1] for the transfer ... of the [tenancy] is the effective remedy for a parent who has not married and who needs the only available home to enable him or her to care for child or children after the final separation of the couple' (per Thorpe J in *Pearson v Franklin* [1994] 1 FLR 246). However, an order can only be made against someone who is a 'parent' of the children for whose benefit the transfer is sought (which does not include a step-father who is not married to the mother: *J v J* [1993] 2 FLR 56).

When considering applications under Sched 1, the welfare principle is not the court's sole consideration. Instead, the court must apply the statutory checklist contained in Sched 1 itself (para 4: *see* Chapter 10). This means that factors such as the father's accumulated entitlement under 'right to buy' legislation, as well as his ability to house himself elsewhere, will be taken into account (*K v K, above*).

Although the point has yet to be taken in a reported case, there are potential difficulties with transferring tenancies in this way, stemming from the limited assignability of secure tenancies under the HA 1985 (the tenancies thought most likely to be affected by this sort of court order). A court order under Sched 1 is not specifically stated to be an exception to the rule that secure tenancies are non-assignable (s 91(1) of the HA 1985), although it may come within s 91(1)(*c*) as an assignment to someone who would qualify under the succession provisions (discussed earlier) had the tenant died immediately before the assignment. It was difficulties of this sort, amongst others, that prompted the Law Commission to propose a wider power to transfer tenancies between cohabitants, discussed earlier.

There may also be some doubt as to whether a tenancy counts as 'property' for these purposes. In the divorce court, the view has been that neither statutory tenancies under the Rent Acts nor public sector tenancies count as 'property' for the purposes of the MCA 1973 and cannot therefore be transferred. There is no reason why the same should not apply to Sched 1 to the CA 1989, which is drafted in very similar terms. Similarly, the divorce court has traditionally been reluctant to order a transfer of a tenancy where there is a covenant against assignment without the landlord's consent (*see Thompson* [1976] Fam 25; *Hale* [1975] 2 All ER 1090; *Regan* [1977] 1 All ER 428). These problems do not arise under Sched 4 to the FHDVA 1995.

## Landlord and tenant law

The previous sections have touched on some of the principles of landlord and tenant law in so far as they are affected by the existence of an occupation order. These principles are now explored in more detail to see how they apply irrespective of an occupation order. Private and public sector tenancies are dealt with separately, although recent changes to housing law have introduced much greater uniformity between the two.

## Private sector tenancies

As a result of s 34 of the Housing Act 1988 (HA 1988) no tenancy created on or after 15 January 1989 can be a protected tenancy under the Rent Act 1977 (RA 1977) except in limited circumstances (eg a contract was made for the tenancy before that date or the tenancy is granted to an existing protected tenant). In addition, the Rent Act was amended by the HA 1988 so that the nature of the protection has been changed. Because a large number of tenancies will remain governed by the Rent Act for many years to come, these are dealt with first under a separate subheading.

### *Tenancies created before 15 January 1989*

The basic structure of the Rent Act's security of tenure provisions is that a tenancy within Pt I of the Act is a protected tenancy where a dwellinghouse is let as a separate dwelling (s 1). On the determination of the contractual tenancy, a so-called statutory tenancy comes into effect so that the tenant is protected if and so long as he occupies the dwellinghouse as his residence (s 2(1)). One important consequence of this is that a court cannot make a possession order against him except as provided by s 98 and Sched 15.

If the tenancy is vested in the parties' joint names and the woman remains in the property after separation then the position is relatively free of difficulty. The man may wish to determine his liability under the tenancy by serving a notice to quit (which he may do unilaterally in the case of a periodic tenancy: *Hammersmith and Fulham LBC v Monk* [1991] 3 WLR 1242). The woman will then remain there as the sole statutory tenant (*Lloyd v Sadler* [1978] 2 All ER 529). Alternatively, the woman may wish to prevent the man from returning and *she* can serve notice to quit, thereby triggering a statutory tenancy. He loses his security of tenure provided he no longer occupies the dwellinghouse as his residence but she then exposes herself to a discretionary (although narrow) ground for possession by the landlord under Case 5, Sched 15. Loss of protection under the Rent Act through absence can often be a difficult issue to determine and we will see *below* that it is possible to be deemed to be occupying although physically absent. On the other hand, if the woman is not disadvantaged by the change in her status from contractual to statutory tenant, there may be something to be gained from serving notice to quit and putting the onus on the man to establish his continued occupation in the event of him deciding to return.

In the case of a fixed term tenancy, a tenancy vested in joint names can only be surrendered by joint tenants acting together (*Leek and Moorlands BS v Clark* [1952] 2 QB 788). Where the tenancy is in the sole name of the departing man, he may try to surrender the tenancy to the landlord unilaterally. Can he do so? In *Colin Smith v Ridge* [1975] 1 All ER 290 the defendant lived with the sole tenant and had two children by him. When the tenant left, the landlord company wished to seek possession and the tenant assisted by executing a deed of surrender. The question turned on whether the tenant was in occupation *through the defendant* and whether he was able to surrender the tenancy in these circumstances. In a previous case the Court of Appeal had been asked to decide whether the tenant, whilst in prison, had remained in possession through his 'mistress' who had lived in the home during some of his absence (*Brown v Brash* [1948] 1 All ER 922). It had been held that to remain in possession whilst physically absent there must be an intention to return ('*animus possidendi*') and some 'visible state of affairs in which the animus possidendi finds expression' ('*corpus possessionis*'). It was said that the longer the tenant was away the harder it became for him to establish these. In addition, the Court of Appeal had held in *Thompson v Ward* [1953] 1 All ER 1169 that the *corpus possessionis*, again a 'mistress', had to be installed *with the function of preserving the premises for his ultimate homecoming*. It would appear therefore that the woman in *Colin Smith v Ridge* had no hope because these conditions were clearly not satisfied.

Counsel argued, however, that whilst these requirements were lacking, a cohabitant could now rely on a series of cases which had held that a *married* tenant was unable to give up actual possession whilst his wife remained there because he was under a duty to provide a roof over her head (*see* eg *Middleton v Baldock* [1950] 1 All ER 708). Counsel argued that 'in these days possession by a mistress who has borne children to the protected tenant is analogous to possession by a wife' (Cairns LJ at 293c). (It will be recalled that spouses do not now need this protection at common law because they are usually better protected by the FHDVA 1995; for an illustration, *see Hoggett v Hoggett* (1979) 39 P&CR 121.)

The Court of Appeal rejected the argument. Lawton LJ said (at 293g):

> 'She was not his wife, so she did not enjoy the special position recognised by the common law for wives; she was his lodger ... He was under no legal obligation towards her.'

*Colin Smith v Ridge* must represent the current law regarding cohabitants. Nevertheless, it might be open to a future Court of Appeal, and it is certainly open to the House of Lords, to hold that some form of occupation duty is owed to a former cohabitant with children and that the reasoning in the case should not be followed.

If there has been no express surrender by the man, a landlord may alternatively argue that the man's departure amounts to a surrender by operation of law. For this to occur, there must be unequivocal conduct which is inconsistent with the continuance of the tenancy. In *Chamberlain v Scalley* (1994) 26 HLR 26, for example, a departing cohabitant (the sole tenant, in this case a woman) was held not to have surrendered her tenancy by unequivocal conduct because she had left most of her possessions in the tenanted premises, including two pet cats, and had not ruled out the possibility of a reconciliation with the man left behind. She had also made it clear in her affidavit that she had no wish to deprive the man of his home.

*Statutory succession on death*

Ironically, perhaps, a former cohabitant may be better off if the sole tenant with whom she was living has died. The first matter to be considered is the nature of the tenancy at the date of death. If the tenancy was contractual then it vests in the personal representatives of the deceased. If the cohabitant is the beneficiary of the tenancy under the will she will remain in the property as the tenant's successor in title. She is then a protected tenant under the Rent Act and the phasing out of protection under the Act by the HA 1988 does not appear to have affected this situation. If she is not in occupation, she should consider moving in before the landlord determines the tenancy (and he could presumably do this by serving notice to quit on the President of the Family Division if a grant of probate has not been taken out in respect of the estate).

If the surviving cohabitant is not the beneficiary of the protected tenancy but she is in occupation then she may qualify as a statutory successor under s 2(1)(*b*) of and Sched 1, para 3 to the Rent Act 1977, as amended. Prior to the HA 1988, these provisions allowed for the succession of the statutory tenancy to a 'person who was a member of the original tenant's family ... residing with him at the time of and for the period of six months immediately before his death'. This wording, without significant alteration, had been used in rent restriction legislation since 1920, although two statutory successions subsequently became possible (Sched 1, para 7). Section 39 of the HA 1988 has now amended the rules on statutory succession in the case of deaths on or after 15 January 1989. The rules are complex and the description here is only meant to be sufficient to cover the position where the sole tenant, not himself a statutory successor, has died.

Under the new rules, if the first succession is to a spouse then the successor will remain fully protected under the Rent Act. Most importantly, 'spouse' is now defined to include 'a person who was living with the original tenant as his or her wife or husband' (para 2 of Sched 4 to the HA 1988, amending Sched 1 to the RA 1977). This means that the cohabitant no longer has to come within the category 'member of the tenant's family' and so she does not have to satisfy the residence period (now extended from six months to two years), provided that they were living together immediately before the tenant's death.

There is a body of case law on statutory succession by cohabitants under the old provisions. This case law may remain relevant to the current provisions but it should now be easier to qualify. The old cases concerning whether a cohabitant was a member of the deceased's family invoked various policy considerations, however veiled, about the recognition of unmarried cohabitation as a kind of family. Now that the legislature has expressly provided that marriage-like cohabitants are to be included within the definition of spouse, the policy hurdles presumably no longer apply. Case law on the cohabitation rule in social security (Chapter 3) and on the DVA 1976, now FHDVB (Chapter 6), will also be relevant. For these reasons, a briefer treatment of the case law on the old Rent Act provisions is now possible.

Over time it became progressively easy for a cohabitant to show that she had been a member of the deceased tenant's family. Whilst in *Gammans v Ekins* [1950] 2 All ER 140 it was possible for Asquith LJ to say that he regarded such a construction of the statute as 'an abuse of the English language' (at 142a) and that it would be anomalous if 'a person can acquire the status of irremoveability by having lived in sin' (at 141h), three years later the Court of Appeal in *Hawes v Evenden* [1953] 2 All ER 737 held that there was a family. The difference between the two cases was thought to be that in the second case the parties had had children. In *Dyson Holdings v Fox* [1975] 3 All ER 1030, however, there were no children but the Court of Appeal held that the woman who had lived with the tenant from 1940 until his death in 1961 had been a member of his family. The process was not uniform and, even with relationships of many years' duration, the courts seemed still to look for signs of (what the judges regarded as) marriage-like behaviour. In *Helby v Rafferty* [1978] 3 All ER 1016, for example, the woman (who was the tenant) had not adopted the man's name and the couple had not encouraged people to regard them as members of a family. According to Stamp LJ (at 1022j): 'Marriage is essentially a public status, which can however be assumed by a couple without the formalities by "living as man and wife". In the present case there is no evidence that such status enjoyed any public recognition … '

Furthermore, there was evidence that the deceased had not wanted to marry R 'because she wished to retain a certain amount of independence and freedom'. It therefore appeared to the trial judge 'to follow inevitably that she was deliberately choosing to avoid permanence in the relationship' (at 1023e) and permanence was, apparently, essential (Roskill LJ at 1024g).

*Helby v Rafferty* is probably out of line with recent decisions (*see Watson v Lucas* [1980] 3 All ER 647, CA and *Chios Property Investment Co Ltd v Lopez* (1987) 20 HLR 120, CA). Whilst it must be true that the longer the relationship then the more likely that there will be a finding of marriage-like cohabitation, and it must also be true that the presence of children will strengthen the claim, there are no actual rules about common names, holding out or requisite intention. Presumably also, the judges must recognise that patterns of behaviour in marriage itself change over time and this recognition will be reflected in the way they approach the question of quasi-marriage.

Absence by the tenant from the property, perhaps because of illness, may mean, on the facts, that the necessary co-residence did not exist 'immediately' before the death (*Gasking & Co v Evans*, unreported, CAT 922, 14 October 1980; [1982] CLY 701). On the other hand, it seems that the tenant's intention is crucial. If the tenant, although absent, intended to return to the property and resume living there with the survivor then that may be sufficient (*Hedgedale v Hards* (1991) 23 HLR 158, CA).

*Tenancies created on or after 15 January 1989*

As a general rule these will be assured tenancies under the new provisions in Chap I, Pt I of the HA 1988. (Assured shorthold tenancies under Chap II are not considered here.)

In most respects for present purposes, assured tenancies in the private sector are similar to secure tenancies granted by local authorities. In particular the procedures for terminating an assured tenancy are similar to those for a secured tenancy, and the possibility of one joint tenant giving effectual notice to quit exists. To avoid duplication, therefore, the reader is referred to the discussion of public sector tenancies *below*. One difference should be noted, however. Section 17 of the HA 1988 provides for succession by an assured tenant's spouse on death if he or she was occupying the dwellinghouse as his or her only or principal home immediately before the death. In line with the amended provisions in the Rent Act, 'spouse' is defined to include a person living with the deceased as his or her spouse (s 17(4)). This differs from the position with secure tenancies where a cohabitant must come within the category of a member of the deceased's family and, as will be seen *below*, a minimum residence period therefore applies.

**Public sector tenancies**

The security of tenure legislation relating to public sector tenancies is now contained in ss 79–117 of the HA 1985, as amended by the HA 1988. A secure tenancy arises where the landlord condition in s 80 and the tenant condition in s 81 are satisfied. Broadly, the landlord condition is satisfied if the landlord is a local authority, a new town corporation, a housing action trust, an urban development corporation or the Development Board of Rural Wales. The tenant condition is satisfied if the tenant is an individual and occupies the dwellinghouse as his only or principal home; or, where the tenancy is a joint tenancy, if each of the joint tenants is an individual and at least one of them occupies the dwellinghouse as his only or principal home.

The nature of the security of tenure is different from that given to old protected tenancies under the Rent Act. Section 79 provides that where in a tenancy under which a dwellinghouse is let as a separate dwelling the landlord condition and the tenant condition both are satisfied then the tenancy is a secure tenancy. Excepted from the section are certain tenancies within Sched 1 to the Act, tenancies that cease to be secure after the death of the tenant and tenancies that cease to be secure in consequence of assignment or subletting.

Section 82 describes the nature of the security. Briefly, a secure tenancy that is either a weekly (or other periodic) tenancy or a tenancy for a term certain but subject to determination by the landlord, cannot be brought to an end by the landlord except by obtaining an order of the court. Section 83 prescribes the form of notice that the landlord must serve upon the secure tenant before commencing proceedings for possession and s 84 contains or refers to the grounds on which the court may order possession.

The security of tenure provisions here work differently from the old Rent Act protection of private sector tenancies because they regulate the method of terminating the contractual tenancy rather than creating a different form of tenancy to come into operation on the determination of the contractual one. Thus, many of the private sector problems of notice to quit, mesne profits and status of the tenant are avoided. The consequence of the secure tenancy provisions for some cohabitants may, however, have been adverse. Prior to the HA 1980 (which introduced secure tenancies), local authorities took what many regarded as a sympathetic and practical approach to family breakdown. They tended to require the production of a court order, usually a custody order, terminated the tenancy of the non-custodian party and granted a new tenancy to the custodian. Subject to what is said *below*, this is no longer possible, but the position of a cohabitant with children may be protected by a transfer of the tenancy under either Sched 4 to the FHDVB or under Sched 1 to the CA 1989 (both discussed earlier).

*Secure tenancy in man's sole name*

As with private sector tenancies, if the tenancy is in the man's sole name then the woman is in a difficult position unless the tenant is prepared to co-operate. If they can come to an agreement then an assignment of the tenancy should be considered. By virtue of s 91(1) a secure tenancy that is a periodic tenancy or a tenancy for a term certain granted on or after 5 November 1982 is not capable of being assigned except in the cases mentioned in subs (3). The relevant exception in that subsection is para (c): an assignment to a person who would be qualified to succeed the tenant if the tenant died immediately before the assignment. We look at succession on death below but at this stage it is enough to say that many cohabitants would qualify.

Section 91(3) only says which secure tenancies are *capable* of assignment. There may, however, be an express provision in the tenancy agreement prohibiting assignment. The effect of an assignment in breach is to make the assignee vulnerable to possession proceedings on the ground of breach of the tenancy under Sched 2 Ground 1, but at least the landlord would have to prove reasonableness.

An alternative to assignment is a surrender of the tenancy by the man to the local authority. This should only be considered where the authority is prepared to grant a fresh tenancy to the woman alone.

If the tenant will not agree to assign the secure tenancy then the woman's only course is either to obtain an occupation order, or a series of occupation orders, under cl 9 of the FHDVB, or to seek a transfer of the tenancy itself (*see above*). The purpose of an occupation order would be to seek to ensure that the man can no longer be said to be occupying the dwellinghouse as his only or principal home (*see above*). The landlord could then serve a notice under s 83 of the HA 1985 and take possession proceedings in the normal way. The tenancy is no longer a secure tenancy and the court would have no discretion in the matter. However, a transfer is probably a more reliable means to the same end.

*Secure tenancy in joint names*

If the parties are *joint* secure tenants then the woman's position may be stronger. If the other party is prepared to co-operate then he may release his interest to the occupier. If not, then a strategy involving notice to quit should be considered, provided of course that the housing authority has been consulted in advance about either granting a new tenancy or re-housing elsewhere.

At common law a joint periodic tenancy can be determined by notice to quit given by one joint tenant acting alone unless there is a provision to the contrary in the tenancy agreement. This rule was applied to secure tenancies by the House of Lords in *Hammersmith and Fulham LBC v Monk* [1991] 3 WLR 1144, a case involving unmarried joint periodic tenants. Here, a woman gave a local authority landlord notice to quit in respect of a secure tenancy, having arranged with the authority to be rehoused elsewhere. The House of Lords held that the notice to quit was valid and brought the tenancy to an end. The authority was granted possession against the man.

This is a convenient rule for housing authorities who wish to manage their housing stock more effectively, and it offers women the opportunity to trade one council tenancy for another: but what is sauce for the goose is also sauce for the gander, and the decision opens up the possibility of a departing male joint periodic tenant pulling the rug from under a woman partner before she has had the opportunity to apply for a transfer of the tenancy under Sched 4 or for an occupation order. If made homeless, a woman may not fall into the category of priority need for rehousing purposes (*see* Chapter 5).

The notice to quit must be an 'appropriate' and effective one, that is, it must give the period of notice required either at common law or by the terms of the agreement. *Monk* was distinguished on this ground in *Hounslow LBC v Pilling* [1993] 1 WLR 1242. Here, an unmarried couple had a joint periodic secure tenancy, under an agreement that obliged the tenants to give the landlord four weeks' written notice, 'or such lesser period as the council may accept when the tenant wishes to end the tenancy'. The woman gave a unilateral notice to quit which, relying on this clause, the council accepted three days after it was given and then sought possession from the man. It was held that three days' notice was insufficient to terminate a weekly tenancy. The relevant provision was construed as a break clause which, on general principles, can only be operated by joint tenants acting together.

It was also held in *Pilling* that s 5(1) of the Protection from Eviction Act 1977 applied to a notice to quit given by a tenant. This, amongst other things, requires a notice to quit to be given not less than four weeks before the date on which it is to take effect. Although the statutory protection can be disapplied by agreement between landlord and tenant, it was held that it could not be disapplied by agreement between a landlord and only one of two joint tenants.

Secure periodic tenancies are conceptually different from protected tenancies and no statutory form of tenancy comes into operation on their termination. The landlord therefore has the right to seek possession at the expiry of the notice. A fresh tenancy can be granted in the woman's sole name and no doubt the local authority would approach the matter in the same way as it did prior to the introduction of security of tenure. If the man refuses to leave then the woman can take possession proceedings against him and these will succeed unless, for example, the man can establish a licence which should not yet be determined (discussed *below*). Alternatively, the woman may propose to the housing authority that she give a notice to quit in return for rehousing elsewhere (as in *Monk*).

There is an argument that the notice to quit strategy exposes the woman to an action by the man for breach of trust. Joint tenants hold the property as trustees by virtue of the co-ownership provisions in s 36 of the LPA 1925. The unilateral determination of the tenancy may be a breach of trust. However, Lord Browne-Wilkinson in *Monk* thought it 'very dubious' that there would be a breach of trust in these circumstances, pointing out that the statutory trusts for sale imposed by the LPA 1925 were not intended to affect beneficial entitlements between co-owners. This was confirmed in *Crawley BC v Ure* (1995) *The Times*, 23 February, where the Court of Appeal held that the duty of consultation imposed on trustees for sale by s 26(3) of the LPA 1925 applied only to 'positive acts' taken by trustees, and that a notice to quit, being in substance merely an indication of unwillingness that the periodic tenancy should continue, was not such a positive act. It was therefore not a breach of trust for one of two joint tenants to give notice to quit without consultation.

*Statutory succession on death*

Where the sole tenant dies then statutory succession of the tenancy is dealt with by s 87 of the HA 1985. A person is qualified to succeed the tenant under a secure tenancy if he occupies the dwellinghouse as his only or principal home at the time of the tenant's death and is either the tenant's spouse or is another member of the tenant's family and has resided with the tenant throughout the period of 12 months ending with the tenant's death. A person is not, however, qualified if the tenant was himself a successor, as defined in s 88. It is important to note that if the deceased was a joint tenant who had become the sole tenant by survivorship then, unlike the case with the Rent Act, the deceased is defined as already being a successor and no further succession is possible. If, however, the deceased was a joint tenant under a joint tenancy which was determined before the other joint tenant's death, and was then regranted a sole tenancy of the same property (so that survivorship has not applied), the deceased will not be treated as a successor: 'it is important not to confuse the property with the tenancy' (per Fox LJ in *Bassetlaw DC v Renshaw and Renshaw* (1991) 23 HLR 603).

Section 113 defines membership of another's family and it expressly includes a couple living together as husband and wife. To be clear, however, the category of 'spouse' remains confined to a married person and is separate from the category of family member. There is therefore a material difference between assured tenancies under the HA 1988 and secure tenancies under the HA 1985. In the public sector, the cohabitant must have been residing with the tenant throughout the period of 12 months ending with the death whereas in the private sector there is no minimum residence period. It has been held that the requirement of residence for 12 months preceding the tenant's death need not be residence exclusively in the property to which succession is claimed (*Waltham Forest LBC v Thomas* [1992] 3 WLR 131, HL): 's 87 does not stipulate that the successor must have resided at a particular house for 12 months but only that he should have resided with the deceased tenant for that period' (per Lord Templeman, at 133C). However, the couple must have lived together as husband and wife *throughout the required period*, so that an unsettled or intermittent relationship may not qualify (*see City of Westminster v Peart* (1992) 24 HLR 389).

## Licences

### Introduction

A cohabitant who does not have the benefit of an occupation order and who cannot establish rights of occupation through the law of landlord and tenant or through beneficial ownership of the property may still have a right to occupy if she can show a licence. In certain circumstances, the creation of a licence may have the effect of establishing a settlement under the SLA 1925 and lead to consequences quite unintended by the parties. A licence may also make the licensee an 'entitled applicant' for the purposes of the FHDVB, but only if the licence takes the form of a contract entitling the licensee to occupy the home (cl 7(1)(*a*)(i)). Some working definitions are necessary.

A *bare licence* at common law is one that can be revoked by the licensor at any time without liability upon giving reasonable notice to the licensee. At the very least, a cohabitant must have been occupying the property as a bare licensee and is entitled to reasonable notice to quit. It may be that a court will find that a short period of notice, say 28 days, is adequate, bearing in mind that no consideration has been given by the licensee but this should not be assumed. A court might be sympathetic if the cohabitation has been of substantial duration and order a longer period. An injunction can be sought to restrain termination of the licence without reasonable notice.

A *contractual licence* at common law is revocable upon giving reasonable notice but the licensor is liable to damages if the revocation is in breach of contract. In certain cases, equity has intervened to protect licences by granting injunctions restraining wrongful revocation (*Winter Gardens Theatre (London) Ltd v Millenium Productions Ltd* [1948] AC 173, HL).

Whereas both the bare licence and the contractual licence depend, strictly, on an agreement between the parties, there are reported cases that do not fit neatly into either category. Most of these were decided by the overt use of estoppel, but there is a residue of cases which seem at least to avoid the language of estoppel. It is possible that a new type of licence is being created by the courts in an *ad hoc* way to deal with cases of injustice where it is not easy to spell out any agreement. This has been called an equitable licence and is to be distinguished from a contractual licence supported by equity. It is a 'licence of which the Court has to spell out the terms' (Lord Denning in *Hardwicke v Johnson* [1978] 2 All ER 935 at 939a). The review of the cases below draws a simple distinction between contractual licences on the one hand and estoppel/equitable licences on the other.

### Contractual licences

Strangely, perhaps, the leading case for our purposes is one where the parties had not actually lived together as husband and wife and where the court did not enforce occupation. It is commonly assumed to be an example of a contractual licence, although it is possible that the language used by Lord Denning suggests the imposition of terms by the court rather than a simple enforcement of what was agreed by the parties. In *Tanner v Tanner* [1975] 3 All ER 776 the defendant became pregnant by the plaintiff. He agreed to buy a house for her, and what turned out to be twins, to live in. The defendant gave up her flat, the tenancy of which was protected by the Rent Act, and moved into the house. She took her furniture and paid £150 towards some more. She also managed the letting of a flat on the first floor. At no stage did the parties live together and after the relationship had broken down the plaintiff took proceedings for possession.

The trial judge ordered the defendant to vacate the premises and she moved out. She appealed claiming a beneficial interest in the property but this claim was dismissed by the Court of Appeal. Instead it was held that she had been entitled to a licence, the terms of which had been breached by the defendant, and she was awarded damages for the breach assessed at £2,000. The judges in the Court of Appeal may have arrived at their decision via different routes. Lord Denning appears to have relied upon equitable principles, playing down the role of agreement, whereas Browne LJ and Brightman J took a more orthodox contractual path. The steps in Lord Denning's reasoning appear to be as follows:

(1) 'This man had a moral duty to provide for the babies of whom he was the father. I would go further. I think he had a legal duty towards them. Not only towards the babies. But also towards their mother ... In order to fulfil his duty towards the babies, he was under a duty to provide for the mother too' (at 779h).
(2) The conclusion to be drawn from the facts, in the light of that duty, was that 'in all the circumstances it is to be implied that she had a licence ... There was, it is true, no express contract to that effect, but the circumstances are such that the court should imply a contract by him—or, if need be, *impose the equivalent of a contract by him*—whereby they were entitled to have the use of the house as their home until the girls finished school' (at 780b–c). [Emphasis added.]
(3) The licence could not be enforced because the defendant now had somewhere else to live but 'it seems to me that this court has ample power, when it revokes an order of the court below, to do what is just and equitable to restore the position as fairly as it can in the circumstances. The plaintiff has obtained an unjust benefit and should make restitution' (at 780f–g).

Browne LJ and Brightman J, while agreeing with Lord Denning's conclusion, cannot be taken as supporting the imposition of a contract. One can, nevertheless, detect the application of equitable principles under the cover of contract law. First, the defendant did not plead the existence of a contract (she was seeking a share in the proceeds of sale). Whilst it is possible to be a party to a contract without even imagining it, such a situation must be rare after professional advice. Second, the measure of damages seems more akin to that used in quasi-contract (unjust enrichment) than contract itself. In the absence of special circumstances, damages for the breach of an implied contract would be the loss to the innocent party arising naturally from the breach (*Hadley v Baxendale* (1854) 9 Exch 341 at 354, Alderson B). In *Tanner*, however, damages were assessed as the sum 'which the plaintiff might reasonably have expected to pay for a surrender of that licence' (Brightman J at 781h).

The plaintiff was therefore not required to compensate the defendant for her loss in finding somewhere else to live and paying rent. Instead, he was made to disgorge the amount by which he was unjustly enriched through having vacant possession of the property.

*Tanner v Tanner* has been extensively discussed here because it gives a glimpse of the range of approaches a court might take. Two later cases on substantially similar facts took a restrictive interpretation of it and claimed to apply ordinary contractual principles. In *Horrocks v Foray* [1976] 1 All ER 737 a differently constituted Court of Appeal regarded it as most definitely involving a contractual licence. Megaw LJ said (at 741j):

> What was decided in *Tanner v Tanner* was very simple. It was decided that on the evidence that had been adduced in that case there was a fair inference to be drawn that the man and his mistress had entered into a contract by which the man had agreed, for consideration, that the house which was being bought by him for the occupation of the woman and her children should remain available to her, with a continuing licence to occupy it so long, at any rate, as the children were of school age.

It seems that Megaw LJ did discern in *Tanner* the element of an imposed contract or equitable licence. He said (at 742c): 'It may be that some other approach to situations of this sort would be preferable. But that is not a matter for us. We have got to take the law as it is and apply it as it stands.'

In *Horrocks v Forray* the defendant had been the deceased's lover for 17 years up to his death (unknown to the deceased's wife). He had, apparently, kept her in style. A year before his death he bought a house for her and their child to live in. He made tentative steps to transfer it to the defendant but did not go through with it. Upon his death, his executors sought possession of the property. Unless the property could be sold with vacant possession the estate would be insolvent and the widow and legitimate daughter would take no benefit. The Court of Appeal stated that the only approach was that of contract law. Megaw LJ found no reason to disagree with the trial judge's decision that the facts did not warrant the inference of a contract. Scarman LJ on the other hand seemed to base his judgment on the parties' lack of intention to create legal relations. He said (at 745f–g):

> In *Tanner* the man and woman were making arrangements for the future at arm's length. The woman was concerned for herself and her children: the man was concerned to limit and define his financial responsibility towards the woman and his children … But how different is this case. Right up to the death of the man there was a continuing, warm relationship of man and mistress. He was maintaining his mistress in luxurious … style, and, as we

now know, in a style beyond his means.

The supposed distinction between the two cases is curious. If a contract is to be inferred it is deemed to operate from the time of the permission to occupy. There is nothing in the Law Report to suggest that the Tanners' relationship was not 'warm' at the time the house was acquired. If it had not been 'warm' one wonders why he bought the house. His later conduct shows that he was not given to philanthropy. The Court of Appeal in *Horrocks v Forray* may have acted out of sympathy for the widow and daughter of the marriage and the distinctions drawn between the two cases are insubstantial. It is quite possible that in neither case was there a contract. In *Tanner*, however, the equities favoured the licensee whereas in *Horrocks v Forray* they favoured the licensor's next of kin. In addition, the court may have taken note of the fact that Mrs Forray (the 'mistress') had 'also had not infrequent sexual intercourse with another man, apparently a great friend of the deceased and, apparently, with his knowledge' (at 739a).

The decision of Jonathan Parker QC, sitting as a deputy High Court judge, in *Coombes v Smith* [1987] 1 FLR 352 may be a further example of extraneous factors affecting the decision whether to find a contract; in this case the excessively ambitious claim made by the plaintiff. Here, the defendant provided a home for the plaintiff and their daughter to live in. Over the years he regularly told her that he would be moving in with them but he did not do so. He visited regularly and in addition to paying all the bills he gave the plaintiff an allowance for herself and the daughter. There was no discussion of marriage. At one stage the plaintiff asked the defendant to put the house into joint names but he refused. The judge found that the defendant said to the plaintiff: 'Don't worry. I have told you I'll always look after you', or words to that effect. The plaintiff redecorated the property several times and caused central heating to be installed, although without the defendant's knowledge. When the relationship broke down the daughter was about ten years old and the plaintiff applied for and obtained an affiliation order (now an order under Sched 1 to the Children Act 1989). The defendant, through his solicitors, agreed to allow the plaintiff and the daughter to continue living in the property until the daughter was 17 and to continue to pay the mortgage instalments. The concession was made again in his defence to the High Court action. The plaintiff's writ claimed that the defendant was contractually bound to provide her with a roof over her head for the rest of her life or in the alternative that he was estopped from evicting her without providing suitable alternative accommodation.

The contractual claim was therefore bolder than the result in *Tanner* because the licence found there was limited to the children leaving school. The judge said that in *Tanner* the Court of Appeal had inferred the existence of a contractual licence and, significantly, he quoted from the judgment of Brightman J rather than Lord Denning. He found that on the evidence before him he was unable to infer an enforceable contract to provide accommodation for life and in the absence of any lesser contract being asserted the claim was dismissed. The estoppel aspect of the case is dealt with *below*.

## Estoppel and equitable licences

It was suggested earlier that some cases cannot easily be explained within the framework of contract law. Whether they are all ultimately explicable by estoppel, constructive trust or by a new form of equitable licence cannot be explored in a text of this nature. Modern appellate court guidance is certainly needed in the area. For present purposes, the cases are reviewed in a way that gives an idea of the range of arguments that might be presented.

*Chandler v Kerley* [1978] 2 All ER 942 is a useful case with which to begin as it seems to mark the boundary between the contractual and the equitable approach. It illustrates the way that equity may intervene to protect what is said to be a contractual licence. Lord Scarman stressed that 'the role of equity is supportive and supplementary' (at 945j). He said that: 'If the legal relationship between the parties is such that the true arrangement envisaged by the parties will be frustrated if the parties are left to their rights at law, an equity will arise which the court can satisfy by appropriate equitable relief.'

In this case the plaintiff bought a house from the defendant and the defendant's husband who were on the point of separating. The plaintiff and the defendant were lovers, although this was not the reason for the breakdown of the defendant's marriage. The idea was that the plaintiff and the defendant would live together in the house with the defendant's children. The defendant asked the plaintiff what would happen if they parted. He replied that he could not put her out. The court inferred that there was a contractual licence that was to be determined on reasonable notice. The notice was set at 12 months by the Court of Appeal. Despite the court's apparent wish to return to orthodox principles, one might doubt whether there was sufficient consideration to justify a contract or, if there was, whether the court enforced the contract's real terms. The consideration for the contract appears to have been the defendant selling the house to the plaintiff at less than the asking price, although one might have thought that it should have been at less than the *market* price before any real consideration moved from the defendant (and her husband). Furthermore, if the representation was that he could not put her out, then this was the term of the contract which the court should have enforced.

In fact, it seems that Lord Scarman quietly dropped the requirement that there be a fully fledged contract which equity can support. He ran into difficulty when he tried to rationalise a series of difficult cases on licences (*Bannister v Bannister* [1948] 2 All ER 133, *Errington v Errington and Woods* [1952] 2 All ER 149 and *Binions v Evans* [1972] 2 All ER 70) and fit them within an orthodox framework. At 945h he said that a contract is necessary before equity can intervene but at 946d he said that the defendant need only 'establish the existence of an understanding or arrangement which though giving rise to no legal right brings into existence an equity'.

This takes us directly to estoppel where equity can intervene and enforce occupation rights without having to pay lip-service to the rules of contract. We start with some general rules which are applicable both to this chapter, which is concerned with occupation rights, and to the next chapter, where proprietary rights are in issue.

*Estoppel generally*

The terminology of estoppel is often confusing. One accepted classification is to make an initial division between estoppel at common law, which is basically a rule of evidence preventing someone from asserting as a fact that which s/he had previously denied (or *vice versa*), and equitable estoppel. In turn equitable estoppel can be divided into promissory estoppel and proprietary estoppel. The former is only available as a defence (in England and Wales, at least) and, as its name implies, operates on a promise or statement of intention. It seems only to have a suspensory effect and the classic occasion of its use is where a creditor, without receiving consideration, agrees to accept smaller instalments (such as a reduced rent) and then attempts to resile without giving reasonable notice. This is unlikely to be an issue with cohabitants and we are more concerned here with proprietary estoppel. Proprietary estoppel can give rise to a cause of action over property, usually land, and can result in an order relating either to occupation or to ownership. Although we deal in this chapter only with those cases where occupation is in issue, the principles are the same for ownership.

An equity arises in favour of A against O if:

(a) A has incurred expenditure or otherwise acted to her or his detriment;
(b) in the belief, actively or passively encouraged by O, that A already owns a sufficient interest in the property to justify the expenditure or that he will obtain such an interest;

(c) in circumstances where O must have known of the expenditure and of the right to interfere.

If these conditions are satisfied and there is no bar to an equity, then the expectations of A will be enforced.

*Cases on estoppel*

Two major cases concerning occupation claims and cohabitants are *Greasley v Cooke* [1980] 3 All ER 710 and *Coombes v Smith* [1987] 1 FLR 352. They illustrate respectively the potential and limitations of estoppel. In *Greasley v Cooke*, the defendant when aged 16 was employed as a maid by a widower who had four children. She later became attached to one of the children, K, and they lived together as husband and wife. The widower died and the defendant remained in the house with K, looking after the other children. One of the children, who was mentally ill, remained in the house until she died, by which time the defendant had cared for her for over 35 years. Following K's death, possession proceedings were taken against the defendant. The trial judge found that the defendant believed that she could remain in the house for as long as she wished and that this belief had been induced by assurances and conduct of K and one of his brothers. He also held, however, that the onus was on the defendant to prove that she had acted to her detriment and that she had failed to discharge it. The Court of Appeal allowed her appeal and granted a declaration that she was entitled to occupy the property rent free for so long as she wished to stay there.

The reasoning of their Lordships is interesting and may be of considerable benefit to a cohabitant who has lived with the owner of the property for a long time and who has given up a career opportunity, for example, to look after her partner and children: a stereotypical quasi-marriage, as it were. Lord Denning's approach seems to go through three stages. First, there must be a statement or conduct calculated (or apparently calculated) to put the defendant's mind at rest; to reassure her of her position. Second, if this is shown, the onus of proof then shifts to the plaintiff to show that the defendant did not rely on the statement or conduct. In other words, there is a presumption that reliance had been placed on the behaviour (and this might be difficult for a plaintiff to rebut). Third, once reliance is established, it must be unjust or inequitable for the party making the assurance to go back on it. This third stage is interesting because the traditional view of estoppel is that the representee must have suffered some detriment, usually expenditure of money. Of course, suffering a detriment is good evidence that it would be unjust or inequitable to allow the representor to go back on the assurance but Lord Denning's approach is wider.

The other two judges in *Greasley v Cooke* were more cautious. Waller LJ confined himself to the onus of proof point and allowed the appeal simply because the trial judge had been wrong. Dunn LJ also claimed to allow the appeal on this narrow point but then appeared to distance himself from Lord Denning's wider view of reliance and said that there 'is no doubt that for proprietary estoppel to arise the person claiming must have incurred expenditure himself or acted to his detriment' (at 715f). Such a division of approach was quite common in cohabitant cases where Lord Denning was involved. He seemed to approach the problem from outside and impose what he regarded as an equitable solution. Some other judges stayed within the problem, as it were, and claimed simply to be giving effect to the understanding of the parties.

If *Greasley v Cooke* suggests the potential of proprietary estoppel in these circumstances, *Coombes v Smith*, assuming it is correctly decided, indicates the limits. The facts are set out *above* under the heading of contractual licences and we have seen that the plaintiff's ambitious contractual claim failed. She had no greater success with estoppel, and by claiming an outright transfer of the property she may also have overstretched herself in this context. Jonathan Parker QC, relying on an old authority (*Willmott v Barber* (1880) 15 ChD 96 at 105–6), said that for the plaintiff to succeed she must show that she had made a mistake as to her legal rights. The fact that she had asked for the house to be put into joint names was taken as evidence that she knew she had no legal right to remain in the house and she therefore had to fail. This seems a little harsh. It is quite possible for someone to believe she has a legal right but to want it formalised so that there is no dispute if things turn sour. In any event, it is not clear that a mistaken belief in a legal right *is* a precondition. Standard textbooks suggest that a belief by the claimant that she *will obtain* an interest will suffice. In a recent authoritative treatment of estoppel, the decision of the Privy Council in *AG of Hong Kong v Humphreys Estate Ltd* [1987] 2 All ER 387, it was not said that there must be such a mistake, although admittedly the plaintiff's awareness that it had no contractual rights was damaging to its case. The plaintiff in *Coombes v Smith* failed on two further principal grounds. First, she had not acted to her detriment. Becoming pregnant and bringing up her child could not be said to be consequent upon any mistake as to her legal position. Second, the defendant had done nothing to encourage her to act to her detriment.

As with many of these cases, the judgment might not reflect the flavour of the evidence at the trial and the submission of the defendant's counsel that if the plaintiff succeeded here then the majority of mistresses (*sic*) might expect a life interest in their home does have some force. Furthermore, the defendant's concession of occupation until the daughter reached the age of 17 (a concession that, in the result, was more generous than the court would have ordered) made it easier for the judge to take a technical line. Nevertheless, other cases seem to have used a broader brush. In *Maharaj v Chand* [1986] 3 All ER 107 the Privy Council used estoppel to enable a cohabitant to remain permanently in the home. The man had represented to her that it would be a permanent home for her and the children and that she would be treated as living there as his wife. In reasonable reliance on the representation she had acted to her detriment by giving up her flat. She used her earnings to pay for household needs and looked after the man and the children. There are, no doubt, many distinguishing factors between this case and *Coombes v Smith* but a mistake over legal rights is not one of them.

*Estoppel and the Settled Land Act 1925*

If the equity necessary for estoppel is established, then it is normally satisfied by enforcing the plaintiff's expectation; either by conferring a right of occupation or by creating ownership rights. *Griffiths v Williams* (1978) 248 EG 947 shows how flexible the powers are. Here the defendant had relied substantially on an assurance that she could stay in a house indefinitely. Goff LJ was anxious not to involve the Settled Land Act 1925, which potentially arises where there are interests in succession not held under a trust for sale. A Settled Land Act settlement would confer a power of sale on the tenant for life which was greater than her expectation. He therefore suggested to the parties that a long non-assignable lease should be granted at a rent below two-thirds of the rateable value of the house, thereby conferring on the defendant a personal right of occupation, secure against purchasers of the freehold, but outside the provisions of the Rent Act.

*Griffiths v Williams* was not cited by Vinelott J in the recent case of *Ungurian v Lesnoff* [1990] 2 FLR 299. Here the woman made major sacrifices in burning her boats, as it was put by the judge, and leaving Poland to live with the man. The man bought a house in his sole name and for the next four years the woman, with the help of her sons, carried out considerable improvements to the property, the man paying for all the materials. He later sought possession of the property and Vinelott J found that the parties had had a common intention that the woman would be entitled to live in the house with her children, sharing it with the man when he was in England, and with any of his children who were in the country for their education (at 313C).

The question for the judge was then whether the common intention and the work done by the woman gave rise 'either to a constructive trust under which Mrs Lesnoff became entitled to a beneficial interest in the house, or to a licence to reside, or to an estoppel preventing Mr Ungurian from denying her right to reside in the house' (at 313E). Vinelott J found that the 'inference to be drawn from the circumstances in which the property was purchased and the subsequent conduct of the parties—the intention to be attributed to them—is that Mrs Lesnoff was to have the right to reside in the house during her life' (at 314A).

The judge seems to have protected this right by the imposition of a constructive trust, and without going through the normal steps of estoppel reasoning. Following *Bannister v Bannister* [1948] 2 All ER 133 he found that a Settled Land Act settlement arose and that the woman was the life tenant entitled to call for the execution of a vesting deed in her favour. In the event of a sale by her she could purchase a substitute property or enjoy the income from the sale proceeds.

The implications of this decision will have to be considered in future cases. It is by no means unheard of to protect occupation by imposing a constructive trust (*see Re Sharpe* [1980] 1 WLR 219; doubted, seemingly on other grounds, by the Court of Appeal in *Ashburn Anstalt v Arnold* [1989] Ch 1) but it is more commonly done by a declaration that the owner is estopped from denying the existence of a certain state of affairs and the making of consequential orders.

One possible virtue of the Settled Land Act settlement is that steps can be taken to regularise the conveyancing position. It was not clear in *Re Sharpe* whether the licence protected by a constructive trust there would bind third parties and the approach in *Ungurian v Lesnoff* at least sits within the orthodox framework of land law. On the other hand, Settled Land Act settlements are usually thought to be cumbersome and inconvenient, perhaps attributable to modern unfamiliarity with the drafting of them. In any event, if in this case the intention was that Mrs Lesnoff was to *share* the occupation, how are the rights of the sharers to be identified and enforced, particularly if the property is sold and the life tenant takes an income from the proceeds?

We have dealt now with the main approaches that might be taken where an occupation dispute is to be decided through the use of licences. Some judges on particular facts prefer to work through the law of contract and appear simply to enforce any contract that they find. Some will look for agreement, at least, and then decide an equitable way of giving effect to it. Others take a more interventionist line and attempt to impose a just and equitable solution. Of course, the fact that the parties in these cases were cohabitants or lovers is not strictly relevant to the rules of estoppel. They are supposedly applied irrespective of the parties' relationship. Further guidance can therefore be obtained from other cases on estoppel involving some kind of family setting: *see*, in particular, *Hardwick v Johnson* [1978] 2 All ER 935, where Lord Denning said at 939a that he was imposing an 'equitable licence of which the court has to spell out the terms' and *Williams v Staite* [1978] 2 All ER 928, where the Court of Appeal was asked to revoke an equitable licence which had been established some time before in the county court.

## Establishing a beneficial interest

The ways in which a beneficial interest in property can be established are dealt with in Chapter 8. For present purposes it is assumed that such a beneficial interest exists (and there is often little dispute about its existence, as opposed to its size).

A cohabitant beneficially entitled to a share in the proceeds of sale has a right to occupy the property (*Bull v Bull* [1955] 1 QB 234). Thus one cohabitant cannot exclude the other if they are both beneficial owners (either as equitable joint tenants or tenants in common). A party who is guilty of expulsive behaviour may be liable to pay an occupational rent to the excluded beneficial owner (*Dennis v McDonald* [1982] FLR 409). The problem under discussion here is where one of the parties wishes to sell the house and the other wishes to remain. This sort of problem has featured for many years in divorce law and a number of solutions have been developed, in particular postponement of sale with certain readjustment of rights and obligations.

The early signs in cases concerning cohabitants are that similar solutions can be found but one must be careful to note that their context is quite different. The solutions can only exist where each cohabitant has a beneficial interest, whereas this is irrelevant in divorce. Furthermore, the divorce powers are much wider than those available to cohabitants; in particular there is power to adjust ownership rights and the court is not limited to enforcing the rights which flow as a matter of law from joint ownership. Even where a court makes an order which appears similar to that which a divorce court might make, there may be underlying differences. For example, liability for outgoings and the non-occupying party's right to move back into the property can only be regulated in an indirect and clumsy fashion (unless there is an occupation order in force, in which case the court has the powers conferred by cl 12 of the FHDVB, discussed *above*).

In this section it is assumed that the dispute is between the owners. Similar disputes over sale may, however, arise in other ways, and the outcomes may be different. For example, if it is a trustee in bankruptcy of one of the owners who requires a sale and the non-bankrupt is resisting it then the matter is decided under well-established principles (*see Re Citro* [1991] 1 FLR 71 and the cases cited there). The outcome will normally be a sale. The provisions in s 336 of the Insolvency Act 1986 which, in effect, give the spouse of a bankrupt one year's grace from sale do not apply to a cohabitant, despite a recommendation from the Cork Committee that they should. If, however, a dependent child of the bankrupt is living in the property then one year's respite may be gained by virtue of the child (s 337).

Where the applicant for a sale is a chargee of the interest of one of the co-owners, then the position is less clear. In *Lloyds Bank v Byrne* [1993] 1 FLR 369, it was held that a chargee was in the same position as a trustee in bankruptcy and was thus entitled to a sale on proof that the debt owed to the chargee could only be discharged if the property were sold, unless there were exceptional circumstances. However, in *Abbey National plc v Moss* [1994] 1 FLR 307, *Re Citro* and the bankruptcy cases were distinguished on the ground that, whereas the bankruptcy of a co-owner brings to an end the collateral purpose for which the property was bought, the mere charging of one co-owner's share may not so that, in accordance with the general principles discussed later, a sale could be refused. *Byrne* was distinguished in *Moss*, but it is not entirely clear how.

### Legal estate vested in one party only

The obvious example of this situation is where the non-legal owner has acquired a beneficial interest in the property by virtue of an implied, resulting or constructive trust in the manner described in Chapter 8. The general view, which is probably now unassailable, is that the legal owner holds the property on a statutorily implied trust for sale for himself and the other party (*Bull v Bull* [1955] 1 QB 234 and *Cook v Cook* [1962] P 235). In the event of a sale another trustee should, technically, be appointed because a sole trustee, other than a trust corporation, cannot give the purchaser a valid receipt for the proceeds of sale. Nevertheless, a purchaser or mortgagee may complete the transaction without ever knowing of the trust and the non-legal owner should urgently consider whether active steps need be taken to protect her position (*see below*). One method of protecting her position is to seek a declaration of beneficial interests under the summary procedure supplied by s 17 of the Married Women's Property Act 1882 (extended to cohabitants by cl 24 of the FHDVB). Another is to apply to the court for the appointment of a second trustee, namely herself. The other party will probably then take the opportunity to ask the court to order sale of the property under s 30 of the LPA 1925.

The section provides as follows:

> If the trustees for sale refuse to sell or to exercise any of the powers conferred by either of the last two sections, or any requisite consent cannot be obtained, any person interested may apply to the court for a vesting or other order for giving effect to the proposed transaction or for an order directing the trustees for sale to give effect thereto, and the court may make such order as it thinks fit.

The section assumes that there is more than one trustee but it presumably applies where this is not so. If the legal owner is not occupying but wishes to sell, he or she applies as a 'person interested' on the basis that a 'requisite consent' cannot be obtained; namely that of the occupying beneficial owner to vacate the premises (per Denning LJ in *Bull*, *above*). The same is true for the non-legal owner who wishes to release capital because he or she is living elsewhere. Whichever way the matter comes before the court, the position will be as *below*.

## Legal estate vested in both parties

Because the property is held on a trust for sale there is a duty to sell the property unless the trustees unanimously decide to exercise their power to postpone sale. Thus, *prima facie*, where one party wishes to sell, the other must concur. If, however, one of the trustees refuses to sell then the legal estate will not shift and the other will have to apply for an order for sale under s 30 of the LPA 1925. This gives the recalcitrant trustee the opportunity to argue that sale should be postponed.

The principles on which a court will decide to postpone sale in a family case short of divorce have, after an uncertain start, begun to emerge from the cases. In *Re Buchanan-Wollaston's Conveyance* [1939] 2 All ER 302 at 308, Lord Greene MR said:

> it seems to me that the court of equity, when asked to enforce the trust for sale, whether one created by a settlement or a will or one created by the statute, must look into all the circumstances of the case and consider whether or not, at the particular moment and in the particular circumstances when the application is made to it, it is right and proper that such an order shall be made. In considering a question of that kind, in circumstances such as these, the court is bound to look at the contract into which the parties have entered and to ask itself the question whether or not the person applying for the execution of the trust for sale is a person whose voice should be allowed to prevail.

In *Jones v Challenger* [1960] 1 All ER 785 at 787 Devlin LJ reviewed the authorities but put the position slightly differently:

> This simple principle that a trust for sale involves a duty to sell cannot

> prevail where the trust itself or the circumstances in which it was made show that there was a secondary or collateral object besides that of sale. It is at any rate wrong and inequitable for one of the parties to the trust to invoke the letter of the trust in order to defeat one of its purposes, whether that purpose be written or unwritten, and the court will not permit it.

One view is that these cases propound a principle that the courts will look to the underlying purpose of the trust and see whether it still exists. If it does, then sale will not be ordered. In fact, *Re Buchanan-Wollastan's Conveyance*, whilst acknowledging that the circumstances at the time of purchase are relevant, seems to require a broader question to be answered: whose voice in equity should be allowed to prevail? Mr John Waite QC, who sat as the judge in *Cousins v Dzosens* (1981) *The Times*, 12 December suggests that these tests amount to the same thing but there may be a difference. The 'underlying purpose' test merely gives effect to the substantive motive of the parties when they bought the house. The 'prevailing voice' test admits circumstances subsequent to the purchase, so that a sale might be postponed if wholly unforeseen events mean that it would cause hardship to the occupier. On balance, a review of the cases indicates that the underlying purpose test is applied but with a rather liberal approach to the interpretation of that purpose. The effect can be to mitigate some of the rigours of the test.

The leading case concerning cohabitants, at least where there are children, is *Re Ever's Trust* [1980] 3 All ER 399. The plaintiff and the defendant began living together and two years later had a child. At about this time the defendant's two children by a dissolved marriage joined them. Two years after this they purchased a house in joint names. Most of the purchase price was provided by mortgage finance and the balance was shared as to £2,400 by the defendant and £1,600 by the plaintiff. A year or so after purchasing the property the relationship broke down. The defendant remained in the home with her three children and the plaintiff applied for an order for sale under s 30 of the LPA 1925. The trial judge held that sale should be postponed until the parties' child attained the age of 16. The judge explicitly referred to the practice of the divorce courts of settling a former matrimonial home and his order was similar to the once fashionable *Mesher* order (*see Mesher v Mesher and Hall* [1980] 1 All ER 126). Ormrod LJ in the Court of Appeal held that divorce cases were not relevant to disputes under s 30 of the LPA 1925, although some of the considerations to be taken into account are common to both classes. He adopted the underlying purpose test and said that the irresistible inference from the facts was that the parties purchased the property as a family home for themselves and the children. He went on (at 403j):

> It is difficult to imagine that the mother, then wholly responsible for two children and partly for the third, would have invested nearly all her capital in the purchase of this property if it was not to be available to her as a home for the children for the indefinite future. It is inconceivable that the father, when he agreed to this joint adventure [*sic*], could have thought otherwise and contemplated the possibility of an early sale without the consent of the mother. The underlying purpose of the trust was, therefore, to provide a home for all five of them for the indefinite future.

Assuming that the presence in the home of four out of the five of them satisfies the underlying purpose test then there was no need for the judge to go further. He did, however, go on to point out that the defendant had provided more capital than the plaintiff, that she was prepared to keep up the mortgage instalments and that the plaintiff had a secure home with his mother. Ormrod LJ, in effect, was addressing the wider question of whose voice in equity ought to prevail so as to evaluate the justice of the underlying purpose test. The Court of Appeal overturned the specific terms of the trial judge's order and simply dismissed the plaintiff's application. Section 30 applications, it was said, can only be decided at a particular moment and in particular circumstances and it would be inappropriate to take an arbitrary date, such as the youngest child's sixteenth birthday. This might give rise to unfortunate uncertainty but the Court of Appeal felt that it could be no more specific than to indicate the sort of circumstance which might justify a further application for sale.

The other fully argued case concerning cohabitants and sale is *Bernard v Josephs* [1982] FLR 178. Here the Court of Appeal found that the beneficial interest was shared equally between the parties, subject to some adjustment for post-separation payments. There were no children and the woman left, allegedly due to the man's violence. He married and remained in the property with his wife. The woman applied for an order for sale so that she could realise her share in the proceeds. In the Court of Appeal the distinction between Lord Denning's interventionist style and the more orthodox approach of other judges is apparent. Lord Denning, while indorsing *Re Evers* claimed there is still discretion to avoid injustice. Even where there are no children, he said (at 168a), the court can refuse to order a sale at the instance of the outgoing party if it would be unduly harsh to require the remaining party to vacate, or it can make an order for sale but suspend it on terms. Griffiths and Kerr LJJ, on the other hand, both took the underlying purpose test. They found that the purpose was exhausted and there was no legitimate ground for refusing sale. In the result, a compromise was reached, largely it seems through a concession by the woman, that a sale would take place if the man did not buy out her interest within four months. Whereas Lord Denning arrived at this result on the premiss that he had power to require it, the other judges expressly said they were indorsing an agreement sensibly reached between the parties.

Remaining cohabitant cases merely apply the principles enunciated in *Re Evers* and *Bernard v Josephs*; with the dichotomy between Lord Denning and the others continuing (*Stott v Ratcliffe* (1982) 126 SJ 310). The approach in *Re Evers* was followed by Purchas J in *Dennis v McDonald, above*, with little discussion and was apparently followed in *Cousins v Dzosens, above.*

This review of the cases suggests that the presence of children will be a central issue in deciding whether sale should be postponed. In the absence of children or other clear evidence that the underlying purpose of the trust still subsists, much may depend on how strictly the judge approaches the matter. For example, if children were born or brought to the home after the property was purchased then it may be difficult to say that the home was bought to accommodate a family. The judge must then decide whether to move to the broader ground of 'whose voice should prevail' and, if so, whether that voice belongs to the occupier. Obvious circumstances to be taken into account would be the respective interests of the parties in the equity, the parties' needs and their housing circumstances. One factor that might be decisive is the ability of the occupier to pay an occupational rent so that the non-occupying owner has some immediate return on his capital and this is dealt with *below.*

## Occupational rent and payment of outgoings

Although the expression 'occupational rent' is used in the cases, it is not strictly accurate. A joint owner has a right to live in the property and cannot be required to pay rent to another joint owner. The payment is more accurately seen either as being for exclusive enjoyment of the property or as interest on the non-occupier's capital.

At first instance in *Dennis v McDonald, above*, Purchas J examined the authorities and held that where one co-owner has been ousted by another then that other can be required to pay compensation. The origin of the power was not fully discussed but the judge appeared to take the view that the court has a general jurisdiction to order the payment and that it does not stem directly from s 30. Presumably a breach of trust is involved and this might provide the authority. At the Court of Appeal stage, the power was not disputed and the issue was how the rent should be assessed. It was decided that the factors in s 70(1) and (2) of the Rent Act 1977 (which are some of the factors relevant to the determination of a fair rent for a private sector tenancy granted before 15 January 1989) should be applied. Thus, regard should be had to all the circumstances (other than personal circumstances) and in particular to the age, character, locality and state of repair of the dwellinghouse. Furthermore, it is to be assumed that the number of persons seeking to become tenants of similar dwellinghouses in the locality on the terms (other than those relating to rent) of the regulated tenancy is not substantially greater than the number of such dwellinghouses in the locality which are available for letting on such terms.

The Court of Appeal held that an annual reassessment would be grossly disproportionate in its cost and inconvenience to the sort of money that would be involved and urged that the respective solicitors attempt to effect agreement. The outcome of the case was that the occupier was ordered to pay to the other one-half of such sum as represents a fair rent, to be assessed under subss (1) and (2) of s 70 without regard to any other provisions of the Act.

Where it is reasonably clear on the facts that an ouster has taken place then this case is clear guidance. What is the position where it is not clear that there has been ouster? If sale is not ordered then it is doubtful that the court has power to make ancillary orders (*see* Kerr LJ in *Bernard v Josephs*, *above*). An indirect method was suggested by Purchas J at first instance in *Dennis v McDonald*. Because it is the occupier who wants sale to be postponed then he or she can be invited to give an undertaking to the court to make payments and it can be made clear that if the invitation is declined a sale will be ordered. This method is presumably not confined to payment of occupational rent. The non-occupier may be concerned about joint and several liability under mortgage covenants and the occupier could also be invited to undertake to pay the mortgage and indemnify the non-occupier against any liability for breach of other covenants.

### Exclusive occupation

In many cases the non-occupier will have found secure accommodation elsewhere and, if the property is not to be sold, may have to be content with occupational rent until sale. What if he decides that he wants to move back in rather than rely on the rent? It is unlikely that the court's power in s 30 to make such orders as it thinks fit extends to ordering *exclusive* occupation for the other party. In any event, as we have seen, that power appears to be contingent on an order for sale being made and we are dealing here with a situation where no order is appropriate. An equivalent jurisdiction open to cohabitants is s 17 of the Married Women's Property Act 1882 (cl 24 of the FHDVB) but, in view of the powers available under the FHDVA 1995 (and before it the DVA 1976) to regulate occupation, cases on occupation have not had to be decided under this section. The Court of Appeal in *McDowell v McDowell* (1957) 107 LJ 184 held that there was no power under s 17 to order exclusive occupation between spouses. In so far as there might be some doubt about this case, the doubt arises because a husband has a duty at common law to provide a roof over his wife's head. It is hardly possible that the courts' powers under s 30 could be more extensive than those under s 17.

The FHDVB could be used in this situation because (unlike the DVA 1976) it extends to *former* cohabitants. Under cl 7, an entitled applicant may apply for an occupation order in respect of a house that is or has been the home of the applicant and an associated person, or was intended by them to be their home (cl 7(1)). For these purposes, an associated person includes a former cohabitant (cl 2(*b*)). A former cohabitant may also apply for an occupation order under cl 9 (cl 9(1)).

## Chapter 8

# Ownership of Property

## Introduction

This chapter considers the ways in which a cohabitant can establish and protect rights of ownership. As in the previous chapters it is assumed that the plaintiff is a woman, although the actions discussed are open to both partners. Chapter 7 was concerned with occupation of the home and some of the themes there are developed further here. The particular focus is on methods whereby one partner can establish and protect an interest in the home despite the absence of any, or sufficient, written evidence that she should have such an interest. If necessary, the reader can refer back to the previous chapter to consider whether a court will order the immediate sale of the property and distribution of the proceeds.

### Development of the law in recent decades

Before the decision of the House of Lords in *Lloyds Bank plc v Rosset* [1990] 2 FLR 155, it was possible to identify two different approaches to the question of informally acquired ownership. One was rooted firmly in the assumed intention of the parties, while the other was more prepared to look also at the overall justice of the case and its consequences. The latter worked through a kind of remedial constructive trust fashioned largely by Lord Denning. The intention approach was certainly in the ascendancy and it now seems to have triumphed in *Rosset* itself. The word 'seems' still has to be used, however. Whilst the House of Lords has undoubtedly disposed of some questions (after, it must be said, an incomplete review of the case law), others have arisen. In particular, it is possible that proprietary estoppel will now develop to take the place of the justice approach previously occupied by the remedial constructive trust.

## Spouses and cohabitants compared

Before proceeding, it may be helpful for someone coming new to the subject to compare the positions of spouses and cohabitants. There are certainly still occasions when the law of trusts (with which this chapter is mainly concerned) is required to resolve problems concerning spouses. For example, the parties may have separated but no petition for divorce or judicial separation is to be presented. Alternatively, the dispute may be between a spouse and a third party, such as a trustee in bankruptcy, chargee or personal representative. Such disputes may have become less common, if only because of the modern tendency for married couples expressly to vest the matrimonial home in themselves as beneficial joint tenants. As will be seen, this is normally conclusive between the parties and, whilst not binding on a third party, seems often to be accepted by trustees in bankruptcy if there is evidence of contributions by both spouses.

The main reason why disputes concerning spouses are rarely resolved by the law of trusts, however, is because of the courts' adjustive powers under the Matrimonial Causes Act 1973 (MCA 1973), available in connection with nullity, judicial separation and divorce suits. Here the court must follow guidelines, principally those contained in s 25 (as amended), but they are guidelines that still leave room for a large degree of discretion and the vested property rights of spouses can be, and very frequently are, overridden.

In contrast, cohabitants can make virtually no use of the family law system devised for spouses. The exceptions concern an engaged couple (who need not, of course, be cohabiting). By virtue of s 2(1) of the Law Reform (Miscellaneous Provisions) Act 1970, on the termination of an agreement to marry (a term that includes agreements that would not have been enforceable at common law: *Shaw v Fitzgerald* [1992] 1 FLR 357) any rule of law relating to the rights of husbands and wives in relation to property in which either or both has or have a beneficial interest is also applicable to property in which either or both of the couple had an interest whilst the engagement was in force. This presumably means, for example, that s 37 of the Matrimonial Proceedings and Property Act 1970 is available (*Bernard v Joseph* [1982] 3 All ER 162). That section deals with contributions to the improvement of property and although purporting merely to be declaratory does arguably create new law, depending on the view one takes of resulting and constructive trusts. Crucially, however, the Law Reform (Miscellaneous Provisions) Act 1970 does not allow a formerly engaged person to invoke the adjustive powers in s 24 of the MCA 1973 (*Mossop v Mossop* [1988] 2 FLR 173).

It follows, then, that on the breakdown of a cohabiting relationship, disputes over property are dealt with in a quite different way than in marriage breakdown. One way of expressing the difference is to say that in cohabitation breakdown the principal question is 'who *owns* the property?' In marriage breakdown it is 'who *should* own the property?'

Matters have improved recently, however. The summary jurisdiction under s 17 of the Married Women's Property Act 1882 (MWPA 1882), previously available only to married couples and to engaged couples within three years of the termination of the engagement, will be extended by cl 26 of the Family Homes and Domestic Violence Bill to cohabitants. This can have procedural advantages (discussed further *below*), as well as giving rise to the exemption in reg 94(*d*)(iii) of the Civil Legal Aid (General) Regulations 1989 whereby the first £2,500 of any property recovered or preserved is exempted from the statutory charge under s 16(6) of the Legal Aid Act 1988.

In addition, there is one jurisdiction to which cohabitants have access on an equal footing with spouses: parental obligations of support towards children. This is discussed in detail in Chapter 10. For present purposes, it need only be noted that the powers available to the courts to transfer property 'to or for the benefit of children' under Sched 1 to the Children Act 1989 may be relevant in sorting out the proprietary consequences of a cohabiting relationship (assuming the presence of children of the man). For example, the courts have been willing to consider transferring tenancies between former cohabitants under these provisions, even though the caring parent would also benefit from the transfer (*see K v K* (1992) Fam Law 396); but the courts are less willing to use these provisions to transfer large amounts of capital that would have the effect of providing for a child beyond majority (*A v A* [1994] 1 FLR 657; *T v S* (1995) Fam Law 11). This is discussed further in Chapter 10.

## Immediate advice on separation

Assuming that no emergency relief is required concerning children or restraint from violence, the first task on the breakdown of the relationship is to obtain as clear a view as possible of the tenure of the family home. If it is rented on a periodic tenancy then it will presumably have no sale value. Reference should be made to the previous chapter because the question may simply be one of deciding who is to continue in occupation. If the home is freehold or held on a long lease then it is likely to have some net capital value and be capable of use as security. It is essential to determine the ownership of that capital and consider whether third parties could acquire rights whilst negotiations or litigation are proceeding.

As noted above, cl 26 of the FHDVB makes available the summary procedure under the MWPA 1882 for determining 'any question arising between cohabitants or former cohabitants as to the title to or possession of property'. The extension of this procedure to cohabitants will have a number of consequences. One is that many more proceedings can be started in the county court, where the procedure is both simpler and cheaper. Another is that the powers of the court to make 'such order as it thinks fit' (s 17 of the MWPA 1882) with respect to the parties' property becomes available. Although it is well established that a court has no power to *vary* (as opposed to declare) property rights under this procedure (*Pettitt v Pettitt* [1970] AC 777), s 17 gives the court a discretion to decide how those rights should be enjoyed (eg by ordering a sale: *see* s 7(7) of the Matrimonial Causes (Maintenance and Property) Act 1958). Finally, there are exemptions from the operation of the legal aid statutory charge, already discussed.

The question of protecting a beneficial interest is dealt with *below* but it is helpful to consider some of the issues here.

*(1) Who holds the legal estate?* The first question is the ownership of the legal estate: who is the grantee under the conveyance or assignment (in the case of unregistered title) or the transferee (in the case of registered title)? If there is any element of doubt, a search of the Index Map and Parcels Index under r 286 of the Land Registration Rules 1925 will reveal whether the title is registered. If it is, then office copies of the register can be obtained (following the opening of the register by the Land Registration Act 1988) which will disclose the registered proprietors. If the land is unregistered, then a solicitor might approach the first mortgagee and, if necessary, apply for the title deeds on the usual undertaking as to safekeeping and return. If the legal estate is in the sole name of the *other* party then the mortgagee will presumably not send the deeds and will say why.

*(2) Express declaration of beneficial interests* If inquiries reveal that the legal estate is in the joint names of the parties then there is no immediate danger of a third party acquiring rights over the land because both estate owners' signatures are required. One then moves on to consider the beneficial, or equitable, ownership, so as to determine the shares in the proceeds of sale. If there is formal written evidence of an express declaration of trust which comprehensively declares the beneficial interests then that is conclusive between the parties unless the document is set aside or rectified, for example as a result of fraud or mistake (*Goodman v Gallant* [1986] 1 FLR 513; *Turton v Turton* [1988] 1 FLR 23).

An express declaration of trust is likely to be found, if at all, in the document conveying the title. If the title is unregistered then one simply looks at the deeds and must assume, in the absence of information to the contrary, that there is no other document declaring the trusts. If the title was first registered as a result of the most recent disposition then the instrument inducing the first registration should be with the deeds for inspection. If neither of the foregoing applies then the Land Registry may send a copy of the last transfer and one should look for an express declaration of trust. The standard declaration in a registered land transfer that the survivor of the transferees can give a valid receipt for capital monies is sufficient to operate as a declaration of a beneficial joint tenancy, even where the transferees have omitted to sign it (*Re Gorman* [1990] 2 FLR 284, overruling *Robinson v Robinson* (1976) 241 EG 153). One must, however, look closely at the terms of any declaration; for example, to see whether it precludes the possibility of a third party having a beneficial interest. Conveyancers are well advised to add extra words to the standard declaration such as 'to hold unto themselves as joint tenants beneficially'; see *Harwood v Harwood* [1991] 2 FLR 274 at 288, CA; *Huntingford v Hobbs* [1993] 1 FLR 736. However, a separate declaration of trust is usually best, with each party having a separate copy.

*(3) Severance of beneficial joint tenancies* If there is an express beneficial joint tenancy (and remembering that an express beneficial tenancy in common is possible) then one must consider whether that joint tenancy has already been severed or should now be severed. The principal consequence is, of course, that rights of survivorship will no longer apply. If this is the client's wish, a will should be considered urgently. Whilst a client will often want her children to benefit, she may still be married to a former partner who might take the whole of the interest as a surviving spouse on intestacy. It can rarely be right to leave the children with a speculative and expensive claim under the Inheritance (Provision for Family and Dependants) Act 1975 (*see* Chapter 9).

The most likely forms of severance will be by written notice (under s 36(2) of the LPA 1925) or by course of dealing (sometimes called severance by 'mutual conduct', ie conduct indicating a common intention shared by both joint tenants to sever). Severance is also possible by a joint tenant dealing unilaterally with his or her share (eg by one joint tenant purporting to mortgage the property and forging the other's signature in order to do so: *Abbey National PLC v Moss* [1994] 1 FLR 307); or by express mutual agreement.

Any notice is likely to have been indorsed on the instrument of grant to the joint tenants (in unregistered title) or appear as a restriction on the register (in registered title). Severance by a course of dealing, or mutual conduct, will be less easily determined. In *Barton v Morris* [1985] 2 All ER 1032, the cohabitants were business partners and the property appeared in the accounts as a partnership asset. It was held by Nicholls J in the Chancery Division that a joint tenancy had continued until the death of one of them so that the survivor took the whole. Normally equity leans against a joint tenancy in the case of a partnership and if jointly owned property is brought into the partnership then severance is presumed. Here, however, the express declaration of a joint tenancy was made when a partnership was in contemplation and because nothing appeared to change subsequently to suggest that there should no longer be a joint tenancy then that joint tenancy was assumed to have continued. In *Burgess v Rawnsley* [1975] 3 All ER 142 an oral agreement to purchase the other's interest was held by the Court of Appeal to be effective to sever the joint tenancy even though the agreement was not evidenced in writing and was subsequently repudiated by one of them (*see also Hunter v Babbage* (1994) Fam Law 675). However, unfinished negotiations between joint tenants with a view to agreeing a severance may not amount to a severance if there is no 'finality or mutuality' between the parties (per Judge Blackett-Ord in *Gore and Snell v Carpenter* (1990) 60 P&CR 456).

If the legal estate is clearly in the sole name of the other party then consideration must be given to the existence of an express, resulting, implied or constructive trust. These are dealt with at length below. Initially, protection of such an interest must be considered (*see below*) and severance might still be relevant. It is quite possible for a resulting or constructive trust to be found under which the sole legal owner holds for them both as beneficial joint tenants. There seems to be nothing wrong in principle with a notice that any beneficial joint tenancy that there might be in the property is hereby severed.

Finally, it should be noted that when severance takes place the parties automatically become tenants in common in equal shares. In other words, there is no scope for argument that contributions had been unequal (*Goodman v Gallant, above*). The only qualification to this is that credit can be given for mortgage repayments and improvements to the property since separation.

## The law of trusts

### Introduction

The simplest way to begin is by reminding oneself *why* the law of trusts has become the principal means whereby disputes over the beneficial ownership of land are decided. The reason can be stated simply. The commonly held view is that the combined effect of ss 34–36 of the Law of Property Act 1925 (LPA) and s 36 of the Settled Land Act 1925 requires co-ownership of land to take place behind a trust for sale unless there is a strict settlement. If no trust for sale is expressed then a statutorily implied one comes into effect. The trust is therefore the vehicle for apportioning shares between co-owners that slots most easily into this statutory framework.

The framers of the legislation appeared, however, to assume that the legal estate would be vested in at least two people or a trust corporation. As a result, the situation common in case law concerning cohabitants where the legal estate is vested solely in one of them but the other has made a contribution to the purchase price was not obviously considered. The Court of Appeal decision in *Bull v Bull* [1955] 1 QB 234 is usually taken as authority for the proposition that a statutory trust for sale arises in such a case and that if contributions to the price are unequal then there will normally be an equitable tenancy in common (subsequently confirmed by the House of Lords in *Williams & Glyn's Bank v Boland* [1981] AC 487).

The awkwardness of fitting family situations into the law of trusts has been recognised by the courts; *see*, for example, Ormrod LJ's remark in *Williams & Glyn's Bank v Boland* [1979] 2 All ER 697 at 707b that 'implied trusts of this type do not fit easily into the scheme of the Law of Property Act 1925'.

*The requirement of writing*

Whatever the exact nature of the trust created, we are clearly within the law of trusts. One turns then to the procedural formalities set out in s 53 of the LPA concerning the declaration of trusts and the disposition of equitable interests. By s 53(1)(*b*):

> a declaration of trust respecting any land or any interest therein must be manifested and proved by some writing signed by some person who is able to declare such trust or by his will.

And by s 53(1)(*c*):

> a disposition of an equitable interest or trust subsisting at the time of the disposition, must be in writing signed by the person disposing of the same, or by his agent thereunto lawfully authorised in writing or by his will.

Clearly, such provisions by themselves preclude the creation or disposition of an equitable interest in the circumstances we are primarily considering here; namely where there is nothing 'on the deeds' about beneficial ownership and where even the legal ownership is quite probably in one name only. Section 53(1)(*b*) appears to require signed written evidence of the creation of the trust and if one is trying to argue that the equitable interests are actually different from what appears in writing then one is faced with the requirement that a disposition of an existing interest must, under s 53(1)(*c*), be effected in writing.

*Exceptions to the writing requirement*

What saves the position is s 53(2) which provides that: 'This section does not affect the creation or operation of resulting, implied or constructive trusts.' Hence, where there is no writing complying with s 53(1)(*b*) or (*c*), a cohabitant can only establish a beneficial interest in land if she can show a resulting, implied or constructive trust in her favour (subject to the question of proprietary estoppel, discussed *below*).

## Resulting, implied and constructive trusts

One of the many sources of confusion in the case law in this area has been the lack of consensus as to what the words 'resulting', 'implied' and 'constructive' are to mean. Some judges have apparently regarded the terms as interchangeable. Even Lord Diplock in the leading House of Lords decision of *Gissing v Gissing* [1970] 2 All ER 780 claimed (at 790a) that 'it is unnecessary for present purposes to distinguish between these three classes of trust'. The history of the case law since *Gissing* suggests that an 'implied' trust has no relevant meaning but that the labels 'resulting' and 'constructive' have been applied indiscriminately. The confusion may be narrowed a little if one begins with the orthodox meanings that 'resulting' and 'constructive' had before the arrival of cases on informal trusts in a family setting.

*Some first principles*

A resulting trust has, historically, arisen in a number of situations. For our purposes the relevant one can be stated like this: When property is bought in the name of A, but B makes a contribution towards the purchase price, a rebuttable presumption arises that it is intended that A should hold the property on trust for A and B in the proportions that they have contributed to the price. A, in this example, holds the property on a *resulting trust* for A and B. To approach the matter from the other direction, B's contribution 'results back' in the form of a share in the property; a share that goes up or down with the value of the property. It places the onus on A to show that B had intended some other consequence.

Thus A might show that the money from B was a gift, a loan or a payment of rent. The basis of the resulting trust, in this context at least, is therefore the presumed intention of the parties. In the absence of some other explanation given by A, it is presumed that the parties intended to share the property in the proportions to which they contributed to the price.

There was one exceptional case where the presumption of a resulting trust was displaced. This was where the presumption of advancement applied. For example, where a husband put property into the name of his wife or paid out money on property already in her name, the presumption of advancement was said to rebut the presumption of a resulting trust with the effect that a *gift* to the wife was presumed unless the husband could come up with a different explanation. The presumption of advancement, founded in a concern to protect married women when their position at common law was precarious, is said to be very weak today (*Pettit v Pettit* [1970] AC 777, Lord Reid at 793, Lord Hodson at 811 and Lord Diplock at 824; but *see Tinsley v Milligan* [1993] 3 WLR 126, where the House of Lords, admittedly *obiter*, treated the presumptions of advancement as still effective). In any event, it does not apply to cohabitants. (One might note in passing that s 3(2) of the Law Reform (Miscellaneous Provisions) Act 1970 provides that the gift of an engagement ring is rebuttably presumed to be an absolute one. Note also that in *Moate v Moate* [1948] 2 All ER 486, the presumption of advancement was held to apply even though completion of the purchase took place shortly before the marriage so that, at the time when A put property into B's name, they were not actually husband and wife. Both of these could, on the facts, apply to a cohabiting couple.)

In a simple case, then, of property being purchased outright for cash and the parties both contributing to the price, the answer is to be found by starting with the presumption of a resulting trust and examining whether it has been rebutted. Outright purchases may be relatively infrequent in the kinds of cases with which we are concerned. The resulting trust can, however, fairly easily be stretched to a more common example where both parties contribute to the so-called deposit: the gap between the purchase price (and associated costs) and the amount raised on mortgage. Here, the presumption will arise that the parties intended to share the equity in proportion to their contributions. If, however, the subsequent mortgage repayments are not also shared in those proportions, we enter the murkier waters discussed *below*. At this stage, the purpose is only to isolate the simple cases.

As for the constructive trust, this too has a long pedigree. Traditionally, a constructive trust is a relationship created by equity in the interests of good conscience and without reference to any express or implied intention of the parties. It is 'constructed' by equity rather than by the parties and so it may or may not give effect to what one or both of them intended. In this jurisdiction, it has mainly been used in defined cases of breach of fiduciary duty or unconscionable conduct (*Belmont Finance Corporation Ltd v Williams Furniture Ltd* [1978] 3 WLR 712). In other words, it has tended to be a response to *particular categories* of wrongdoing. In the United States, however, the constructive trust has been used as a more general remedy in cases of unjust enrichment. Some of the English cases in the 1970s and 1980s probably exhibit a tendency in that direction also.

A simple example of a constructive trust being applied in a situation that might plausibly arise with cohabitants is this. At the time of the purchase, the parties expressly agree that the property is to be shared beneficially even though the legal estate is to go into one name only and the other is making no contribution to the price. The agreement is made in the presence of impeccable witnesses and there is no difficulty in proving it. Without more, the agreement will lack effect because the requirement of writing is not satisfied and because a resulting trust does not arise (the promisee not having contributed to the price). Equity does not assist a volunteer. If, however, the promisee materially changes her position in reliance on the agreement, perhaps by making regular contributions to the mortgage repayments or by improving the property, she will no longer be a volunteer. The assertion by the man of absolute beneficial entitlement in these circumstances would be unconscionable. The man's conscience is now bound by the agreement and equity will enforce it. A trust has been constructed by the court. Whilst the constructive trust here gives effect to the intention of the parties, that is simply because of the particular circumstances. A constructive trust on other facts can arise irrespective of intention. For example, a solicitor who runs off with his client's money is a constructive trustee of it, but that is the last thing he or she intends.

As with the example given of a resulting trust, this was a simple case. Unfortunately, events do not usually happen like this. Once the facts depart from these situations one runs into all kinds of doctrinal problems. Both of the examples dealt with matters beginning with the time of purchase: either contributions to the price or an express agreement right at the outset. Suppose, however, that the parties had not met at the time of purchase. Suppose she moved in with him and he then said that the house is to be shared. Or, to make it more realistic, it was not said in so many words, but some kind of understanding existed. She may have started to share in the mortgage repayments. Or she may have started to contribute to other outgoings in a way that she would not have done had there been no such understanding. These cases can be difficult enough. If one overlays them with evidentiary problems then they become very complex indeed. When matters come to a head on the breakdown of the relationship, each tells a different story; whether genuinely or otherwise. To make it worse, there is often no clear documentary evidence to support either party's case. If any departure from the position with the legal estate is to occur, it will be based on the credibility of the witnesses and inferences to be drawn from what seem to be the facts. The whole process of drawing inferences can be infused with the values of the interpreter. In particular, if one has to ask the question 'would she have done this without some understanding that she was to share in the home?', then there is plenty of scope for ideas about what women are conventionally expected to do without proprietary reward.

These issues are now largely side-stepped in cases of marriage breakdown because the divorce court can decide who is to own the property *in the future* without regard to the current ownership. No doubt the similarity between some married and unmarried couples has tempted judges to try to use the law of trusts to produce similar outcomes in cohabitation breakdown. It is this difficult zone between the clear case of the resulting trust and the clear case of the constructive trust of which we must now try to make some sense.

### *Lloyds Bank v Rosset*

The starting point for considering the modern law is the House of Lords' decision in *Lloyds Bank v Rosset* [1990] 2 FLR 155. As we shall see, this decision preserves both the resulting trust and constructive trust approaches outlined *above*; but in doing so, has stamped a rigid conceptual scheme on the area and raises more questions than it answers about the relationship between implied trusts and other concepts, especially proprietary estoppel.

Ironically, perhaps, *Rosset* concerned a matrimonial home. The house in question had been bought with money paid from a trust fund in which Mr Rosset was a beneficiary. An overdraft with Lloyds Bank was arranged in order to pay for renovations to the property and secured by a legal charge. The house was vested in Mr Rosset's sole name because, as Mrs Rosset knew, the trustee had required that to be the case. The couple separated, leaving Mrs Rosset in occupation, and the bank sought possession because its demand for repayment had not been met. Mr Rosset did not resist the claim. Mrs Rosset argued that her beneficial interest was an overriding interest which bound the bank because she was in actual occupation at the relevant time (*see below*).

The trial judge held that Mrs Rosset had a beneficial interest in the property, the extent of which was to be determined at a future hearing. Although Mrs Rosset had made no financial contribution to the property, she had spent considerable time in making it habitable. At the time of the purchase the property had not been occupied for seven or eight years and required major renovation. The parties were allowed a key before exchange of contracts and Mrs Rosset supervised and co-ordinated the building work, on her own or with her husband. She redecorated some of the property. These and other actions led the trial judge to conclude that Mrs Rosset must have reduced the cost of renovation and thus indirectly contributed to the acquisition of the property, albeit to a small extent (at 162C).

The House of Lords disagreed. Lord Bridge summarised the law in the following passage:

> The first and fundamental question which must always be resolved is whether … there has at any time prior to acquisition, or exceptionally at some later date, been any agreement arrangement or understanding reached between them that the property is to be shared beneficially. The finding of an agreement or an arrangement to share in this sense can only, I think, be based on evidence of express discussions, however imperfectly remembered and however imprecise their terms may have been. Once a finding to this effect is made it will only be necessary for the partner asserting a claim to a beneficial interest against the partner entitled to the legal estate to show that he or she has acted to his or her detriment or significantly altered his or her legal position in reliance on the agreement in order to give rise to a constructive trust or proprietary estoppel.
>
> In sharp contrast with this situation is the very different one where there is no evidence to support a finding of an agreement or arrangement to share, however reasonable it might have been for the parties to reach such an arrangement if they had applied their minds to the question, and where the court must rely entirely on the conduct of the parties both as the basis from which to infer a common intention to share the property beneficially and as the conduct relied on to give rise to a constructive trust. In this situation direct contributions to the purchase price by the partner who is not the legal owner, whether initially or by payment of mortgage instalments, will readily justify the inference necessary to the creation of a constructive trust. But, as I read the authorities, it is at least extremely doubtful whether anything less will do.

We can see here traces of a constructive trust in the first of these categories and of resulting trust in the second. Applying these formulae to the facts in *Rosset*, the House of Lords held that Mrs Rosset had no interest: there was no evidence of an 'agreement' to qualify Mrs Rosset for a share under the first paragraph; and her contributions, which Lord Bridge found to be '*de minimis*', were not sufficiently 'direct' to qualify under the second.

The significance of *Rosset* lies in the pre-eminence accorded to the parties' intentions. The courts must first ask whether the parties reached any informal agreement about ownership and, if they did, whether there has been the required reliance on that agreement. If they did not, then the courts can only infer that intention on the basis of a narrowly defined range of direct financial contributions to the acquisition of the property. This seems to close off the possibility of the courts imposing trusts on the basis of 'justice' or 'good conscience' wherever property has been acquired by the parties by joint effort for joint use (as suggested, for example, by Lord Denning in *Eves v Eves* [1975] 1 All ER 768, relying on a dictum of Lord Diplock in *Gissing v Gissing* [1970] 2 All ER 780). However, the reference to proprietary estoppel in Lord Bridge's formulation of his second category has sown the seeds of what may become a similar justice-based approach. This is discussed in detail *below*.

We turn now to a more detailed consideration of Lord Bridge's formulae.

*The first category: express but informal agreements to share ownership*
According to Lord Bridge, the first question is whether there has been any 'agreement arrangement or understanding' between the parties concerning property ownership. This must normally be shown to have existed at the date of acquisition: evidence of post-acquisition agreements will only be admitted in exceptional cases. What if, as often happens, one of the parties moves into the house of the other after purchase and they then come to an oral agreement or understanding? Unless this is an exceptional case—and Lord Bridge gives no guidance as to what that is—then presumably it must either be dealt with in the second category (*see below*) or one must turn to proprietary estoppel (*see below*).

Leaving that problem on one side for the moment, we must first consider the questions of evidence and proof raised by Lord Bridge's first category. According to Lord Bridge, there must be evidence of express discussions, 'however imperfectly remembered'. These must be pleaded 'in the greatest detail, both as to language and as to circumstance' (per Waite J in *Hammond v Mitchell* [1991] 1 WLR 1127). If proceedings are brought in the Family Division, the claimant's affidavit is the key document, and must contain the required particulars in sufficient detail (if only because it will stand as her evidence in chief, on which she will not be allowed to enlarge orally before cross-examination: per Waite J).

But what must be proved? First of all, there must be evidence that the parties have communicated their intentions about ownership to each other. It is not enough that the parties were quietly thinking the same thoughts without communicating them: 'our trust law does not allow property rights to be affected by telepathy' (per Steyn LJ in *Springette v Defoe* [1992] 2 FLR 388). However, the discussion need not demonstrate a sophisticated lawyer's understanding of the implications of joint ownership. In *Savill v Goodall* [1992] 25 HLR 588, for example, a couple who were living in a former council house acquired under the 'right to buy' legislation were held to have evinced a common intention to share ownership during a conversation that centred on the need to provide the male claimant with a 'secure home'. This was treated as an express discussion about joint ownership sufficient to found a claim under Lord Bridge's first category.

What must the express discussions be about? Lord Bridge's formulation suggests that the courts are exclusively concerned with 'agreements arrangements or understandings': that is, evidence of some subjective meeting of minds between the parties. The cases suggest, however, that the courts will range more widely than this. In *Eves* (*above*) and *Grant v Edwards* [1986] Ch 638, both of which Lord Bridge described as 'outstanding examples' of his first category, the (male) property owner had offered the claimant an excuse for not putting the property into joint names (in *Eves*, that the claimant was too young and in *Grant*, that it would prejudice her claims against her former husband in ancillary relief proceedings). In neither case could it be said that the man 'agreed' that there should be shared ownership: indeed, their subjective intention was probably precisely the opposite. Nevertheless, they had certainly generated that expectation in the claimant and were (rightly) obliged to give effect to it.

However, an expectation of property ownership in the mind of the claimant is not enough in itself. In *Rosset*, for example, the trial judge found clear evidence that Mrs Rosset believed that the house was jointly owned, but the House of Lords nevertheless dismissed her claim on the ground that there was no evidence of any *specific* conversation about ownership having taken place between the parties to which this expectation could be attributed (*see also Springette v Defoe* and *Savill v Goodall*, both *above*). Mrs Rosset had merely assumed (wrongly) that jointly used property would be jointly owned.

The position seems to be, then, that there must be evidence of some specific statement or conversation about ownership, even though what was said lacked a full grasp of the legal niceties of co-ownership—or that it was a trick, deceit or otherwise not representative of the speaker's true intentions. What is required, in other words, is a specific expectation-generating statement (and this will not always be easy to prove). If this is correct, then the phrase 'agreement arrangement or understanding' is not a totally accurate description of what is needed. For example, a unilateral declaration of intent, entailing no consensus *ad idem* between the parties, may also qualify for these purposes: *see Hammond v Mitchell, above*, where the man's spontaneous declaration of an intent to share ownership was enough to found a claim; *see also Risch v McFee* (1991) 61 P&CR 42, where a man's statement that 'a common law wife is as good as a "proper" wife' helped the woman claimant establish her claim.

The next step is to show that the claimant has *relied* on the specific statement. The acts of reliance and the statement must be linked (per Brightman J in *Eves, above*): but how? Again, Lord Bridge offers no guidance, so we must turn to earlier case law. Unfortunately, no consistent judicial approach emerges. This is evident from *Grant v Edwards* (*above*), in which all three members of the Court of Appeal offered slightly different views on the question of linkage. For Nourse LJ, the test is a causal one: the claimant must show that she would not have performed the acts in question but for the man's statement. For Mustill LJ, it is a question of looking at what the parties have agreed the claimant is to do in return for fulfilment of the expectation (although this may require the court to reconstruct the terms of the bargain).

Although Browne-Wilkinson VC agreed with Nourse LJ's approach (by holding that payments used to discharge a mortgage, directly or indirectly, will be assumed to have been induced by the man's statement), he went on to hint at a broader approach, drawing on the analogous doctrine of proprietary estoppel, in the following terms:

> ... once it has been shown that there was a common intention that the claimant should have an interest in the house, any act done by her to her detriment relating to the joint lives of the parties is, in my judgment, sufficient detriment to qualify. The acts do not have to be inherently referable to the acquisition of the house ...

This approach supplies the necessary linkage by casting the burden of proof on to the man to show that, once the necessary 'common intention' has been proved, any detrimental acts 'relating to the joint lives of the parties' were not a result of the common intention. Otherwise, the necessary link will be inferred. This approach has yet to be developed in the cases, although Lord Bridge's fleeting reference to proprietary estoppel suggests that the House of Lords may be sympathetic in the future to estoppel-based analysis. This is considered further *below*.

These differences of approach could have important practical consequences. This can be tested by considering the treatment of, for example, housework and child care under these different approaches. A causal test leaves room for assumptions about what women can or cannot be expected to do in the ordinary run of things: it leaves the way open for judges to discount domestic activities on the ground that they would have been done anyway. Under a bargain-based test, on the other hand, it would be open to the parties to stipulate expressly that such contributions are not given freely but are instead consideration for a promise of property ownership (*see* Chapter 11 on cohabitation contracts). For reasons given above, Browne-Wilkinson VC's approach is the most generous from the claimant's point of view, always assuming that domestic contributions could be regarded, *prima facie*, as detriment incurred in relation to the parties' joint lives.

*The second category: direct financial contributions*

If no 'agreement' can be proved, then the claimant will be forced to rely on Lord Bridge's second category by showing that she has made 'direct financial contributions' to acquisition. Such contributions perform the dual role of proving, first, the existence of a common intention concerning ownership as well as, second, reliance by the claimant on that intention. Contributions to the purchase are required, either initially (in cash) or subsequently through making mortgage repayments. For these purposes, a tenant's statutory entitlement to a discount under 'right to buy legislation' will count as the equivalent of an initial cash contribution to purchase (*see Marsh v Von Sternberg* [1986] 1 FLR 526; *Springette v Defoe* and *Savill v Goodall*, both *above*). Improvements to property are probably outside the scope of this principle, unless they can be characterised as related to acquisition, since English law does not grant an improver a right to compensation in the absence of an agreement to that effect (*Thomas v Fuller-Brown* [1988] 1 FLR 237).

According to Lord Bridge 'nothing less [than direct financial contributions to acquisition] will do'. So, for example, substantial financial contributions to general household expenses *other than* the mortgage will not suffice, even though (it seems) the mortgage could not be paid without those contributions. Such contributions may count as detrimental reliance under the first category, but only (as we have seen) if there have been prior specific discussions about ownership between the parties.

Lord Bridge's formula takes a much narrower view than earlier authority of what kinds of contribution count. There was, for example, some pre-*Rosset* support for rewarding substantial but indirect financial contributions to household expenses without the need to show an informal agreement between the parties (per Fox LJ in *Burns v Burns* [1984] Ch 317). After *Rosset*, this no longer seems possible except under the first category. This in turn suggests that cases will (and should) in future be pleaded under the first category where possible, with the evidentiary quagmire that first category cases bring in their wake.

*Quantification of interests*
Assuming that enough has been done to establish some degree of sharing in the equity, how are the actual shares to be determined? If the case falls within the first category—ie where there has been an express understanding which has been sufficiently relied upon—then that understanding is presumably to be given effect, even if it entails the claimant receiving more than she has contributed in her reliance. By analogy with contract law, a court will not be concerned with the adequacy of the consideration. The only alternative to quantification on this basis is for the court to exercise a discretion in fixing shares on the basis of what seems just at the time: this was certainly Lord Denning's approach in *Eves*, but it did not command enthusiastic support from the other members of the same court

There is, conceptually, nothing wrong with an agreement that the ultimate shares in the equity are to be determined in the light of the actual contributions which the parties make. This deferred ascertainment method was mentioned by Lord Diplock in *Gissing*, alluded to by the Court of Appeal in an unreported case, *Burgess v Burgess* 15 December 1977, and repeated in *Passee v Passee* [1988] 1 FLR 263, CA and *Stokes v Anderson* [1991] 1 FLR 392. By extension, therefore, it must also be possible in a 'second category' case for one to infer from the parties' conduct that there was a common intention that the ascertainment of their interests should be deferred. Alternatively, although there may be evidence of an agreement to share ownership, the parties may not have agreed the proportions. In either case, it is possible that one moves back, at the quantification stage, to Lord Denning's attempt to impose a fair result. In *Stokes v Anderson* the Court of Appeal reduced the trial judge's award of a half-share in the property to that of one-quarter with Nourse LJ saying:

> [A]ll payments made and acts done by the claimant are to be treated as illuminating the common intention as to the extent of the beneficial interest. Once you get to that stage, ... there is no practicable alternative to the determination of a fair share. The court must supply the common intention by reference to that which all the material circumstances have shown to be fair.

The only firm conclusion to be drawn from this, it seems, is that quantification of interests under the first category will not depend on the value of the claimant's contribution: other factors take over. Once arrived at, the parties' shares will usually be treated as subsisting in the 'equity' of the property, that is, the amount by which the market value of the property exceeds any outstanding mortgage debt. In a case where both parties have assumed liability under the mortgage during the relationship, this will be the normal method of calculation (subject, if necessary, to post-separation adjustments, discussed later).

However, complications may arise if the terms of the informal understanding between the parties show that the claimant's share was conditional on her undertaking sole liability to repay the mortgage. Here, it appears from *Savill v Goodall* (which concerned a male claimant) that the shares will not be calculated as subsisting in the equity, as described *above*, but instead in the market value of the house: but the claimant will then be obliged to redeem the mortgage from her share of the proceeds (which could, of course, substantially diminish the value of her share). The principle at work is that where the claimant's 'assumption of liability to discharge the legal charge was [according to the terms of the agreement] the *quid pro quo* for his acquisition of a half share in the property ... equity will not allow him both to assert a claim to his half share and to deny the liability subject to which it was acquired' (per Nourse LJ).

Turning to the second category, it might be thought that problems of quantification disappear. After all, once a direct financial contribution has been identified, it should be possible to calculate it as a percentage of the total. Two particular problems arise. The first is what is to count as 'the total' for the purposes of calculation: the 'equity' or the property's market value (ie the net or gross proceeds of sale)? The second is how to treat contributions by way of mortgage repayments. An example may illustrate the uncertainties.

Suppose that a house is purchased for £50,000. W contributes £37,500 in cash, the balance of £12,500 is from a mortgage (so that the cash : mortgage ratio is 75 : 25). Both M and W are jointly formally responsible for paying the mortgage, but they agree between themselves that M is in fact to take sole responsibility for making the payments (which, to make things easy, we will assume are of interest only). M pays £2,500 before the relationship breaks down. The mortgage still stands at £12,500, the property's value having risen to £75,000 (ie leaving an 'equity' of £62,500). (For the sake of simplicity, we leave out questions of entitlement to endowment policies or other collateral, but assume that any estate agent's fees would be deducted from sale proceeds whichever method is used.)

In these circumstances, how much credit should M be given for undertaking to pay the mortgage? Should it be the interest he has actually repaid (£2,500); the whole mortgage sum (£12,500); or half the mortgage sum (£6,250)? And once we have decided that, is M's share to be calculated as a percentage of the net sale proceeds; or of the gross proceeds? And is M to be treated as responsible for discharging the mortgage out of his share, or not?

If we pursued the approach outlined in *Savill v Goodall*, then there would be a *quid pro quo*: M would be credited with contributing the whole mortgage sum, giving him a 25 per cent share, but he would be obliged to repay the mortgage out of his share. This means that he would be credited with 25 per cent of the gross sale proceeds (ie £18,750) from which he would have to repay the mortgage (£12,500) leaving him £6,250. W's share would be 75 per cent of the gross proceeds, ie £56,250.

An alternative would be the method adopted in *Huntingford v Hobbs*, the facts of which closely resemble the example given *above*. Here, M was credited with contributing the full mortgage amount, (which, on our example, would again entitle him to a quarter share), which was then calculated as follows: the amount outstanding on the mortgage was credited to W and deducted from the 'equity', leaving £50,000 (ie £62,500 – £12,500). M's quarter-share was then calculated in this remaining £50,000, giving him £12,500. On this calculation, therefore, M gets double what he would get under the *Savill* method (although if the cash : mortgage ratios were 50 : 50, both methods would produce the same result).

This discussion does not exhaust the potential complexities in valuation, but is intended to illustrate them. They are, perhaps, more acute under the second category than the first, given the emphasis in the first category on the fulfilment of expectations as opposed to the strict calculation of direct contributions under the second; but they may surface even there.

*Date of quantification*

There has been some controversy over the date at which the respective shares are to be valued. In a period of house inflation (or deflation) this can be a crucial question because there is frequently a gap of months or years between separation and litigation. If the beneficial interests are to crystallise at the time of separation, with the party who remains paying the mortgage and benefiting from all the subsequent increase in value, this would often produce a quite different result than if the respective shares were to remain constant to the date of trial but with one party receiving a cash credit for payments made after separation (*see below*). In *Hall v Hall* [1981] FLR 379 the Court of Appeal held that in cases involving unmarried couples a judge is entitled to hold that the trust under which the beneficial interests are held was extinguished at the date of separation; in other words the departed party does not obtain the full benefit of post-separation inflation (if any).

From a doctrinal point of view, this was a curious notion which received a little implicit support (*Gordon v Douce* [1983] 2 All ER 228,

CA) but was not generally followed (*Cousins v Dzosens* (1981) *The Times*, 22 December). The Court of Appeal in *Turton v Turton* [1987] 2 All ER 641 has declared *Hall* to be wrong on the grounds that the majority of the House of Lords in *Gissing* held that there is no discretion in the matter. There is presumably nothing wrong, however, with an agreement *at the outset* which provides for the crystallisation of a share at the date of any separation.

*Adjustment for post-separation contributions*

The question of adjustment for contributions made after the date of separation is a difficult one. If there is an express agreement as to deferred ascertainment then post-separation contributions will continue to affect the respective shares, unless the agreement itself provides otherwise. If the trust is based on inferred common intention but it is still found that the parties must have intended deferred ascertainment then presumably the same will apply. If, however, the trust is based solely on inferred common intention and no understanding about deferred ascertainment can be extracted then the parties' shares are presumably fixed at the date of acquisition (their subsequent conduct being relevant only as evidence of what the common intention was). Here, therefore, some adjustment in cash terms may be necessary to take account of post-separation events.

One school of thought was that the party remaining in occupation would be credited with half of the *capital* that she had repaid, but not with repayments of interest, because that was the price that she must pay for exclusive occupation of the property (*Suttill v Graham* [1977] 1 WLR 819; on occupation rents generally, *see* Chapter 7). In *Re Gorman* [1990] 2 FLR 284, however, Vinelott and Mervyn Davies JJ held that this practice (although convenient and likely to save costs) is not a rule of law to be applied in all circumstances. Following the Court of Appeal decision in *Bernard v Josephs* [1983] FLR 179, it was held that one-half of the *whole* instalments could be credited to the parties in occupation who had been paying the mortgage.

The reason for this was that making interest payments was necessary to relieve the property of the charge. The debit side, however, is that the question of an occupation rent is determined separately: the occupier's share will be credited with half of the post-separation mortgage repayments but debited with a half of the appropriate occupation rent. This means that if the mortgage was low but the rental value of the property was high then she might have to account for more occupation rent than she was notionally being credited with in respect of mortgage payments.

Inquiries will have to be made as to the likely rental value, and the amount of post-separation repayments, in order to conduct this calculation: but if it looks as though the likely rent figure is going to be very close to the interest element of the mortgage repayments, the courts may be willing to revert to the *Suttill v Graham* approach and simply treat repayments of interest as equivalent to an occupation rent, so that the occupier is credited only with an appropriate proportion (probably half) of the capital repayments (per Millett J in *Re Pavlou (A bankrupt)* [1993] 2 FLR 751).

Adjustments to the parties' shares may also, it seems, be made on the basis of post-separation repairs and improvements to the property by the occupier. The occupier will be entitled to claim whichever is the lesser of (a) the amount expended or (b) the increase in value in the property thereby realised. This principle applies whether the beneficial interest is held on a joint tenancy or tenancy in common (per Millett J in *Re Pavlou, above*).

*Only the legal estate is in joint names*

The factual settings of the cases discussed so far involved the legal estate being vested in one party's name alone. It is possible that the legal estate is vested jointly but that there is no declaration as to the equitable interests. It is conceivable that this might be done intentionally. For example, one party has provided all the price or 'deposit' but the property is going into joint names in order to afford some security to the other: her or his signature would still be required for a disposition. The intention might be that, initially at least, the parties are content to let the presumption of a resulting trust apply so that the provider of the price takes all of the equity but that some flexibility is left open in the event of the other improving the property or paying some mortgage instalments. Even here, however, it is highly desirable for the agreement to be reduced to writing as a result of the narrow limits set by *Rosset.*

The absence of an express declaration may also be the result of an oversight. One assumes that this is more likely to be overlooked in the case of unregistered land where the conveyance might simply make no reference to them. With registered land, a transfer to joint proprietors will call for some consideration of the survivorship declaration printed in the standard forms. As was seen earlier, a declaration that the survivor can give a valid receipt for capital money may operate as a declaration of a beneficial joint tenancy so that on severance the parties hold as tenants in common in equal shares (*Re Gorman* [1990] 2 FLR 284), but this is by no means assured (*see Harwood v Harwood* [1991] 2 FLR 274). Presumably a solicitor will be negligent if he or she fails to advise about and obtain instructions on the destination of beneficial interests.

If, one way or another, the documentary evidence of title is silent about the equity then, in theory, the position is the same as if the legal estate were vested in only one of the parties. In practice, however, the *fact* that the legal estate was taken in joint names, especially when coupled with joint liability under a mortgage, will require explanation. The most obvious one is that there was some intention to share (*see* eg *Crisp v Mullings* (1975) 239 EG 119 and *Walker v Hall* (1984) 14 Fam Law 21; *Springette v Defoe, above*). Attention will then focus on quantification of the contributions, which will be governed strictly by the size of the parties' respective direct financial contributions, unless there is clear evidence of an actual common intention to share ownership in different proportions. The mere fact of joint legal ownership, even when coupled with joint mortgage liability, will not lead inexorably to equal beneficial shares (*Springette v Defoe, above*).

## Proprietary estoppel

The general rules relating to proprietary estoppel were discussed in Chapter 7. It was mentioned there that proprietary estoppel can give rise to orders about both ownership and occupation rights. This section concentrates on cases concerning the former. They are by no means confined to those involving cohabitants, although they do often involve co-residence. The claim might be by a housekeeper or younger relative who is disappointed by the absence of any provision in a will (eg *Greasley v Cooke* [1986] 1 WLR 1306). In principle, such cases can offer guidance but, as with the law of trusts, the kind of relationship between the parties can affect the inferences of fact that are drawn from conduct.

The role of proprietary estoppel, and its relationship with the constructive trust, has been put in question by the comment of Lord Bridge in *Rosset* that his first category may give rise to a constructive trust *or* to a proprietary estoppel. This reflects judicial statements in earlier cases to the effect that constructive trusts and estoppel, or the principles underlying them, should in some way be assimilated (eg Browne-Wilkinson VC in *Grant v Edwards*; Nourse LJ in *Stokes v Anderson* [1991] 1 FLR 391). There does indeed seem to be a thread of detrimental reliance on a belief induced by the legal owner that is common to both.

However, there are a number of differences. First, the constructive trust is concerned with agreements, whereas estoppel seems to catch a wider range of unilateral representations (although we have queried whether the courts in constructive trust cases are really concerned with agreements at all). Second, there seems to be more discretion available to a court in satisfying the equity raised by an estoppel (per Scarman LJ in *Crabb v Arun DC* [1976] Ch 179 at 198). Although the starting-point for both is the fulfilment of expectations, the courts seem more willing to tailor estoppel remedies to suit the particular circumstances of the case (*see Burrows and Burrows v Sharpe* (1991) Fam Law 67, where the fulfilment of the original intentions of the parties was not practicable and the court 'had to do the best it could'). This often results in a form of protected right of occupation rather than a share in the beneficial ownership (eg *Matharu v Matharu* [1994] 2 FLR 597). Indeed, a constructive trust in the sense we are using here can *only* result in a beneficial share, while estoppel may result in a wide range of proprietary or personal rights. Third, the effect of the remedies *vis-à-vis* third parties may differ (this is discussed at the end of this section). Finally, the burden of proof may be different: in constructive trusts, the claimant must establish that the acts of reliance were linked to the common understanding, whereas in estoppel the courts seem to cast the onus on to the legal owner once the representation has been proved (*Greasley v Cooke*, *above*; *Wayling v Jones* [1993] EGCS 153). This also seems to imply a more generous view of what counts as an act of reliance. It may be premature, therefore, to regard the two as interchangeable: but the possible shift towards estoppel presaged by *Rosset* may indicate a willingness to treat claims more generously than under constructive trust doctrine, but at the same time temper the outcome with greater remedial flexibility.

The leading case concerning cohabitants is *Pascoe v Turner* [1979] 2 All ER 945 where the male plaintiff, who held both the legal and beneficial interests in the house, lived with the defendant from 1965 until he moved out in 1973. It was found that he had assured the defendant on several occasions that the house and its contents were hers. Relying on this, she spent money on the property totalling about £1,000, which represented a substantial proportion of her capital. In April 1976 the plaintiff wrote to the defendant giving her two months' notice of the termination of her licence. She refused to leave and he sued for possession.

The trial judge found that the plaintiff had made a gift of the contents of the house and that the beneficial interest in the house itself had passed under a constructive trust inferred from the words and conduct of the parties. The plaintiff appealed. The Court of Appeal affirmed the judge's finding that the contents passed as a gift. Cumming-Bruce LJ, however, giving the judgment of the court, said that '(t)here is nothing in the facts from which an inference of a constructive trust can be drawn' (at 948g). It was held instead that there had been a purported gift of the house which was imperfect (not being in writing under seal). Nevertheless, an equity had arisen in the defendant's favour and the only way to satisfy the equity in this case was by perfecting the gift and ordering the conveyance of the property to the defendant. In effect the defendant received a £16,000 house for £1,000. The case could be seen as belonging to a well-known application of proprietary estoppel where equity perfects an imperfect gift. Here there had been an attempt at a gift which had failed. Had there simply been a *promise* to give then the court might have exercised its discretion more sparingly.

The Court of Appeal's reasons for rejecting the imposition of a constructive trust are not very clearly presented. In any event, many decisions prior to *Rosset* must now be viewed with caution. One might speculate, however, on what the result would be following *Rosset*. It is possible that the facts fall within the first category of cases mentioned by Lord Bridge, although there was not so much an express *agreement* here as an express attempt at a gift. Leaving that aside, Lord Bridge said that only exceptionally could the agreement be effectually made after the acquisition of the property, as had happened here. Unless, therefore, *Pascoe v Turner* is such an exceptional case, it would still have to be decided under estoppel.

In *Re Basham* [1987] 2 FLR 264 Edward Nugee QC, sitting as a High Court judge in the Chancery Division, seemed to treat proprietary estoppel as an example of a constructive trust, in the company of the equitable principles which apply to secret trusts and mutual wills.

The plaintiff was the stepdaughter of the deceased who was claiming that the whole of the deceased's estate should be transferred to her. The facts are set out at considerable length in the judgment. Suffice it to say that the evidence was clear that the plaintiff had been led to understand she would inherit all of the deceased's property and that, relying on the understanding, she had acted to her detriment in the way that she had looked after the deceased. An unusual factor in the case was that the largest item of value in the estate was a cottage in which the plaintiff had never lived. Counsel for the administrators submitted that for estoppel to operate there must be a mistaken belief as to a legal right. Because the plaintiff had not lived in the cottage she could not claim that she thought she had a legal right to remain there.

The plaintiff succeeded as to the whole of her claim. Edward Nugee QC said that he knew of no case that supported counsel's main submission for the defendants, that the belief on which the claimant relies must be related to an existing right. (In fact, the decision in *Coombes v Smith* [1987] 1 FLR 352 was almost wholly dependent on this alleged requirement but that case, whilst decided, had not been reported at the time.)

Another unusual factor in *Re Basham* was that the plaintiff was claiming the whole of the estate (whatever it might contain) and not just a specific item. In fact, the cottage formed only about one-half of the estate, the balance being in cash. In *Layton v Martin* [1986] 2 FLR 227, another case not cited in *Re Basham*, Scott J had seemed to rule out proprietary estoppel for anything other than specific assets.

A more recent case, *Wayling v Jones* (*above*), is another striking illustration of the potential of estoppel. This was a claim brought against an estate by the deceased's former chauffeur, companion and unpaid business assistant of 16 years. The deceased had promised the claimant that he would leave the claimant a hotel (the chief business asset) in his will, but he failed to do so. The claimant successfully showed that the deceased had made a promise on which the claimant had relied, the reliance being inferred from the claimant's unpaid work in the deceased's various catering businesses. The Court of Appeal was prepared to cast on to the deceased's estate the onus of proving that the claimant had not relied on the promises.

The tentative conclusion that one can reach on the present state of the law is that, in the absence of special circumstances such as an imperfect gift or virtual lifelong devotion to the property owner, the equity raised in proprietary estoppel is more likely to be satisfied by an order relating to occupation, whereas the constructive trust gives rise to an interest in the land and, consequentially, in the proceeds of sale. Whereas with a constructive trust the court is concerned with giving effect to the common intention which it claims to have found, in estoppel something less than this may be sufficient to prevent the legal owner from unconscionably asserting her or his rights at law.

This is only a tentative conclusion and an authoritative statement from the House of Lords on the true relationship between constructive trusts and proprietary estoppel is still awaited. One practical reason why clarification is needed, quite apart from the desirability of certainty, concerns the protection of interests against third parties. If a *trust* is established then, subject to what is discussed below, it will date back to the time when it was created and may have priority over subsequent charges. If a share in the beneficial interest is awarded simply as a way of discharging an estoppel, however, one imagines that an interest in the land only comes into existence at the time of judgment. Before judgment, the estoppel claim is 'inchoate' and, as such, will probably not bind third parties unless the third party has actual notice of the circumstances giving rise to the equity (*Ives Investments Ltd v High* [1967] 2 QB 379; *Ashburn Anstalt v Arnold* [1989] Ch 1) or the third party is a volunteer donee.

If, however, court proceedings have been initiated to assert an estoppel claim, at least where a proprietary right is being sought as a way of satisfying the equity, a pending land action should be registered (in unregistered land) or a caution entered, by analogy with a wife's claim under s 24 of the MCA 1973: *Perez-Adamson v Perez-Rivas* [1987] Fam 89. Otherwise, there seems no obvious registration mechanism for an inchoate equity in unregistered land. In registered land, it is possibly registrable as a minor interest by caution; but it is unlikely that it would qualify as an overriding interest (per Dillon LJ in *Canadian Imperial Bank v Bello* (1992) 64 P&CR 48 at 52, who was, admittedly, referring to a claim in promissary estoppel).

Where the claim is against a deceased's estate, it seems that an inchoate estoppel will bind both the estate and any legatees or intestate beneficiaries (*Re Basham, above*). If it were necessary to freeze the assets pending resolution of the claim (if, for example, the personal representatives were proposing to sell an important asset which the claimant wishes to retain *in specie*), consideration might be given to an interlocutory injunction, the availability of which may turn on the balance of convenience. If the asset is land and proceedings have been commenced, a pending land action should be registered, or a caution entered, as the case may be.

## Protecting a beneficial interest

If a cohabitant has a beneficial interest in land but is not a legal estate owner, then she should consider whether her interest requires protection in the event of a disposition by the legal estate owner. Such a disposition might be the creation of a second or further charge or even an attempted sale.

Because the creation of a legal interest or the conveyance of the legal estate does not require her signature, a third party might be unaware of the cohabitant's existence. The cohabitant will be concerned in case a chargee obtains priority over her interest or, in the case of a sale, that she does not receive her share in the proceeds of sale. Merely being left with a personal action against her former partner for breach of trust is usually inadequate.

If the parties were married, the first consideration would often be the entry of a Class F land charge or a notice on the register under the MHA 1983 but that is not possible where the parties are unmarried. (In any event, an entry under the Act only protects occupation and may not be an adequate step even to protect a spouse. For example, a bank that takes security for an existing debt without carrying out a search of the register would have difficulty in obtaining possession but might still have priority over the wife's beneficial interest.)

## Unregistered title

In the case of unregistered title, an equitable interest arising under an implied, resulting or constructive trust does not appear to be registrable as a land charge under the Land Charges Act 1972. It follows that priorities are governed by the old doctrine of notice.

Notice can be actual—ie where it is truly within the proposed purchaser's knowledge—or constructive—ie where it *would* have been within the proposed purchaser's knowledge if such inquiries and inspections had been made as ought reasonably to have been made by him or his solicitor or other agent (LPA, s 199(1)(ii)(*a*) and (*b*)).

*Constructive notice and occupation*

The main disputes, naturally enough, concern constructive notice and the sort of evidence that should have put a purchaser on inquiry. The question has tended to concentrate on whether a purchaser should have made inquiries of a person *occupying* the property. The traditional view was in the affirmative (*Hunt v Luck* [1902] 1 Ch 428) but this was not applied by Stamp J in *Caunce v Caunce* [1969] 1 All ER 72. Here the judge held that the doctrine of constructive notice does not extend to cases where the presence of the wife was wholly consistent with the title offered by the husband. Furthermore, it was said, *obiter*, that the doctrine does not extend to any other person 'eg, the Vendor's father, his Uncle Harry or his Aunt Matilda, any of whom, be it observed, might have contributed money towards the purchase of the property' (at 728E). Stamp J said that the reason for this 'is that the vendor being in possession, the presence of his wife or guest or lodger implies nothing to negative the title offered' (at 728F). This view was criticised by the Court of Appeal in *Hodgson v Marks* [1971] 2 All ER 684 and the House of Lords in *Williams & Glyn's Bank v Boland* [1980] 2 All ER 408, but both cases concerned registered title where, as will be seen *below*, the rules are different.

Although all commentators seem to regard *Caunce* as no longer authoritative, so that occupation of unregistered land will normally constitute constructive notice, the only decision directly in point seems to be that of Judge John Finlay QC sitting as a High Court judge in *Kingsnorth Trust Ltd v Tizard* [1986] 2 All ER 54. The material facts were that the legal estate of the matrimonial home was in the husband's sole name but the wife undoubtedly had a beneficial interest by virtue of contributions. The marriage had broken down and Mrs Tizard normally slept at her sister's house nearby, returning every day to give the children their breakfast. When Mr Tizard was away working she would sleep in the house. The husband applied for a mortgage advance and described himself as a single man on the application form. The surveyor inspected the property on a Sunday and Mr Tizard told him that his wife had left many months previously and that she was living with someone nearby. The judge found that the wife remained in occupation of the house, an arguable finding but not one that concerns us here, and that guided by the comments on *Caunce* in *Hodgson v Marks* and *Williams & Glyn's Bank Ltd v Boland* the lenders had constructive notice of Mrs Tizard's beneficial interest. In other words, he impliedly held that *Caunce* should no longer be followed. The result of this was that the lender could not escape the clutches of constructive notice by arguing that the wife's interest was not discoverable by reasonable inquiry; it was enough that it was reasonable in the circumstances known to the lender to expect the lender to make more careful or further inquiries than it had in fact made.

*Appointing a second trustee for sale*

It is probably safe to say that for so long as a beneficial owner is incontrovertibly in occupation of unregistered land then it is not imperative to take further steps to protect the equitable interest. On the other hand, if she has left the property, or might have to leave at short notice, or if it is not clear that she is in occupation, positive steps should be taken. The safest course is for her to request the legal estate owner to appoint her as another trustee and for the notice of appointment to be indorsed on the conveyance to him. If he refuses, an application can be made to the court under s 41 of the Trustee Act 1925 for the appointment of another trustee, namely her, and, if necessary, for a vesting order under s 44. Notice of the application should be registered as a pending action under s 5 of the Land Charges Act 1972. If there is no time for this—perhaps because a disposition is imminent and the purchaser might be protected by the priority period conferred by an Official Certificate of Search—an application can be made for an injunction restraining completion pending the appointment of the other trustee (*Watts v Waller* [1967] 1 WLR 451). If a deposit has been paid then one might consider an injunction restraining its release because the deposit may represent a large part of the equity in the property. Notice to the deposit holder warning of a possible breach of trust might be sufficient to prevent its release for fear of being fixed with personal liability.

The purpose behind this strategy is to bring about the situation where the beneficiary's signature is required for any disposition. Strictly, neither the legal estate owner nor the court need appoint her as a second trustee and a third party could be chosen. Whilst this ought to be sufficient a conveyance by two trustees will nevertheless overreach the beneficial interests, leaving the beneficiary only with a personal remedy if she does not receive her share (*City of London Building Society v Flegg* [1988] 1 FLR 98, HL).

*Beneficial owner aware of charge being created*
Even where a beneficial interest has not been overreached, it may still be vulnerable to a third party's charge. This is especially the case where the occupier either knew (or, possibly, ought to have known) of the chargee—perhaps a first mortgagee who lent the money to assist with the initial purchase.

It now seems well established in the cases that, in these circumstances, the occupier will not ordinarily have priority over the mortgagee, although a confusing variety of conceptual reasons have been given for this result. One is that it flows from the nature of the occupier's beneficial interest itself which, because of the occupier's actual or deemed knowledge of the charge, has had 'carved out of it in anticipation a recognition of the rights of the mortgagees whose finance was intended to bring the purchase into being' (per Mustill LJ in *Equity and Law Home Loans Ltd v Prestidge* [1992] 1 WLR 137; *see also Bristol & West Building Society v Henning* [1985] 2 All ER 606). Another is that the occupier's implied authority to the legal owner to encumber the property operates to estop the occupier from denying the mortgagee's priority (per Sir Christopher Slade in *Skipton BS v Clayton* (1993) 66 P&CR 223); or that it grants the legal owner an ostensible authority as an agent on which the lender is entitled to rely (per Lord Oliver in *Abbey National Building Society v Cann* [1990] 2 FLR 122). If the occupier is bound by the first mortgage then it seems s/he is also bound by a mortgage which replaces it (even if the occupier knew nothing about the replacement) at least to the extent of the first loan (*Equity and Law Home Loans Ltd v Prestidge, above*).

Whatever the explanation, it seems that knowledge of a charge on the part of a beneficial co-owner will affect priorities *vis-à-vis* the chargee, and that this doctrine is not confined to unregistered title (although there are other techniques available in registered land, discussed *below*, to achieve the same effect). The boundaries of this doctrine are uncertain: for example, must the knowledge of the charge be actual or constructive? If the latter, will the construction be made only in respect of first mortgages, or might it apply also to second mortgages (as distinct from remortgages: *see above*)? Authoritative answers to these questions are awaited.

**Registered title**

Priority between interests in registered land is governed by quite separate rules although some semantic similarity with the rules of notice can cause confusion. Here the doctrine of notice to a purchaser is strictly irrelevant. Under the land registration scheme interests are divided into overriding interests and minor interests. Put briefly, overriding interests are the broad equivalent of legal estates and interests in unregistered land, affecting purchasers irrespective of notice. They are set out in s 70 of the Land Registration Act 1925. Minor interests are a residual category of interests which only bind a purchaser for value if they are protected by an entry on the register.

A beneficial interest arising under a trust for sale is a minor interest and thus should be protected, at the least, by the entry of a caution under s 54 of the Act. This should ensure that a cohabitant will be warned of any prospective dealing with the land and be given the opportunity to assert her interest regardless of whether she is occupying the property. In other words, there is an appropriate entry under the Land Registration Act, which is not the case with the Land Charges Act 1972. For this reason, whilst applying to be made a trustee of the legal estate is still a counsel of perfection it is less important than in the case of unregistered title.

*Actual occupation*

This leads to what has been a controversial issue in recent years—whether protection is afforded by mere occupation and without an entry on the register. In other words, is there an equivalent to the rule in *Hunt v Luck* in the land registration scheme? The House of Lords in *Williams & Glyn's Bank v Boland* [1980] 2 All ER 408 held that s 70(1)(*g*) of the Land Registration Act 1925 applies in these circumstances and that the occupier's interest is therefore overriding. This paragraph includes as an overriding interest: 'The rights of every person in actual occupation of the land or in receipt of rents and profits thereof, save where inquiry is made of such person and the rights are not disclosed.'

*Boland* was the registered land equivalent of *Caunce v Caunce*. The husband was the sole registered proprietor of the matrimonial home but it was common ground that the wife had a half-share in the equity by virtue of a resulting trust. The husband charged the property to the bank and the dispute was whether the bank took subject to the wife's interest.

The first matter to be decided was whether the wife's interest was only in the proceeds of sale (as the equitable doctrine of conversion would suggest) or also in the land itself. This is because, *inter alia*, the opening words of s 70(1) refer to registered land being subject to a list of overriding interests 'subsisting in reference thereto'; ie in reference to the land. The House of Lords held that the wife's interest was, for present purposes, in the land and was potentially an overriding interest. The wife had an interest in the land, she was occupying, there had been no enquiry and consequently no failure to disclose, and so her interest was an overriding one. Whilst the case concerned the rights of a wife in actual occupation of property in which she had a beneficial interest, there is no reason to confine the case to spouses. Indeed, there was an argument that s 70(1)(g) had always applied to non-spouses in these circumstances and that the doubt had only really existed where the occupier was married to the registered proprietor.

*Date for determining actual occupation*

It has now been conclusively decided that the relevant date for determining whether an interest in registered land is protected by actual occupation (and is therefore an overriding interest) is the date of the completion of the rival transaction, not of its registration (*Abbey National Building Society v Cann, above*). The non-legal owner will therefore have no priority against a first mortgagee in the ordinary circumstances of purchase and contemporaneous mortgage because she will not have been in actual occupation at the moment when the charge was created. Even if the facts are otherwise, it seems she will be in no position to complain because of the implied consent she gave to the creation of the charge, as discussed earlier.

*What is 'occupation'?*

Finally, there is no clear guidance as to what will amount to occupation for these purposes. In *Abbey National Building Society v Cann* (*above*) Lord Oliver said that it is a finding of fact (at 141H):

> It is, perhaps, dangerous to suggest any test for what is essentially a question of fact, for 'occupation' is a concept which may have different connotations according to the nature and purpose of the property which is claimed to be occupied … It does, in my judgment, involve some degree of permanence and continuity which would rule out mere fleeting presence.

*A special rule for first mortgages?*

We have seen that a beneficial interest may be vulnerable to a first mortgage in a number of ways: through consent, agency or estoppel and, in registered land, the definition and timing of 'actual occupation'. This has been underlined by the ruling of the House of Lords in *Cann* (*above*) that where a purchase is being financed by a mortgage executed on the property purchased, the two transactions are to be regarded as indivisible, so that any equitable claim there might be against the purchaser of the legal title will always be demoted in priority to the lender's charge. In technical language, there is no notional *scintilla temporis* ('moment in time') between the two transactions in which the equitable interest can take effect against the title. In effect, the land is already mortgaged at the moment of purchase, thereby squeezing out any claims adverse to the lender.

This is a highly convenient doctrine from a lender's point of view, but it will not assist where there is a real temporal gap between purchase and mortgage. Here, the lender will have to rely, if at all, on the doctrines of consent, etc, discussed earlier.

## Protection for legal co-owners against chargees

Where legal title to property is jointly owned, both co-owners must execute any documents relating to the title. This ensures joint control over dealings. However, this protection will be illusory where one co-owner misrepresents the nature or effect of a transaction to the other, or pressurises the other to execute the document in question. The classic example is where a man is self-employed and wishes to raise finance on the security of the family home; he requires his female partner's signature on the mortgage documents, and obtains it by lying about the true significance of the documents, or by making her life a misery until she signs. In such cases, assuming that there has been a misrepresentation or undue influence by the man, can the bank enforce the security?

This issue has attracted much judicial activity in recent years. The problem has been explaining why a bank should be affected by a defect in a transaction for which it was not responsible. After all, it is not the bank itself, through its employees, that is responsible for the man's actions. Nevertheless, banks have been held unable to enforce their security in a number of cases. Different theories had been advanced for this, including agency or a special rule of equity protecting wives (not cohabitants). However, in *Barclays Bank v O'Brien* [1994] 1 FLR 1 the House of Lords offered a new explanation for the bank's vulnerability, based on the doctrine of notice. The doctrine has been sufficiently widely drawn to include cohabitants.

The *O'Brien* case conformed closely to the classic pattern outlined above. The husband, a businessman, needed to raise finance for business purposes. The bank offered him an increased overdraft facility, to be secured by a second charge over the matrimonial home, which was jointly owned with Mrs O'Brien. She signed a second charge and an explanatory side letter without reading either document, relying on the husband's (false) assurances that the security was limited in both amount and time. The bank failed to ensure that the wife knew what she was signing; nor, in breach of its own procedures, did it advise her to obtain independent legal advice. The husband's indebtedness increased and the bank in due course sought possession of the home under the terms of the charge. The wife argued that the charge was unenforceable. The House of Lords agreed (although, it seems, only on condition that Mrs O'Brien pay back the amount she *thought* had been secured by the charge).

The key concept in Lord Browne-Wilkinson's speech is the doctrine of notice. A wife who had been induced by undue influence or misrepresentation to stand as surety for the husband's debts (as Mrs O'Brien had been) had an equity as against the husband to set the transaction aside. According to Lord Browne-Wilkinson, a bank will not be able to enforce its security if it has notice, actual or constructive, of the vitiating factor giving rise to that equity. A bank will be put on inquiry if two factors are present: (a) the transaction is not on its face advantageous to the surety; and (b) the relationship between the principal debtor and the surety is one of emotional closeness and trust, giving rise to the risk that the principal debtor has exploited the trust and emotional involvement of the other. If these two factors are present, then the bank will be fixed with constructive notice unless it takes steps to advise the surety, at a separate interview, of the nature of the transaction and advises the surety to seek independent legal advice.

A number of points may be made about this doctrine. First, it is not confined to wives, but includes cohabitants, whether hetero- or homosexual. The underlying principle is the recognition of 'the risk of one cohabitant exploiting the emotional involvement and trust of the other', a risk which is unrelated to the presence of a marriage ceremony. Indeed, the protected class may go wider than this: it has been held in *Midland Bank v Massey* [1994] 2 FLR 342, for example, that it includes those who are in non-cohabiting, yet stable and long-standing, emotional and sexual relationships.

Secondly, not all lending transactions are covered. In *CIBC v Pitt* [1994] 1 FLR 17, the House of Lords drew a distinction between surety transactions on the one hand and joint loans, such as second mortgages or remortgages, which are ostensibly for a purpose from which both parties derive an equal benefit, on the other. There is nothing about the latter type of transaction to raise the bank's suspicions, even though (unknown to the bank) actual undue influence has been exercised by one borrower over another. This distinction between different forms of lending may not always be easy to draw, however. For example, a loan may contain elements of both surety and joint loan (eg under an 'all moneys' mortgage securing both types of borrowing). Here, it seems that the transaction will be treated *prima facie* as falling on the surety side of the line (*Midland Bank v Greene* (1994) Fam Law 676). However, in such a case, the complainant may not be able to have the whole loan set aside, but only that attributable to the surety element (*ibid.*).

Thirdly, there must be proof of a vitiating factor as between surety and the principal debtor. For these purposes, there is no automatic presumption of undue influence between spouses or between cohabitants; but if it can be shown that the complainant reposed trust and confidence in the wrongdoer, then a presumption of undue influence will arise (per Lord Browne-Wilkinson in *O'Brien*). Further, it seems likely (though not expressly decided in *Pitt*) that a complainant will not have to prove that the transaction was to her manifest disadvantage (as some earlier cases had suggested she would): disadvantage will be inferred from lack of any clear advantage (*see Midland Bank v Greene, above*). Once established, the effect of this presumption of undue influence is powerful, since it will entitle the complainant to have the transaction set aside unless it can be shown that there was no undue influence (*see Goode Durrant Administration v Biddulph* [1994] 2 FLR 551). This may present lenders with considerable difficulties of proof.

Fourthly, the steps a bank must take to avoid constructive notice need not conform precisely to those outlined by Lord Browne-Wilkinson. In *Midland Bank v Massey* (*above*), it was held that it did not matter that the bank had not interviewed the woman on her own: the bank had otherwise discharged its duty of ensuring that the woman understood what she was signing by *requiring* her to seek independent legal advice: 'it is the substance that matters' (per Steyn LJ). What matters is that the court is satisfied that genuinely independent advice has been received and that the surety knew what she was signing. Further, the bank is not responsible for the nature and extent of the solicitor's advice, which is a matter for the professional judgment of the solicitor. A bank can assume that a solicitor who gives advice has done so honestly, competently and without conflict of interest (*Bank of Baroda v Rayarel and others* (1995) *The Times*, 19 January; *Banco Exterior Internacional v Mann* [1995] 1 FLR 602; but *see TSB Bank plc v Camfield* [1995] 1 FLR 751, where *incorrect* legal advice given to a wife by a lawyer meant that the bank was fixed with notice).

Finally, there is some doubt as to the terms on which relief, if any, is granted. There is now post-*O'Brien* authority that both supports and denies the proposition that a surety is entitled to have the whole transaction set aside. In support of this view is *TSB Bank plc v Camfield* (*above*). The other view is that, at least in cases of misrepresentation, the surety can have it set aside only to the extent that the amount secured exceeds what she has been led to believe (*see Midland Bank v Greene, above*; *Castle Phillips Finance Co Ltd v Piddington* (1994) NLD 12).

## Personal property

### Chattels

Developments within the law of trusts and proprietary estoppel are, of course, of great significance for cohabitants and will remain the most important legal devices for handling disputes on separation (unless statute intervenes). Nevertheless they have their limitations. They are commonly imposed upon specific property, generally land rather than chattels. Whilst the home is the major asset in most families, a cohabitant may feel entitled to a share in other assets (which may have been built up precisely because a home has not been purchased). A non-express trust cannot easily arise over fluctuating assets and the courts are reluctant to find an estoppel in these cases (*Layton v Martin* [1986] 2 FLR 227) although in *Re Basham* [1987] 2 FLR 264 proprietary estoppel was applied over the deceased's whole estate, whatever it comprised.

Trusts and estoppel aside, the ownership of a chattel will accrue initially to the partner who pays for its purchase. There is no presumption of advancement between cohabitants, although there is nothing to stop them making gifts to each other, which will vest ownership in the donee. A gift from a third party will also vest ownership in the donee; who that is depends on the donor's intention. Income belongs to the earner. These simple rules may be complicated if the purchase money comes from a bank account (*see below*).

It is worth bearing in mind that, when matters come to court, 'the parties must expect the court in ordinary cases to adopt a robust allegiance to the maxim that "equality is equity", if only in the interests of fulfilling the equally salutary maxim that "*sit finis litis*"' (per Waite J in *Hammond v Mitchell* [1992] 1 FLR 229, at 242). His Lordship went on to say that if it is really necessary to bring disputes over ownership of household goods to adjudication, it should be by a claim for a declaration as to the beneficial interests rather than by way of an action for conversion or detinue.

### Bank accounts

It is quite possible for a bank account to be subject to a trust. Although the balance in the account might vary, the subject matter is the account itself and is therefore sufficiently certain for the law of trusts to apply. Formally, the only difference from the law that has already been discussed in the context of the home is that the requirements of writing in s 53 of the LPA 1925 do not apply to personalty.

If the bank account is in the *sole name* of one cohabitant, there can still be an express or implied trust in favour of the other. In *Paul v Constance* [1977] 1 All ER 195 one partner opened an account in which to place a sum of money awarded as damages for personal injuries. It was found as a fact that on many occasions he assured the woman that the account was as much hers as his. The Court of Appeal held that there was an express trust over half the fund so that on the man's death his widow only succeeded to the other half on intestacy. The case is principally concerned with the degree of certainty of intention required to distinguish a declaration of trust from an attempted gift and it might be relatively rare for an express trust to be found.

In the absence of express words, it would presumably be possible to find a resulting trust although the circumstances are likely to be rare where one would be warranted. Presumably, if a cohabitant pays money into the other's account then it is capable of resulting back in the form of a share in the account or in an item bought from the account. In *Paul v Constance* a tenancy in common in equal shares must have been found as otherwise the plaintiff would have succeeded to the whole of the account by virtue of survivorship. One assumes that equal contributions into the account with evidence that survivorship was to apply could give rise to an equitable joint tenancy.

It is likely that *joint* bank accounts will give rise to more frequent problems on separation. These problems rarely surface on marriage breakdown because of the discretionary jurisdiction of the divorce court, although a court sometimes adjusts an order it would otherwise have made to compensate for unequal drawings out of an account.

The common law rules on joint accounts seem to be as follows. In the absence of express words sufficient to declare the terms of a trust the court looks first at whether there has been a genuine pooling of resources. Only if there has been will the account be treated as a common fund. The pooling need not be equal provided each party has contributed substantially. The consequence of there being a common fund is that property bought out of the fund normally belongs to the party drawing on the account (*Re Bishop* [1965] Ch 450) but if there is evidence that the property is intended to be held in the same way as the fund (ie jointly) then co-ownership will apply (*Jones v Maynard* [1951] Ch 572). At first sight this rule appears odd: one would expect automatic joint ownership of assets bought out of a joint account. The essence of a joint tenancy, however, is that each is the owner of the whole (as opposed to a tenancy in common where there are distinct shares). A related apparent oddity is that a party can, in the absence of a contrary agreement, withdraw in excess of her or his deposits because, once pooled, the origin of the money is irrelevant. It is not, therefore, automatically wrong for a lawyer to advise a client to draw out all the contents of a joint account when the relationship has broken down. It might even be prudent to do so if the purpose is to preserve the funds while a settlement is reached.

It follows from the *above* that there can be a joint account *without* there being a common fund. For example, all the money is paid in by one cohabitant but the account is in joint names so as to give the other drawing rights in respect of current spending or in the event of the account-holder's death. The basic position here is that the money in the account and the items bought from it belong to the account-holder by virtue of a resulting trust. This is particularly the case where the account has been opened for convenience only (*Simpson v Simpson* [1992] 1 FLR 616). A resulting trust is, however, based on presumed intention and the circumstances might rebut it. For example, drawings by the other for obvious personal use and with the knowledge of the account-holder are likely to be treated as perfectly constituted gifts but these will depend on the circumstances of each debit. As the parties are unmarried there is no question of a general presumption of advancement (*Mossop v Mossop* [1988] 2 FLR 173). Similarly, the Married Women's Property Act 1964, which applies a tenancy in common to housekeeping allowances made by a husband to his wife, can have no application unless the couple are engaged to each other and s 2(1) of the Law Reform (Miscellaneous Provisions) Act 1970 is held to apply to the 1964 Act.

**Insurance and pensions**

The ownership of the proceeds of an insurance policy will depend on the parties' intentions. For example, in *Smith v Clerical and Medical and General Life Assurance* [1993] 1 FLR 47 it was held that the surplus proceeds of an endowment policy, payable on the death of one of two cohabitants, belonged to the survivor. The policy had been entered into in order to finance the redemption of a mortgage on a property jointly owned by the parties. The Court of Appeal construed the parties' intentions as being to ensure that if either partner died, the mortgage would be paid off and the house would vest in the survivor by survivorship. The fact that the house had been sold and the mortgage paid off without drawing on the proceeds of the policy did not affect that intention: the survivor was entitled to the policy proceeds as against the deceased's personal representatives.

Cohabitants cannot take advantage of the rule contained in s 11 of the MWPA 1882 that a policy of life insurance effected by a spouse on her or his own life, expressed to be for the benefit of the assured's spouse or any or all of her or his own children, creates a trust in favour of the assured's spouse and children.

Entitlement to pension benefits will depend on the rules of the scheme concerned. Thought should be given to nominating a cohabiting partner as the beneficiary of death in service or dependants' benefits (*see* Chapter 9 *below*).

## Chapter 9

# Inheritance and Succession

This chapter deals with the major financial consequences that follow from the death of a cohabitant, although the discussions in Chapter 4 of inheritance tax and in Chapter 7 of succession to tenancies are also relevant. The chapter begins by looking briefly at some inheritance rules that relate specifically to cohabitants and it then considers applications for financial provision out of the deceased's estate under the Inheritance (Provision for Family and Dependants) Act 1975 (the 1975 Act). This is followed by further consideration of contract law. Finally, some relevant aspects of the Fatal Accidents Acts are dealt with.

It should be remembered that a cohabitant need only be concerned with the contents of this chapter if the beneficial ownership of property to which she makes a claim is not already vested in her. This means that if she can establish a beneficial interest in specific property under a resulting, implied or constructive trust in the manner described in Chapter 8 then she can enforce it against the personal representatives of the estate. If she is in occupation of the property then it is probably not essential to take immediate steps to protect her interest, for the reasons discussed *above*. Until a grant is taken out, it is unlikely that a disposition having priority over her beneficial interest could be effected. Nevertheless matters should obviously be sorted out as soon as practicable and regard should be had to the limitation period for applications by the next of kin under the 1975 Act; normally six months from the grant.

## Wills and intestacy

### The need for a will

As is usually the case, many problems can be avoided if a well-drafted will is made, but this is particularly true in the case of cohabitants because there is no entitlement under the intestacy rules. A good example of this is *Stott v Ratcliffe* (1982) 126 SJ 310. Here the home had been vested in the joint names of the cohabitants as beneficial tenants in common, meaning that neither would automatically succeed to the other's interest. The deceased had said that he would leave his share to the defendant in his will but he failed to do so. His widow, from whom he had been separated for many years, succeeded on intestacy and although she failed in her application for an order for immediate sale, the whole dispute could have been avoided by a simple will.

For many years the courts have tended to protect bequests to cohabitants and have recognised a moral obligation between testator and beneficiary. For example, bequests have been protected against the claims of a widow for financial provision out of the estate (*Re Joslin* [1941] Ch 200; *Re Charman* [1951] 2 TLR 1095 and *Re E* [1966] 1 WLR 709; but *see also Re Thornley* [1969] 1 WLR 1037). Furthermore, considerations of public policy have been surprisingly absent from many cases. In *Re Lovell* [1920] 1 Ch 122 the testator had bequeathed an annuity to his cohabitant provided she was living with him at the time of his death and provided and so long as she did not return to live with her husband and provided and so long as she should not remarry. This was held by Lawrence J in the Chancery Division not to be void for public policy because the object was not to induce the cohabitant to remain apart from her husband or not to remarry but to maintain her until one of those events took place. Further advice on will drafting and rules of construction will be found in Chapter 11.

## Occupational pension schemes

It is important always to inquire whether the testator is a member of an occupational pension scheme carrying death benefits. If so, the terms of the scheme should be examined. Schemes normally provide for the trustees' discretion, in order that the benefits do not pass through the deceased's estate, but they also normally allow the member to nominate a beneficiary by way of guidance to the trustees. In this case the cohabitant might be nominated. Some schemes automatically include cohabitants but the definition should be looked at closely. A reference to living together 'as husband and wife' is different from a reference simply to a dependant and it avoids examination of relative economic positions on death. If the scheme provides for nominations subject to the trustees' consent then a properly nominated benefit will not be vulnerable to a claim by, say, the deceased's widow because it will not form part of the net estate for the purposes of the 1975 Act; *see Re Cairnes* [1983] 4 FLR 225.

*Intestacy*
In the absence of a will, a cohabitant does not inherit on intestacy because he or she is not within the lists in s 46 of the Administration of Estates Act 1925. The Law Commission has recommended that this position continue (Law Com No 187, *Family Law: Distribution on Intestacy* (1989)). If no provision is made in a will, or if there is a total intestacy, the survivor must therefore claim under the 1975 Act. Of course, if the couple had a child or children then they may benefit on intestacy and, assuming there was no surviving *de jure* spouse, they will take the whole residuary estate. In respect of deaths occurring before the entry into force of s 18 of the FLRA 1987 (4 April 1988), but after 1 January 1970, illegitimate children had the same rights of succession on the intestacy of their mothers or fathers as legitimate children. On the other hand, they did not enjoy intestacy rights *through* their parents so that, for example, an illegitimate child could not take on the intestacy of her or his maternal grandmother. Section 18 of the Family Law Reform Act 1987 (FLRA 1987) applied the general principle in s 1 of the Act to Pt IV of the Administration of Estates Act 1925 (the 1925 Act) so that the marital status of a child's parents is now irrelevant in deducing relationships. Accordingly, all children have the same rights to inherit from their relatives. Section 18(2) preserves the presumption that an unmarried father has not survived his child unless the contrary is shown; in other words, the presumption that such a father will not take on his child's intestacy.

In the event that there is no one entitled to take under the intestacy rules so that the estate falls *bona vacantia* it is understood that the Crown will apply the benefit towards a former cohabitant of the deceased on an *ex gratia* basis exercising its powers under s 46(1)(vi) of the 1925 Act.

## Inheritance (Provision for Family and Dependants) Act 1975

This Act, which applies in the case of deaths on or after 1 April 1976, enables a cohabitant, in certain circumstances, to apply for financial provision from the estate of the deceased. It has been said that at the end of the day the court must ask itself the question: 'What testamentary provision would a reasonable man in the position of this deceased have made for the plaintiff in all the circumstances … ?' (Dunn LJ in *Harrington v Gill* [1983] 4 FLR 265 at 271C). Whilst this approach might be a useful way of standing back and evaluating a hypothetical result, and may indeed be a pragmatic way of deciding disputes that so often involve small estates and large legal costs, there is no substitute for carefully charting one's way through the scheme of the Act. It is assumed in what follows that the survivor is a woman but the Act is neutral between the sexes and some claims have been by men.

### The scheme of the Act

Section 1(1) sets out the list of family and dependants (to borrow the terms from the Act's title) who can apply for financial provision. With the enactment of the Law Reform (Succession) Act 1995 there are now two classes of applicant relevant for our purposes.

*Eligible applicants*

The first of these can be called, for want of a better term 'spouse-like cohabitants'. This category was introduced in 1995 and is inserted in s 1(2)(ba) of the 1975 Act:

> (ba) any person (not being a [spouse or former spouse]) to whom subsection (1A) applies.

Subsection (1A) provides:

> This subsection applies to a person if the deceased died on or after 1st January 1996 and, during the whole of the period of two years ending immediately before the date when the deceased died, the person was living—
> (a) in the same household as the deceased, and
> (b) as the husband or wife of the deceased.

The second category of applicant, which has been in the 1975 Act from the beginning, can be called the dependant and is described in s 1(1)(*e*) as:

> any person ... who immediately before the death of the deceased was being maintained, either wholly or partly, by the deceased.

The dependant is further defined in s 1(3):

> For the purposes of subsection (1)(*e*) above, a person shall be treated as being maintained by the deceased, either wholly or partly, as the case may be, if the deceased, otherwise than for full valuable consideration, was making a substantial contribution in money or money's worth towards the reasonable needs of that person.

At the time of writing, the 1995 Act is not in force. All of the case law is therefore on the second category, the dependant, and much of the discussion below is oriented to that category. Separate subheadings have been introduced to keep the two classes of applicant separate, where necessary. At this stage it should be noted that a dependant does not have to have been living with the deceased at the time of the death, nor at all. In addition to cohabitants, relatives and housekeepers have made applications for financial provision as 'dependants'. The new category of applicant must, however, have had a spouse-like relationship with the deceased for at least the two-year period immediately before the death. One can therefore expect bereaved cohabitants to continue to apply under s 1(1)(*e*) (the 'dependant' category) where:

(a) the deceased died before 1 January 1996;
(b) the applicant and deceased did not live in the same household;
(c) they did not do so as husband and wife; or
(d) they did not do so for the whole of the two-year period leading up to the death.

One might expect that applicants who have lived in a same-sex relationship with the deceased will constitute a growing number of people who come within (c) *above*.

Applicants under either category apply to the court for an order under s 2 on the ground that the disposition of the deceased's estate effected by his will, or the law relating to intestacy, or the combination of his will and that law, is not such as to make reasonable financial provision for her. 'Reasonable financial provision' for all applicants other than a surviving spouse is defined in s 1(2)(*b*) as 'such financial provision as it would be reasonable for the applicant to receive for his maintenance' whereas a more generous standard, not linked to maintenance, is provided in s 1(2)(*a*) for a surviving spouse.

*The court's powers*

If the applicant is eligible under s 1 then the court may make an order under s 2. The precise terms of the section must be considered but basically the powers are similar to those of a divorce court; namely powers to make orders for periodical payments, lump sums, transfers of property, settlements of property and variations of settlements. In addition, an order can be made for the acquisition out of property in the estate of such property as may be so specified. A divorce court cannot do this; at least not directly.

*Criteria*

In deciding whether existing provision for the applicant is adequate and, if not, what provision should be made the court must basically have regard to all the circumstances which it considers relevant, including those listed in s 3(1)(*a*)–(*g*). Again these bear a strong similarity to those to which a divorce court must have regard (*see* s 25 of the Matrimonial Causes Act 1973) and are:

(a) the financial resources and needs which the applicant has or is likely to have in the foreseeable future;

(b) the financial resources and financial needs which any other applicant for an order under section 2 of this Act has or is likely to have in the foreseeable future;
(c) the financial resources and financial needs which any beneficiary of the estate of the deceased has or is likely to have in the foreseeable future;
(d) any obligations and responsibilities which the deceased had towards any applicant for an order the said section 2 or towards any beneficiary of the estate of the deceased;
(e) the size and nature of the net estate of the deceased;
(f) any physical or mental disability of any applicant for an order under the said section 2 or any beneficiary of the estate of the deceased;
(g) any other matter, including the conduct of the applicant or any other person, which in the circumstances of the case the court may consider relevant.

There then follow criteria specifically relevant to each class of applicant. In the case of spouse-like cohabitants (using our terminology), subs (2A) provides:

> Without prejudice to the generality of paragraph (g) of subsection (1) above, where an application for an order under subsection (2) of this Act is made by virtue of section 1(1)(ba) of this Act, the court shall, in addition to the matters specifically mentioned in paragraphs (a) to (f) of that subsection, have regard to—
> (a) the age of the applicant and the length of time of the period during which the applicant lived as the husband or wife of the deceased and in the same household as the deceased;
> (b) the contribution made by the applicant to the welfare of the family of the deceased, including any contribution made by looking after the home or caring for the family.

In the case of dependants, s 3(4) provides:

> Without prejudice to the generality of paragraph (g) of subsection (1) above, where an application for an order under section 2 of this Act is made by virtue of section 1(1)(*e*) of this Act, the court, shall, in addition to the matters specifically mentioned in paragraphs (a) to (f) of that subsection, have regard to the extent to which and the basis upon which the deceased assumed responsibility for the maintenance of that applicant, and to the length of time for which the deceased discharged that responsibility.

The steps one must go through involve asking the questions in the subheadings below.

### What is the net estate?

This is arguably the first question because if it appears that the net estate for the purposes of the Act is very small then the costs of a claim (beyond an initial overture to see how the land lies) might form such a large proportion of the estate as to rule out any further action. Increasingly the courts are urging practitioners to ask, in effect, whether the whole thing is worth the candle and one can expect more reluctance to order that the costs should come out of the estate where the matter has been handled unreasonably.

The 'net estate' is defined in s 25 and one should look at the exact provisions. Basically, it is what one would expect the gross estate to be, less funeral, testamentary and administration expenses, debts and liabilities (including inheritance tax): but there are also some unusual provisions. Property nominated under any enactment is treated as part of the net estate, as is a *donatio mortis causa* (s 8). More significantly, under s 9(1) a beneficial joint tenancy can, in effect, be retrospectively severed by the court 'for the purpose of facilitating the making of financial provision for the applicant'. Retrospective severance is not really an accurate way of looking at the section because the applicant only receives the deceased's severable share to the extent that appears to the court to be just in all the circumstances of the case. The balance of that share still goes by survivorship.

Section 9 was considered by Wood J in *Kourkgy v Lusher* [1983] 4 FLR 65. A literal reading of the section and in particular the words 'for the purposes of facilitating the making of financial provision' would indicate that one can only use s 9 when one has already decided that the existing financial provision is unreasonable. Wood J took a broader view and held that one can take into account the possibility of bringing back into the estate the severable share when deciding on the reasonableness of the existing provision.

A neat point of construction of s 9 arose in *Powell v Osbourne* [1993] 1 FLR 1001. The deceased and his cohabitant had owned a property as joint tenants. The property was heavily mortgaged but there was a collateral endowment policy providing that a sum equal to the mortgage debt would become payable on the first death. The deceased's widow, from whom he had separated three years previously, made a claim under the 1975 Act and sought to have half the life assurance moneys counted as falling within the deceased's net estate, relying on s 9. The wording of the section allows the court to order that the deceased's severable share of property held under a joint tenancy shall be treated as part of the deceased's net estate 'at the value thereof immediately before his death'. Because the endowment policy was taken out only shortly before the death, it had little or no surrender or sale value, if valued immediately before the death. At the *moment* of death, however, it became valuable because the life cover was activated. The Court of Appeal held that the deceased's share in the policy should be valued on the assumption that death was imminent and inevitable. Half the money due under the policy (ie the deceased's severable share) should therefore be treated as part of the net estate. For further discussion of s 9, in an unusual case involving a deceased who had two families, each being ignorant of the other, *see Jessop v Jessop* [1992] 1 FLR 598.

### Is the applicant eligible?

*Spouse-like cohabitants*
Although the word 'cohabitant' is not used in the Act, the particular class of applicant referred to is defined in similar ways to the definitions in social security legislation (*see* Chapter 3), domestic violence legislation (*see* Chapter 6) and legislation concerning the transfer of tenancies (*see* Chapter 7). The tradition of minor discrepancies between definitions has also been continued; for example, under the Family Homes and Domestic Violence Bill, also the product of a Law Commission Report, the cohabitants must have 'lived together' but, unlike some other categories of associated persons, need not have done so in the same household. In the same year, however, the Law Reform (Succession) Act 1995 uses a household test for family provision purposes.

In the absence of case law on the 1995 Act, guidance on the meaning of the definition can be found in the chapters referred to *above*.

*Dependants*
This category can be expected to comprise a diminishing number of applicants because many surviving cohabitants will be eligible to apply under s 1(1)(ba). Nevertheless, as was pointed out above, the surviving partner from a same-sex relationship or from a relationship that did not subsist for a continuous period of at least two years leading up to the death will have no alternative but to apply under s 1(1)(*e*).

It will be recalled that para (e) refers to a person who immediately before the death was being maintained, wholly or partly, by the deceased. Section 1(3) goes on to say that a person shall be treated as being maintained in these circumstances if the deceased, otherwise than for valuable consideration, was making a substantial contribution in money or money's worth towards the reasonable needs of that person.

One could argue that two classes of dependants were envisaged here; those who are dependants within s 1(1)(*e*) and those who are not but who are to be treated as such by virtue of s 1(3). In *Re Beaumont* [1980] 1 All ER 266 at 271a, Megarry VC held that there is only one category and this has since been affirmed. For example, Stephenson LJ said in

*Jelley v Iliffe* [1981] 2 All ER 29 at 34h that s 1(3) exhaustively defines the claimant in s 1(1)(*e*). If one consolidates s 1(1)(*e*) and s 1(3), three questions on eligibility are raised.

(*1*) *Did the deceased make a substantial contribution in money or money's worth towards the reasonable needs of the applicant?* This question was considered in *Jelley v Iliffe, above*. Here the man had gone to live with the woman in a house that had been conveyed to her by her children on the understanding that she would leave it to them on her death. They lived together for eight years and when she died he applied for financial provision. It was held by the Court of Appeal that the benefit of rent-free accommodation was a significant contribution to a person's reasonable needs and in the case of an old age pensioner (as here) was a substantial contribution. A similar view of rent-free accommodation was taken by the Court of Appeal in *Harrington v Gill* [1983] 4 FLR 265.

(2) *Was the contribution by the deceased for full valuable consideration?* This has arguably been the hardest question to answer in many of the cases. The fundamental issue is whether the deceased contributed more to the applicant than he received from her. Only if he did can one say that the applicant was dependent upon the deceased. One thing is clear. Contributions by the applicant do not have to have been made under a contract with the deceased in order for them to constitute full valuable consideration for the support received (*Re Wilkinson* [1977] 3 WLR 514 and *Re Beaumont, above*). The scope for disentitling the applicant is therefore widened.

Some of the important decisions on this issue have been made in cases concerning applications to strike out claims for failing to disclose a cause of action (which is a convenient way for the estate to clear off a hopeless application). This means that the judgments tend to talk in terms of whether there is an arguable case rather than draw firm conclusions. The common way of looking at it is to ask which way the balance of the relationship tipped in terms of money or money's worth. If in the applicant's favour then the applicant should be treated as having an arguable case and the claim should not be struck out. If it was equal, which in practice is a totally unrealistic conception (Purchas J in *Re Kirby* [1982]) 3 FLR 249 at 254G), or in the *deceased's* favour then the applicant's claim discloses no cause of action.

The facts in *Re Kirby* involved the difficult situation of interdependence where the joint resources had effectively been pooled.

The plaintiff and deceased had lived together as husband and wife but had never married. The deceased had contributed about 50 per cent more income into the pool and it was held that there was a triable issue.

The Court of Appeal in *Jelley v Iliffe* also referred to tipping the balance, but this was another striking out case. The metaphor of tipping the balance is presumably helpful in establishing that less than full valuable consideration was given for what was received but if the balance is only slightly tipped then one cannot say that the deceased's contribution towards the applicant's needs was *substantial*.

The question was recently approached directly by the Court of Appeal in *Bishop v Plumley* [1991] FLR 121. Here, with one short interruption, the couple lived together from 1973 until the deceased's death ten years later. For most of the time they lived in straitened circumstances. In 1974, during a brief period of separation, the deceased made a will leaving his property to his son and daughter and he did not revoke or amend the will when he resumed cohabitation with the applicant. In 1983, the deceased inherited some money from a relative and purchased a house outright. As the deceased became progressively ill, the applicant looked after him and did everything within the house. She did 'everything a natural wife would do' (at 124D).

After his death, the applicant sought financial provision from the deceased's estate. The beneficiaries under the will relied on an unattractive defence. They said, in effect, that the devotion the applicant had shown to the deceased amounted to full valuable consideration for the support she received in being able to live rent-free in the deceased's house during the latter part of the relationship. This argument succeeded before a registrar and on appeal to a judge but failed in the Court of Appeal. Butler-Sloss LJ said (at 123C):

> The object of the legislation is to remedy, wherever reasonably possible, the injustice of one who has been put by a deceased person in a position of dependency upon him, being deprived of any financial support, either by accident or by design of the deceased after his death see per Stephenson LJ in *Jelley v Iliffe* ...

Her Ladyship then said (at 126B) that in determining whether or not the deceased was making a substantial contribution, one must look at the problem in the round, applying a common-sense approach, and avoiding fine balancing computations involving the value of normal exchanges of support in the domestic sense.

She accordingly allowed the appeal and remitted the matter back to the registrar for consideration under ss 2 and 3. It is difficult to judge the significance of this case. It develops no new principle of law. On the other hand, it signals that the courts should be slow to interpret the Act so that altruism is penalised.

(3) *Was the deceased's contribution continuing immediately before the death?* Because the dependant must have been maintained wholly or partly immediately before the death of the deceased, the estate can argue that any cessation of maintenance before the death bars the applicant's claim. In *Re Beaumont, above*, Megarry VC postulated the results that might flow if such an argument were successful and he refused to accept it. He said (at 272b):

> If at the moment before the death of the deceased there is some settled basis or arrangement between the parties as regards maintenance, then I think that s 1 should be applied to this rather than to any *de facto* variation in the actual maintenance that may exist at that moment.

This view was indorsed in the Court of Appeal in *Jelley v Iliffe, above*, but the first case to apply it fully was *Kourkgy v Lusher* [1983] 4 FLR 65. The facts of the case are complicated and are set out at great length in the judgment. In brief, the deceased left his wife and went to live with the plaintiff. He continued to return to the former matrimonial home because he practised from there as a chiropodist and his wife was the receptionist and secretary. After three years the relationship between the deceased and the plaintiff began to deteriorate and intermittently the deceased returned to live with his wife. In the months leading up to his death he provided money for the purchase of a house for the plaintiff but at the time of his death he was living with his wife. Wood J, analysing the evidence closely, drew the inference that at a point several months before the deceased died he wished to divest himself of financial responsibility of 'a capital nature, and lasting nature' and that by his death the deceased had abandoned that responsibility.

The relevance of an assumption of responsibility is discussed *below* but the concept enters into several of the stages of reasoning through which one must go to establish a claim. For present purposes we can say that the court looks to the general state of affairs immediately before the death, what Ormrod LJ called the 'norm of this relationship' in *Re Dymott* (unreported, 15 December 1980), and if it is one of maintenance then the applicant satisfies the condition unless there is evidence that the deceased had in fact abandoned responsibility for further maintenance.

**Is the existing financial provision for the applicant reasonable for her maintenance?**

Having now established that the facts of the case make the applicant eligible to apply, one then turns to whether the financial provision for the applicant effected by the deceased's will, the intestacy rules, or a combination of both is reasonable. The standard of reasonableness which the existing financial provision must reach is what is reasonable in all the circumstances for the applicant to receive for her maintenance. Were the applicant a surviving spouse, the standard would be higher.

At this stage it becomes difficult to follow a linear path of reasoning because the statutory factors to which the court must have regard apply both here and in deciding what financial provision, if any, to order. In other words the factors guide a judge in deciding two different questions: whether he or she *can* make an order and whether he or she *should* make one. It is possible to find that the existing provision is not reasonable for the applicant's maintenance but that no other provision should be ordered. Some judges have clearly separated the two issues and the separation can be highly significant for the purposes of an appeal. In *Re Coventry* [1979] 3 All ER 815 Goff LJ said (at 821d):

> The second part of that composite problem is clearly a question of discretion, but I think the first is not. It is a question of fact, but it is a value judgment, or a qualitative decision, which I think ought not to be interfered with by us unless we are satisfied that it was plainly wrong.

On the other hand, the problem has been regarded as indivisible in later cases. In *Harrington v Gill*, as was mentioned earlier, Dunn LJ said (at 271C):

> The scheme of the Act, as set out in the sections, is a little complicated but at the end of the day the court must ask itself the question: 'What testamentary provision would a reasonable man in the position of this deceased have made for the plaintiff in all the circumstances, including the matters set out in s 3'.

The opening words of s 3(1) make it clear that the factors in the subsection (which were described *above*) must be considered when deciding whether the *existing* financial provision is reasonable for the applicant's maintenance as well as when deciding how, if at all, the powers are to be exercised. In so far as one can allocate the cases to the first hurdle of existing provision rather than the second hurdle of whether anything should be done, it seems that the key question in applications by dependants under s 1(1)(*e*) has been the responsibility that the deceased assumed for the applicant. We have seen that if at the time of his death the deceased had divested himself of a responsibility that he had assumed then the applicant will be ineligible. What is less clear is whether there must have been an assumption of responsibility in the first place. The discussion that follows is primarily directed to applications by dependants, because of the specific requirement in s 3(4) that the court have regard to the assumption of responsibility by the deceased for the applicant's maintenance and because, accordingly, all the case law deals with this situation. Nevertheless, applications by the new category of spouse-like cohabitant might still involve an analysis of assumption of responsibility; first, because s 3(1)(*d*) (which applies to *all* applicants) refers to 'any obligations and responsibilities which the deceased had towards any applicant for an order' and secondly because the court might find that assumption of responsibility is a feature of many husband and wife relationships.

Section 3(4) specifically directs the court to have regard to the extent to which and the basis upon which the deceased assumed responsibility for the applicant's maintenance, but nowhere in the Act does it say that an assumption of responsibility is a prerequisite.

The issue was first discussed at length in *Re Beaumont* [1980] 1 All ER 266. Here the plaintiff and the deceased lived together as husband and wife for some 30 years or more. Mrs Beaumont died leaving a will which did not mention the plaintiff (who was aged about 77) and he applied for reasonable financial provision under the Act. The plaintiff had paid the deceased a weekly sum in return for accommodation and also made contributions towards the weekly shopping bill. Each nursed the other through bouts of sickness. The claim failed, ostensibly on the basis that the plaintiff had given full valuable consideration for any maintenance received, but the crucial finding was that the deceased must assume responsibility for the plaintiff before a claim can succeed. Megarry VC said (at 276a):

> The whole picture presented by the plaintiff is one of two people, each with their own earnings and, latterly, their own pensions, who chose to pool such of their individual resources as were needed for them to be able to live with each other without either undertaking any responsibility for maintaining the other. The deceased seems to have been a woman of some independence of character, concerned to make it clear that her bungalow and all improvements to it were hers alone ... It may be that in some cases where there is neither a negation of responsibility nor a positive undertaking of it, it will be possible to infer from the circumstances attending the fact of maintenance that there has indeed been an undertaking of respons-

> ibility ... But it is for the plaintiff to establish here that there has been an assumption of responsibility.

This passage shows Megarry VC found that not only was an assumption of responsibility a prerequisite to entitlement but also indicates (by the use of the phrase 'it may be that in some cases') that such an assumption will not normally be presumed from the fact of maintenance. The Court of Appeal in *Jelley v Iliffe* disapproved of this construction. There Stephenson LJ said that he did not question Megarry VC's opinion that there must be an assumption of responsibility (which is possibly less than wholehearted agreement with it) but held that substantial maintenance gave rise to the presumption that responsibility had been assumed; a presumption that might be rebutted by circumstances including a disclaimer of any intention to maintain (at 35h). Furthermore, it was not necessary to show that the deceased had intended that responsibility to continue after his death. The object of the legislation, he said (at 36a):

> is surely to remedy, wherever reasonably possible, the injustice of one, who has been put by a deceased person in a position of dependency on him, being deprived of any financial support, either by accident or by design of the deceased, after his death. To leave a dependant, to whom no legal or moral obligation is owed, unprovided for after death may not entitle the dependant to much or indeed any financial provision in all the circumstances, but he is not disentitled from applying for such provision if he can prove that the deceased by his conduct made him dependent on the deceased for maintenance, whether intentionally or not.

To sum up the position so far one can say that, in the absence of very special circumstances, if the norm of the relationship at the time of the death was substantial maintenance of the applicant by the deceased then that will empower the court to make an order provided there has been no express or implied disclaimer by the deceased of the assumption of responsibility that is inferred from the mere fact of the maintenance (and provided, of course, that there has not been full valuable consideration in return).

### What order, if any, should be made?

The statutory factors in s 3 must now be revisited for the purpose of deciding whether the powers should be exercised and, if so, to what extent. The text that follows is geared to applications by dependants, owing to the absence of any case law on the new category of cohabitants.

The cases already cited should be read to give an impression of the sorts of things that weigh heavily with a court. A divorce practitioner might approach a case in the same way as a dispute over financial provision in divorce. Instead of the other spouse, there are beneficiaries liable to be disappointed and because the standard to be achieved for a dependant is only that of maintenance one could take the divorce analogy further and consider what might be ordered after a short marriage. In the absence of special circumstances, a short marriage will not give rise to a major redistribution of resources. At first sight the short marriage comparison appears inappropriate in a case under the 1975 Act where the dependency has been of long standing, and of course it might actually be inappropriate on the facts, but the Act does provide for a higher standard (similar to the divorce standard) in the case of surviving spouses and some practical effect has to be given to a distinction drawn by a statute.

In *Re McC* (1979) 9 Fam Law 26 the applicant moved in with the deceased on the basis that she would be his 'common law wife'. At the request of the deceased she placed her illegitimate daughter for adoption and the couple had a planned child. The applicant received no wages but was given money for housekeeping. The deceased died leaving all his estate, valued at between £25,000 and £35,000, to his son by a previous marriage. Sir George Baker P awarded the applicant £5,000, with the remainder of the estate to be divided between the son and the child of this union. The order was based on the grounds that the relationship had been a stable one, with the applicant being described as a *de facto* wife, and everything pointed to a family unit. The marriage-like quality of the relationship was also stressed by Dunn LJ in *Harrington v Gill* [1983] 4 FLR 265 and in *Re Kirby* [1982] 3 FLR 249 Purchas J said that the association was a marriage in all but formality. He also specifically linked the quality of the relationship with the assumption of responsibility factor, saying (at 251E):

> In this case the responsibility assumed by either or both of the parties to the long association cannot for practical purposes be distinguished from those accepted by a married couple towards each other. The only distinction is that in a marriage the obligations to support are formal whereas those in this association were informal but none the less effective for that.

The category of dependant in s 1(1)(*e*) is not, however, confined to cohabitants, let alone marriage-like ones, and so-called 'mistresses' who have not actually lived with the deceased have been successful. In *Malone v Harrison* [1979] 1 WLR 1353 a lover obtained a lump sum of £19,000 from the net estate of £480,563. She had been wholly maintained by the deceased for the 12 years immediately preceding his death and had received sizeable gifts from him. One interesting feature of the case was that the plaintiff's principal opponent was the deceased's '*de facto* wife' who had lived with the deceased for over 18 years and who was a beneficiary under the will. The trial judge, Hollings J, accepted that no order should be made at the expense of the *de facto* wife and therefore the lump sum was taken from the legacy to the deceased's brother.

This review of the 1975 Act indicates that the Act can be a major source of financial provision for a bereaved cohabitant. Although one or two of the early cases suggested that an unduly technical approach might be taken by the courts—for example Megarry VC's analysis of assumption of responsibility—more recent decisions show that once substantial net contributions by the deceased up to the date of death are established then the court will look at the whole situation in the round and try to balance the competing claims fairly. The principal weakness of the Act, which no amount of judicial creativity can overcome, is the need for a net contribution by the deceased to the applicant. In a case where there is no doubt that the balance of advantage was in favour of the deceased so that there was owed, morally at least, a debt of gratitude to the applicant then the Act cannot be used. If such a debt is enforceable at all it will be under non-statutory remedies.

## Agreements for testamentary provision

### Express agreements

Express promises to provide for a cohabitant on the promisor's death may be more common than 'cohabitation contracts' made at the commencement of the relationship as the latter require a rather greater awareness of the legal implications of cohabitation: for a discussion of cohabitation contracts *see* Chapter 11. In particular, when one of the parties is considerably older than the other it is easy to imagine a promise being made along the lines of 'if you look after me until my death, I will leave you all my estate', or a specific part of it. For legal effect to be given to such an agreement one must either establish a contract or rely on a discretionary or equitable remedy based on unjust enrichment or estoppel.

*Agreement*

For there to be a contract there must have been an offer, capable of being accepted, which was actually accepted by words or conduct. There must also have been consideration moving from the promisee, unless the agreement was under seal. The terms of the contract must be sufficiently certain, although this may say nothing more than that there has to be an offer capable of acceptance, and any statutory formalities must be observed.

An example of the difficulties faced by a plaintiff can be found in

*Layton v Martin* [1986] 2 FLR 227. Here the plaintiff had a relationship with the deceased for about eight years and the deceased then asked her to come and live with him. In a letter he said that he would never let her down in any way. He wanted her to be his wife in everything but name 'until something happens' to his wife, who was in poor health and living abroad. He offered the plaintiff financial security during his life and on his death. The plaintiff did not in terms respond to the offer but she did come to live with him some months later. On his accountant's advice, the deceased paid her a wage of £100 a month and a housekeeping allowance.

Scott J found that the services that the plaintiff was expected to provide, and did provide, were to all intents and purposes those of a wife. The relationship ran into difficulties after five years and the deceased gave her written notice of dismissal. A formal settlement was reached whereby she kept the car he had provided, in return for a small payment in full and final settlement of all claims arising out of the contract of employment.

The deceased died two years later and the plaintiff made no claim against the estate until the following year when the deceased's solicitor wrote to her asking for some information about the deceased's assets. The plaintiff could obviously not claim under the Inheritance (Provision for Family and Dependants) Act 1975 because, *inter alia*, she was not being maintained by the deceased immediately before his death. She based her claim on three foundations; constructive trust, estoppel and contract. She failed on all three grounds primarily because, on the facts, it could not be said that she had been influenced in any material respect at all by the offer of financial security and her going to live with him could not be construed as an acceptance of the offer. Scott J was concerned to go further, however, so that other defendants did not find themselves at their own expense having to resist similar untenable claims. On the contract point he said that the deceased's letter was not sufficiently certain to amount to an offer and was not capable of acceptance. It was impossible to know what was involved in an offer of financial security.

*Intention to create legal relations*

Apart from difficulties in proving the agreement and its terms, there is the question of intention to create legal relations. Classically, it has been assumed that the parties to a 'domestic agreement' or 'family arrangement' do not intend to create a contract. The cases have normally concerned spouses (*see* eg *Balfour v Balfour* [1919] 2 KB 571 and *Gould v Gould* [1969] 3 All ER 728) but not always (*see Jones v Padavatton* [1969] 2 All ER 616, where a contract between mother and daughter was found but only on the basis of special facts).

Cases involving cohabitants, although arguably now 'family' cases, might well be treated differently in view of the absence of any special statutory procedure for resolving disputes between them and any common law maintenance obligations. On the other hand, express reference to the rule was made by May LJ in *Burns v Burns* [1984] 1 All ER 244 at 257. Scott J dealt with this point in *Layton v Martin* (at 239E), although having already dismissed the case on its facts he was now speaking *obiter*:

> Further, in family or quasi-family situations there is always the question whether the parties intended to create a legal binding contract between them. The more general and less precise the language of the so-called contract, the more difficult it will be to infer that intention.

*Writing requirements for contracts concerning land*

If the subject matter of the promise is a disposition of an interest in land, then it must ordinarily comply with the new requirements of writing made by the Law of Property (Miscellaneous Provisions) Act 1989. The old requirement in s 40 of the Law of Property Act 1925 that, to be enforceable by action, a contract for the sale or other disposition of an interest in land had to be evidenced by a written memorandum signed by the party to be charged, has been repealed. Now the contract must actually *be* in writing, signed by both parties, and incorporate all express terms. The old doctrine of part performance has gone, being predicated on the fact that an oral agreement was nevertheless a valid contract which was simply unenforceable by action through want of written evidence. Now, if the requirement of writing is not satisfied, reliance would have to be placed upon resulting, implied or constructive trusts, the operation of which is expressly preserved in s 2(5) of the 1989 Act. Alternatively, a claim might be framed in proprietary estoppel (*see* eg *Greasley v Cooke* [1980] 3 All ER 710, discussed in Chapter 7).

It has now been determined that a death-bed gift of land can be effective if dominion over the title deeds has fully been parted with (*Sen v Headley* [1992] 2 FLR 449). It had previously been thought that a *donatio mortis causa* could not operate to transfer real property.

If an enforceable contract can be established then the property which is the subject matter, or a sum of money representing the damages for breach of contract, may be immune from a claim under the Inheritance (Provision for Family and Dependants) Act 1975 if, *inter alia*, the promise was not made with the intention of defeating an application for financial provision under the Act; *see* s 11.

**Implied contracts**

These are, of course, valid in the same way as express contracts but are inferred from the conduct of the parties. If the claim concerns land, then it can only be dealt with through the law of trusts or estoppel because, being based on an implied agreement, it cannot have been reduced to writing sufficiently to satisfy s 2 of the Law of Property (Miscellaneous Provisions) Act 1989 (*see above*).

It seems unlikely that the courts will be willing to find an implied contract to make testamentary provision of personalty unless there are cogent reasons for inferring an agreement relating to specific property. This is because such a contract would evade the strict requirements of the Wills Act 1837. Even if some form of agreement can be inferred, the terms may be too vague to constitute a contract (*MacPhail v Torrance* (1909) 25 TLR 810).

*Quasi-contract and estoppel*

In so far as one can satisfactorily draw distinctions between legal devices within the law of restitution one can say that quasi-contract imposes an objectively just result irrespective of subjective intentions whereas proprietary estoppel gives effect to a belief that the plaintiff was led reasonably to hold.

Although some Commonwealth jurisdictions seem increasingly to be enforcing debts of gratitude and other promises not enforceable as contracts, there is little evidence of a similar trend here. As long ago as 1963, in the Canadian case of *Rowe v Public Trustee* (1963) 38 DLR (2d) 462, a long-standing fiancée succeeded in recovering on a *quantum meruit* a sum for the services she had performed for the deceased after they had reached an understanding that she would benefit from the estate. Whilst the approach was not followed by the Supreme Court of Nova Scotia in *Re Spears and Levy* 52 DLR (3d) 146 the court there still imposed a constructive trust in favour of a woman who wrongly thought she would inherit under the intestacy legislation so that the same result was achieved. In New Zealand, s 3 of the Law Reform (Testamentary Promises) Act 1949 (as amended), which supplements the family provision legislation there, enables a claim to be made against an estate based upon the rendering of services on an express or implied promise. The claim is permitted by s 3(2), 'whether the services were rendered or the work was performed before or after the making of the promise'. 'Services' have been interpreted loosely and the provision of companionship and the atmosphere of a home have been held sufficient (*Bennett v Kirk* [1946] NZLR 580 at 583).

It is impossible to say whether English courts will move in this direction. Whilst *Re Basham* [1987] 1 All ER 410, a case discussed in Chapter 8, might be an indication that they will, the claimant there was awarded the whole estate only on the basis of fairly clear representations that she was to inherit everything. The case is only a first instance decision and did not refer to all the relevant authorities. In particular, it did not refer to *Layton v Martin, above*. There Scott J held that the proprietary estoppel claim, based on representations contained in a letter from the deceased, failed because estoppel could only arise against specific assets. The essence of estoppel was a representation that the representor would not insist on his legal rights. It followed that there must be specific property over which he, or his estate, could be estopped from enforcing a legal claim. *Re Basham* and *Layton v Martin* do not in fact conflict in their result because although in *Re Basham* one could not know in advance how large the estate would be, at least it would be possible to ascertain it when the time came. In *Layton v Martin* it was impossible to say with precision what would amount to financial security.

## Fatal Accidents Act 1976

If the deceased's death was brought about by the fault of another so that a cause of action arises, usually in negligence, then a cohabitant can receive some financial benefit from the tortfeasor through two routes. First, if she is a beneficiary of the deceased's estate then she might share in any damages that the estate is awarded when suing in the deceased's name. Second, she may now be treated as a dependant within the Fatal Accidents Act 1976 and be compensated for the loss of maintenance that she will suffer as a result of the death. The two actions are now quite separate so that anything she takes in her capacity as beneficiary of the deceased's estate is not taken into account when assessing her claim under the Fatal Accidents Act.

A claim under the 1976 Act by the executor or administrator of the deceased is made on behalf of one or more of the dependants, as defined in the Act. Prior to the Administration of Justice Act 1982, a cohabitant was not a dependant although in latter years the courts seemingly tried to find an indirect route through which she could benefit. In *K v JMP Co Ltd* [1975] 1 All ER 1030 the dependants were the three children of the deceased who were still living with their mother. Before the death, they had all lived together as a family. The court had the normal task of working out the multiplicand and had to decide how much expenses should be deducted before applying the multiplier. Naturally, an element was deducted for the deceased's own expenses but the question arose whether a further deduction should be made in respect of the mother's. The Court of Appeal held that those expenses now covered by social security should be deducted but the remainder of her expenses (which had formerly been met by the deceased) were not deducted and therefore the figure to be multiplied for each child was higher.

The decision can be seen solely from the children's point of view. Unless provision was made for the mother to do the things that their father used to do (such as taking them to Ireland to see relatives) then they could not be done by the children alone. It is clear from the judgment however that the Court of Appeal wanted the extra portion of the award to go to the mother; in other words she was claiming through the children (*see* eg Cairns LJ at 1034b).

Section 3 of the Administration of Justice Act 1982 inserted a new s 1(3) into the Fatal Accidents Act 1976 and included as a dependant, for the purposes of the Act:

> (b) any person who—
> (i) was living with the deceased in the same household immediately before the date of the death; and
> (ii) had been living with the deceased in the same household for at least two years before that date; and
> (iii) was living during the whole of that period as the husband or wife of the deceased.

The definition here is very similar to that used in the Law Reform (Succession) Act 1995 (*see above*).

A new s 3(4) of the 1976 Act further provides that in a claim by this dependant:

> there shall be taken into account (together with any other matter that appears to the court to be relevant to the action) the fact that the dependant had no enforceable right to financial support by the deceased as a result of their living together.

According to the Lord Chancellor in a parliamentary debate on this provision, its purpose was to make clear to the court that one of the factors which it ought to take into account when applying the multiplicator was that the relationship was one which could be determined by the will of either party without legal proceedings and without giving rise to any obligation on the part of the other. It was not intended to give rise to merely token awards.

The amended Act is clearly of importance to a bereaved dependent cohabitant whose partner's death was caused by the tortious act or omission of another. *K v JMP Co Ltd* has not, however, been rendered completely redundant because of the way that a cohabitant is defined in the Act. There must have been a spouse-like relationship for the two years immediately preceding the death. If, for example, the couple had separated prior to the death and the survivor was looking after children of the relationship then there would have been no spouse-like relationship immediately before the date of the death and the Act could not be used. Similarly, the cohabitation might have lasted less than two years but there might nevertheless have been dependency because the couple had already had a child. It may therefore still be necessary to argue that the award to the children should be calculated in such a way as to tack on an element for the mother's dependency.

## Chapter 10

# Children

## Introduction

Whether or not a child's parents are, or were, living together is normally irrelevant in the law of children, although it may well affect the way that the rules are applied. This chapter deals only with those aspects of children law that might be expected to impinge directly on cohabitation and its aftermath. Reference to specialist texts on the law of children may still be necessary. The emphasis here tends to be on the unmarried father, not because the writers have any particular concerns in this regard but because, in practical terms, it is the different legal position of the father that signifies the main differences between marital and non-marital families.

### Illegitimacy at common law and statutory reforms

The general rule at common law is that a child born to parents who are not married to each other is illegitimate, regardless of whether the parents are or were living together. The policy of English law since at least the Family Law Reform Act 1969 has been to remove the legal distinctions between legitimate and illegitimate children. It is a policy that has been implemented hesitantly and is not yet complete.

The Family Law Reform Act 1987 (FLRA 1987) made a number of procedural and substantive changes of importance to cohabitants. The changes were first recommended in the Law Commission Report on *Illegitimacy* (Law Com No 118) in 1982, which departed from an earlier tentative view that the 'status' of illegitimacy should be removed. This would have had the effect of giving all fathers the same parental rights but many people objected to an improvement in a father's position irrespective of whether he had had any real contact with the child. The 1982 Report therefore favoured removing as many distinctions as possible, in so far as they affected children, but retaining the central principle that a putative father had no parental rights over his child unless he had been granted them by a court or he had been appointed a testamentary guardian.

In an effort to remove pejorative labels it was recommended that the expressions 'marital' and 'non-marital' should replace 'legitimate' and 'illegitimate'. In 1986 a Second Report was published (Law Com No 157) annexing a draft Bill which was substantially enacted in the FLRA 1987. It was pointed out in the Second Report that even the terms 'marital' and 'non-marital' drew unwarranted attention to distinctions between children and the final proposals referred, when strictly necessary, to whether the child's parents were married to each other at the time of the birth.

Section 1(1) of the FLRA 1987 now states the general position as follows:

> In this Act and enactments passed and instruments made after the coming into force of this section, references (however expressed) to any relationship between two persons shall, unless the contrary intention appears, be construed without regard to whether or not the father and mother of either of them, or the father and mother of any person through whom the relationship is deduced, have or had been married to each other at any time.

Subsection (2) then introduces the concept of 'a person whose father and mother were not married to each other at the time of his birth' which, in effect, replaces the expression 'illegitimate child'. Subsection (4) provides that the time of a person's birth shall be taken to include any time during the period beginning with:

(a) the insemination resulting in his birth; or
(b) where there was no such insemination, his conception, and (in either case) ending with his birth.

Section 1 had prospective effect only, applying the new rule of construction to measures introduced after the Act. At the same time, however, s 2 of the Act applied the new general principle (that the parents' marital status is *prima facie* irrelevant) to a number of statutes then existing which dealt with the liable relative provisions in social security, maintenance of wards of court, custodianship and the Guardianship Acts 1971 to 1973. Specific provision was also made for the continuation of legitimation under the Legitimacy Act 1976 (FLRA 1987, s 1(3)). Adoption of a child whose parents were not married to each other also continues to have the effect of legitimating the child.

The Children Act 1989 (CA 1989) has taken the process of eliminating distinctions between children a step further, although more by improving the position of the natural father than by removing any remaining consequences of illegitimacy which affect the child directly.

The CA 1989 amounts to a major overhaul of the law of children. A comprehensive description of the Act is beyond the scope of this text but some concepts and rules need introduction here. The Act applies to any 'child'. This is defined in s 105 as a person under the age of 18, but the definition is without prejudice to provisions relating to financial relief (which, as under the previous law, can continue beyond 18 in some circumstances). In many instances the age of 16 marks a change in the legal position because of specific provisions in the Act.

*The welfare principle*

Section 1 of the CA 1989 re-enacts, with modifications intended to make it more intelligible, the welfare principle. Its centrality to many of the matters dealt with in this chapter cannot be exaggerated and its placement in this introduction is meant to emphasise, not diminish, its continuing relevance in the chapter.

> 1(1) When a court determines any question with respect to—
> (a) the upbringing of a child; or
> (b) the administration of a child's property or the application of any income arising from it, the child's welfare shall be the paramount consideration.

Further provisions in the same section give guidance on determining the child's welfare and also reflect a second principle in the legislation, the principle of non-intervention. In any question with respect to a child's upbringing, the court shall have regard to the general principle that any delay in determining the question is likely to prejudice the welfare of the child (s 1(2)). In addition the court must have regard to a number of circumstances when considering whether to make, in contested proceedings, a contact order, prohibited steps order, residence order or specific issues order or (whether or not in contested proceedings) orders concerning care and supervision by a local authority (s 1(3) and (4)). The circumstances are, in summary form:

(a) the ascertainable wishes and feelings of the child concerned (considered in the light of the child's age and understanding);
(b) the child's physical, emotional and educational needs;
(c) the likely effect on the child of any change in circumstances;
(d) the child's age, sex, background and any characteristics considered relevant;
(e) any harm that the child has suffered or is at risk of suffering;
(f) the capability of the parents and other relevant people of meeting the child's needs; and
(g) the range of powers available under the Act.

*The non-intervention principle*

The non-intervention principle is expressed in s 1(5) as follows:

> Where a court is considering whether or not to make one or more orders under this Act with respect to a child, it shall not make the order or any of the orders unless it considers that doing so would be better for the child than making no order at all.

It will be seen that the marital status of the child's parents does not feature in the matters mentioned above: nor, indeed, do those provisions refer to whether the parents are, or have ever been, living with each other. Marital status does, however, have an important bearing on the position of the father.

The remainder of the chapter deals with the most important provisions of the CA 1989 in so far as they are relevant to cohabitation and separation. For the sake of economy of expression, the terms 'unmarried mother', 'unmarried father' and 'unmarried parents' are used. In practice, of course, they might be married to someone else so that, to use the language of s 1 of the FLRA 1987, one should strictly be talking about a father or mother who were not married to each other at the time of the child's birth.

## Parental responsibility for a child

This section deals first with the position concerning parental responsibility in the absence of any court order or agreement with the mother. It then considers two methods whereby parental responsibility might come to be shared. It concludes by mentioning how parental responsibility can be lost.

### The initial position concerning parental responsibility

While married parents each have parental responsibility, s 2(2) deals differently with unmarried parents:

> (2) Where a child's father and mother were not married to each other at the time of his birth—
>
> (a) the mother shall have parental responsibility for the child;
>
> (b) the father shall not have parental responsibility for the child, unless he acquires it in accordance with the provisions of this Act.'

Using different terminology, this repeats the position at common law and the later statutory reflection of it in s 85(7) of the Children Act 1975. Some of its consequences will be explored under various headings in the remainder of the chapter.

'Parental responsibility' seems like a new legal concept but it is defined in familiar terms by s 3(1) and (2):

> (1) In this Act 'parental responsibility' means all the rights, duties, powers, responsibilities and authority which by law a parent of a child has in relation to the child and his property.
>
> (2) It also includes the rights, powers and duties which a guardian of the child's estate (appointed, before the commencement of section 5, to act generally) would have had in relation to a child and his property.

The initial position, then, is that the unmarried mother has all of what used to be called the parental rights and duties and the father has none. *Prima facie*, the mother has the exclusive legal right to determine such matters as place of residence, place and type of education, course of medical treatment, choice of religion, the child's surname, administration of property and consent to marriage between the ages of 16 and 18. Furthermore, the child's nationality and immigration status continue to be determined by that of the mother (*see* s 50(9) of the British Nationality Act 1981 and *R v Immigration Appeals Adjudicator, ex p Crew* (1982) *The Times*, 26 November, CA) as does his domicile. (In so far as the justification for continuing this distinction between children lies in the difficulty in proving paternity in immigration matters then the introduction of DNA profiling techniques, discussed *below*, makes it look distinctly thin.)

Some of the above remarks are subject to one proviso of uncertain scope which may affect a cohabiting unmarried father. By s 3(5):

> A person who—
>
> (a) does not have parental responsibility for a particular child; but
>
> (b) has care of the child,
>
> may (subject to the provisions of this Act) do what is reasonable in all the circumstances of the case for the purpose of safeguarding or promoting the child's welfare.

Although this was enacted mainly with a foster parent in mind, it would apply also to an unmarried father who has care of, but not parental responsibility for, the child. The subsection is not, however, very helpfully expressed and so in the cases where there is likely to be some dispute, such as those involving health and education authorities, it is unclear what, if any, authority the father enjoys.

The reference in s 3(5) to provisions of the Act is to provisions like those in s 10 (starting proceedings without leave) and s 13 (changing the child's surname). In addition, the carer is presumably also subject to any order of the court in someone else's favour. This is because a person *with* parental responsibility cannot act in any way which would be incompatible with an order made under the Act (s 2(8)) and it is hard to imagine that a person without it could be in a better position.

## Parental responsibility orders

Section 4 of the FLRA 1987 introduced a procedure whereby an unmarried father could apply to a court for an order that he should have all the parental rights and duties with respect to the child. If successful, he shared them with the mother of the child, if still alive, or any guardian appointed under the Guardianship of Minors Act 1971. As will be seen *below*, the parental rights and duties order in its relatively brief life was the subject of some controversy in the courts. Much, but not all, of this has been rendered redundant by the CA 1989.

Section 4(1) of the CA 1989 now allows a court, on the application of the father, to make a parental responsibility order in his favour. The meaning of 'parental responsibility' was considered *above*.

The intention behind the old parental rights and duties order was that, in many cases, the application would be made with the consent of the mother. In that way, unmarried parents could choose to be put on the same footing as married parents. The new s 4 order is likely only to arise where the mother cannot be found or in cases of conflict, either between the father and mother or between the father and third parties. This is because, as will be seen shortly, the CA 1989 now allows the parents to make an enforceable agreement which does not have to be converted into a court order.

### *When granted*

There is now a substantial case law on when parental responsibility orders will be granted. Cases decided under s 4 of the FLRA 1987 remain authoritative (per Waite J in *Re CB* [1993] 1 FLR 920). The following principles emerge. First, the governing criterion is the child's welfare, since it is a matter that relates to the child's upbringing (*D v Hereford and Worcester* [1991] 1 FLR 205; *Re G* [1994] 1 FLR 504). Secondly, it will be assumed to be in the child's interests to make an order where the father can establish (a) that he has shown a degree of commitment to the child; (b) that there is a degree of attachment between the father and the child and (c) that the father's motives in applying for the order are not demonstrably wrong or improper (*Re H (No 2)* [1991] 1 FLR 214; *Re G, above*). However, these factors are not exhaustive. As Ward J put it in the *Hereford and Worcester* case (*above*), quoting from Lord MacDermott in *J v C* [1970] AC 688: 'all the relevant facts, relationships, claims and wishes of the parents, risks, choices and other circumstances are taken into account and weighed'.

Thirdly, it is no objection to making an order that it confers no practically useful rights, or rights that are not immediately enforceable. In *Re H (No 2)* (*above*), an order was made even though the children were about to be freed for adoption, since the order would at least confer on the father the 'residual rights' contained in ss 19 and 20 of the Adoption Act 1976 (to receive reports and to apply to revoke the freeing order). Similarly, in *Re C* [1992] 1 FLR 1, an order was made even though the father was unlikely to play an immediate part in the lives of his children owing to the mother's implacable hostility towards him. According to Waite J, an order would confer 'a status carrying with it rights in waiting, which it may be possible to call into play when circumstances change with the passage of time' (at 4). Fourthly, and allied to the last point, the question of parental status is to be considered quite separately from questions of contact or residence. Thus, it is open to a court to refuse a father's application for contact or residence but still to make a parental responsibility order (*Re H* [1993] 1 FLR 484; *Re CB* [1993] 1 FLR 920).

The only reported case to date in which an order has been refused is *Re T* [1993] 2 FLR 450, where the father had been convicted of assault on the mother and of 'callous cruelty' to the child by removing the child from its mother for nine days following a contact visit.

*Consequences of a parental responsibility order*

Even without an order, an unmarried father has certain rights and responsibilities. For example, he can apply as of right for the full range of s 8 orders, without leave (*see below*). He is also liable to support the child whether he has parental responsibility or not (*also below*). Once made, therefore, an order simply places the father in the same legal position as his married counterpart (except that an unmarried father's parental responsibility is more easily terminated: *see below*).

In practical terms, this means that, among other things, the father would have a formal status with respect to the child's school and may be able to consent to medical treatment on the child's behalf. It does not, however, enable a father to interfere with day-to-day decisions made by the child's mother (per Wilson J, *Re P* [1994] 1 FLR 578), not least because of the principle that each person with parental responsibility may act alone and without the other (or others) in meeting that responsibility (s 2(7)) (subject, of course, to the terms of any order in force with respect to the child: s 2(9)). A father with an order has no power to override a mother's decision. Any specific disagreements would have to be resolved by court order.

The general rules relating to parental responsibility also apply. First, the mother's parental responsibility continues. Section 2(6) says that a person does not lose parental responsibility solely because another person acquires it. Second, the father is not entitled to act in any way that would be incompatible with any order made with respect to the child under the Act (s 2(9)). Third, the father may not surrender or transfer his parental responsibility but he may arrange for some or all of it to be met by one or more persons acting on his behalf (s 2(9)). The delegate, for want of a better term, can be someone who already has parental responsibility (s 2(10)). The father, by making a delegation, is not absolved of liability for any failure to meet any part of his responsibility.

An alternative method whereby an unmarried father may acquire parental responsibility is by his appointment as the child's testamentary guardian (*see below*).

### Parental responsibility agreements

The CA 1989 provides that parental responsibility can be *shared* by agreement between unmarried parents. Section 4(1)(*b*) specifically provides for a parental responsibility agreement to be made in the form, and recorded in the manner, laid down by regulations made by the Lord Chancellor. The Parental Responsibility Agreement Regulations 1991 (as amended by the Parental Responsibility Agreement (Amendment) Regulations 1994) provide that a parental responsibility agreement is to be in the form set out in the Schedule. It is to be filed, together with two copies, in the Principal Registry of the Family Division of the High Court. The copies are sealed and the Principal Registry sends one to each parent. The form provides that each parent's signature is to be witnessed. The form contains a statement that the agreement will not take effect until it has been filed.

Once a parental responsibility agreement has been filed the consequences are the same as if an order under s 4 had been made (*see above*).

If no parental responsibility agreement has been made, the mother may still appoint the father to be the child's guardian after her death (*see below*).

### Residence orders

An unmarried father will acquire parental responsibility when a residence order is made in his favour. This is a consequence of s 12(1), which requires a court to make a s 4 order when making a residence order in favour of an unmarried father who does not already have parental responsibility. As Waite J pointed out in *Re CB* (*above*):

> there is an unusual duality in the character of a parental responsibility order: it is on the one hand sufficiently ancillary by nature to pass automatically to a natural father without inquiry of any kind when a residence order is made in his favour; and, on the other, sufficiently independent, when severed from the context of a residence order, to require detailed consideration upon its merits as a free standing remedy in its own right (p 929).

An unmarried father does not require leave in order to apply for a residence order. Residence orders are discussed later.

### Losing parental responsibility

A basic principle in the Act is that parental responsibility continues after the separation of the parents and despite the subsequent making of orders that cut down the possibility of fully discharging it: despite, for example, a residence order that provides for the child to live with someone else. This principle is modified in the case of unmarried fathers. Short of the child's adoption, the only way in which the father's parental responsibility can be brought to an end is by an order of the court made on the application of another person with parental responsibility or, with leave of the court, the child (s 4(3)). This means that even where the father has acquired parental responsibility by entering into an agreement with the mother, the responsibility can only be ended by a court. Furthermore, whilst an unmarried father has a residence order his parental responsibility cannot be brought to an end (s 12(4)).

## Establishing parentage

The general principle in s 1 of the FLRA 1987 that, *prima facie*, parental marital status is irrelevant does not, of course, dispense with the prior question of whether there is parentage. In various proceedings under the CA 1989 and the Adoption Act 1976 paternity in particular will still have to be proved formally where it is not admitted. If authority is needed for this proposition then one should note the Court of Appeal decision in *Re W* [1990] 2 FLR 86 where it was held that there was no power to make a custody order under the Guardianship of Minors Act 1971 unless and until it had been determined that the putative father was the father of the child. There is no reason to suppose that the position is different under the CA 1989.

### Declarations

Prior to the Family Law Act 1986 paternity could only be proved in other proceedings; ie incidentally in a dispute. It was not possible to obtain a bare declaration of paternity (*Re JS* [1980] 1 All ER 1061, CA), although declarations of legitimacy and validity of marriage could be sought under s 45 of the Matrimonial Causes Act 1973. Section 56 of the 1986 Act made further provision for declarations in family cases and this was amended by s 22 of the FLRA 1987 concerning declarations as to legitimacy or legitimation. The result is that any person may apply to a court for a declaration that a person named in the application is or was his parent or that he is the legitimate child of his parents. Paternity can therefore now be proved in isolation from other proceedings but only on the application of the child. If the child is under the age of 18 then the application will have to be made through her or his next friend. It is theoretically possible, therefore, for an adult to seek to resolve the matter through the child.

Section 58(1) of the 1986 Act provides that, where the truth of the proposition to be declared is proved to the satisfaction of the court, the court shall make the declaration unless to do so would manifestly be contrary to public policy. It is not clear that any disadvantages to the child which arise because a declaration would have the effect of showing her or him to be illegitimate involve *public* policy considerations. It should be noted for completeness that there can be no declaration of illegitimacy (s 58(5)(*b*)).

Section 27 of the Child Support Act 1991 has provided another occasion when a bare declaration of parentage can be sought. The new legislation is discussed *below*. Briefly, the Secretary of State or a person with care of the child may apply to the court for a declaration as to whether or not the alleged parent is one of the child's parents. A declaration under the section has effect only for the purposes of the Child Support Act and applications for 'top-up' maintenance under s 8 of the CSA 1991 (s 27(3) of the CSA 1991).

## Presumption of legitimacy

Paternity disputes do of course arise between spouses but there is a common law presumption of crucial importance. This is that where a child is born to a married woman the child is presumed to be the legitimate child of her husband unless there was a decree of judicial separation in force at the date of conception (*Ettenfield v Ettenfield* [1940] P 95).

The law has had to adapt to changes in reproductive technology. Section 27 of the FLRA 1987 made provision for cases of birth following artificial insemination of a married woman using the sperm of someone other than her husband. The child was to be treated in law as the child of the parties to the marriage unless it was proved to the satisfaction of the court that the husband did not consent to the insemination. This provision has now been replaced and its successor deals also with other reproductive techniques involving donated sperm or embryos (s 28(2) of the Human Fertilisation and Embryology Act 1990). Now, however, the presumption of paternity is preserved even where the husband can show that he did not consent to the treatment. He will therefore have to disprove paternity in the same way as other husbands, ultimately by using DNA testing (*see below*).

*Rebutting the presumption*

Although, technically, a presumption is merely an evidential device to switch the onus of proof to the party denying it, a court can sometimes make life very difficult for that party. If evidence in rebuttal could only be provided by blood tests, it may refuse to order them so that the child's existing beliefs are not disturbed (*Hodgkiss v Hodgkiss* [1984] FLR 563, CA). It may also decline to give the husband leave to appeal out of time, even if medical evidence could now establish conclusively that he is not the father (*Edwards v Edwards* [1981] 2 FLR 401 and *Clark v Clark* [1981] 2 FLR 405 but *see also Dixon v Dixon* [1983] 4 FLR 99). The policy behind the first two of these decisions was to avoid 'bastardising' the children but this is a policy that must be increasingly questionable today.

If the situation is the other way round, so that it is the *mother* who denies that her husband is the father, then the admission of the man whom she claims to be the father can be sufficient to rebut the presumption of legitimacy (*R v Kings Lynn Justice, ex p M* [1988] 2 FLR 79).

*No presumption of paternity arising from cohabitation*

Whilst the common law presumption is, in theory, one of legitimacy only, in practice it operates as a presumption of paternity. The Law Commission decided against creating a formal presumption of paternity where the parties were cohabiting at the time of conception. This is despite the fact that such a presumption appears to operate satisfactorily in other jurisdictions (*see* s 10(3) of the Children (Equality of Status) Act 1976 in New South Wales, s 8(6) of the Status of Children Act 1974 in Tasmania and now s 66Q of the Family Law Act 1975 (Cth)). Nevertheless, parental cohabitation is evidence from which paternity can be inferred so that little other evidence may, in practice, be required.

*Human Fertilisation and Embryology Act 1990*

This Act now makes provision for cases where an unmarried couple receive treatment from a person to whom a licence applies under the Act.

If the man's sperm is not used then he may nevertheless be treated as the father of the child *provided* that the common law presumption of legitimacy does not apply (ie provided that the woman's husband is not presumed, in effect, to be the father); *see* s 28(3). The purpose of this provision is to ensure that the child has two people to support her or him (although the Act does, in fact, make it possible for a child to be 'legally fatherless'). In the usual case of an unmarried woman receiving treatment with her partner, however, the partner is regarded in law, for all purposes, as being the child's father even though his sperm was not used (s 29(1)).

*Admissible evidence*

This leads us away from presumptions and to the more general questions of what evidence is admissible and what standard of proof is required in order to show parentage.

The Family Law Reform Act 1987 recognised that recent scientific advances have been made and that new techniques may be more reliable than conventional immunological blood tests. Section 23 of the Act (not yet in force) will amend s 20 of the FLRA 1969 so that a court may order 'scientific tests' and the taking of 'bodily samples' in place of the current powers which are limited to directing blood tests. 'Bodily sample' means a sample of bodily fluid or bodily tissue and 'scientific tests' means tests made with the object of ascertaining the inheritable characteristics of bodily fluids or bodily tissue.

Until s 23 is in force (if at all) the courts are confined to ordering tests on blood, but a much more exact procedure is available as a result of DNA profiling. DNA testing techniques have been publicly available since 1 June 1987. Disputes over paternity can now, for the first time, be positively resolved beyond reasonable doubt because DNA testing is to be distinguished from conventional blood tests which generally act negatively; ie to exclude a man from possible paternity, rather than to identify the father conclusively. Nevertheless, blood testing is also becoming more sophisticated in estimating the likelihood that a particular man is the father sufficient to dispel any reasonable doubt.

Section 89 of the CA 1989 also made amendments to s 20 of the FLRA 1969 (in respect of children under the age of 18) by adding two new subsections. These new subsections, as clarified by Sched 16, para 3 to the Courts and Legal Services Act 1990, take into account that there are now two methods of testing paternity, with immunological testing, costing under £50, and DNA profiling, costing over £300. Parties can choose which method they prefer but the court will retain its overriding discretion to refuse the order sought. (*See*, further, the Blood Tests (Evidence of Paternity) Regulations 1971 as amended by SI 1989 No 776, SI 1990 No 359, SI 1990 No 1025 and SI 1992 No 1369; *see also* the Magistrates' Courts (Blood Test) Rules 1971.)

The court has no power to compel anyone to submit to the taking of a blood sample. The court's power is to 'direct' blood tests, and a party is free to ignore the direction (but runs the risk of adverse inferences being drawn: *see below*). The consent of a child over the age of 16 is required before samples of their blood can be taken. If under the age of 16, the consent of the person with 'care and control' (presumably residence rather than parental responsibility) of the child is required (FLRA 1969, s 21(3)).

The refusal of any person to consent, either on their own or on a minor child's behalf, will enable the court to draw such inferences as may appear proper in the circumstances (s 23(1) of the FLRA 1969; *Re CB* [1994] 2 FLR 762). The court's power to draw inferences is unlimited (*Re A* [1994] 2 FLR 463). For example, a man's refusal to undergo tests will lead to the 'virtually inescapable' inference that he is the father; at the very least, he will have to advance 'very clear and cogent reasons' for refusing to be tested (*Re A, above*). The reason for this is that, in view of advances in techniques of blood testing, 'any man who is unsure of his own paternity ... has it within his power to set all doubt at rest by submitting to a test' (per Waite LJ in *Re A*).

Inferences may also be drawn against a custodial parent who refuses to comply with a direction. The same applies where the custodial parent refuses to comply with a direction that *the child* be tested (per Wall J in *Re CB, above*): but where this intention is declared in advance, a direction will not normally be made for a blood test on a child (*see below*). Nor will the courts make a direction they know will be ignored solely in order to draw an adverse inference (per Balcombe LJ in *Re F* [1993] 1 FLR 598). However, although not strictly permitted by statute (which allows an inference to be drawn only where a direction has been made), it has been suggested that the courts *will* nevertheless draw an adverse inference against the custodial parent where a direction has been refused on the grounds of the custodial parent's declared intention not to comply with it (per Wall J in *Re CB, above*).

The doctrine of *res judicata* does not apply in affiliation proceedings. If, therefore, an application failed for lack of scientific evidence, this does not preclude a later application which is based on modern methods of establishing paternity; *see H v O* [1992] 1 FLR 282.

In addition to blood tests and inferences drawn from cohabitation, admissions by the man will also be relevant. In *R v Bournemouth Justices, ex p Grey & Rodd* [1987] 1 FLR 36 it was held that a social worker could be summoned as a witness to give evidence of the man's admission as there is no public interest immunity. Furthermore, the man's consent to being registered as the child's father will be *prima facie* evidence (s 34(2) of the Births and Deaths Registration Act 1953 and *Brierley v Brierley and Williams* [1918] P 257).

*When will blood tests tests be directed?*

The starting-point for deciding when to direct that blood tests be taken is that the interests of justice will normally require that available evidence is not suppressed and that the truth is ascertained whenever possible (per Lords Reid and Morris in *S v McW* [1972] AC 24). Thus a court need not be satisfied that the outcome of the test will be for the benefit of a child; although a test will not be ordered if there is evidence that it would be against the child's best interests (*ibid*).

Within this general principle, a number of patterns relevant to unmarried fathers emerge from the cases. First, a test is more likely to be ordered at the instance of a married father seeking either to uphold or rebut the presumption of legitimacy, than on the application of an unmarried man seeking to deny a husband's paternity. In *Re F* (*above*), a man's application for a test was refused on the ground that the child in question was living happily with its (married) parents and that it was not in the child's interests that its secure family unit be disturbed. In addition, the fact of paternity would make no difference to the outcome of any proceedings with respect to the child. Similarly, in *Re CB* (*above*), a direction was refused partly on the ground that the purpose for which it was sought was to enable a 'stranger to the marriage' to rebut the presumption of legitimacy. In such cases, the presumption in favour of discovering the truth seems to be replaced by a presumption in favour of suppressing the truth (and thereby indirectly preserving the presumption of a husband's paternity) unless there is some clear advantage to the child in directing a test.

These cases can be contrasted with *S v McW* (*above*, where tests were ordered on the application of husbands seeking to rebut the presumption of legitimacy); and with *Re G* [1994] 1 FLR 495, where a husband's application for a direction in support of his own claim of paternity was granted even though the mother had formed a stable new relationship. In both cases, the presumption in favour of ascertaining the truth was asserted. In *Re G*, *Re R* (*above*) was distinguished on the ground that the application in the latter case 'was wholly intrusive in the context of what had become once again a happy and settled marriage'.

The second principle to emerge is that a test on a child will not be directed where the custodial parent refuses to comply (per Balcombe LJ in *Re F*, above). This principle may, again, have less force where the applicant is a husband (*see Re G, above*, where the mother declared her opposition to a test, which was directed nevertheless). If a test is refused on this ground, however, the court is still at liberty to draw inferences adverse to the caring parent, as discussed earlier.

*Standard of proof*

The exact standard of proof required to establish paternity cannot be stated with precision. Traditionally, it was the higher criminal standard of 'beyond a reasonable doubt'. This reflected the serious consequences that were said to follow from a court's finding that a child was illegitimate. Section 26 of the FLRA 1969 then provided that it was not necessary to achieve this standard in order to rebut any presumption of law as to the legitimacy or illegitimacy of any person in any civil proceedings: evidence that it is more probable than not that that person is illegitimate or legitimate will suffice. Understandably, this was taken as meaning that the normal civil standard of 'the balance of probabilities' applied but it has been suggested that there is an intermediate standard (*see Serio v Serio* [1983] 4 FLR 756; *W v K* [1988] 1 FLR 86; *Re JS* (1991) Fam Law 22).

In *Re A (above)*, Waite LJ summarised the effect of these authorities in the following three propositions (at p 470):

(1) The question raised by an issue of paternity is a serious one: more serious in the scale of gravity than, for example, proof of debt or minor negligence.
(2) The balance of probability has to be established to a degree of sureness in the mind of the court which matches the seriousness of the issue.
(3) The weighing process involved in (2) must not be over-elaborate. The court should not attempt in a precise—almost mathematical—way to determine precisely what degree of probability is appropriate to the gravity of the issue. There is still ample scope for the influence of common sense and the insight gained from first impression.

## Registration of birth

Sections 24–25 of the FLRA 1987 inserted new ss 10 and 10A into the Births and Deaths Registration Act 1953 and these have been further amended by the CA 1989 (Sched 12, para 6).

The sections deal with the registration of the birth of a child whose parents are not married to each other. The father is, in certain circumstances, a qualified informant concerning the birth of the child so that by him giving information about the birth and signing the register any other qualified informant is discharged from the duty (s 10(2)).

For the man's name to appear on the register as the child's father there must either be a joint request by him and the mother or one of the following conditions must be satisfied:

(1) The mother declares the man to be the father and produces a statutory declaration by the man stating himself to be the father.
(2) The man declares himself to be the father and produces a statutory declaration by the mother stating him to be the father.
(3) Either parent produces a parental responsibility agreement and declares that the agreement complies with s 4 of the CA 1989 and has not been brought to an end by court order.
(4) As for (3) but a parental responsibility order under s 4 is produced.
(5) Either parent produces a financial provision order under Sched 1 to the CA 1989 and declares that the order has not been discharged.
(6) Either parent produces a certified copy of a court order under s 4 of the FLRA 1987, s 9 of the Guardianship of Minors Act 1971 or s 4 of the Affiliation Proceedings Act 1957 and declares that the order has not been brought to an end or discharged by a court.

## Changing the child's name

Because the parents were not married to each other at the time of the birth, the mother initially has sole parental responsibility (*see above*). She may therefore choose the child's surname although, as the child becomes mature enough to decide the matter, this parental power may taper away under the principle commonly taken to have been established by the House of Lords in *Gillick v W Norfolk and Wisbech Area Health Authority* [1986] 1 FLR 224.

If the parents have come to share parental responsibility, either by court order or agreement under s 4 of the CA 1989, then either of them may take steps as a result of which the child is known by another name because of the normal rules concerning shared parental responsibility in s 2(7). Any disagreement would be resolved judicially, applying the welfare principle. The position changes, however, where a residence order (*see below*) is in force with respect to the child. No person may then cause the child to be known by a new surname without either the written consent of every person who has parental responsibility for the child or the leave of the court (CA 1989, s 13(1)).

## Consent to marriage

The FLRA 1987 amended the Marriage Act 1949 to take into account the new procedure whereby an unmarried father could obtain parental rights and duties. Further amendments have been necessary to take into account the changes in the CA 1989.

The consents now required to the marriage of a person between the ages of 16 and 18 are contained s 3(1A) of the Marriage Act (inserted by Sched 12, para 5 to the CA 1989). They are, in shortened form:

(a) each parent of the child who has parental responsibility and each guardian;
(b) the person or persons with whom the child lives as the result of a residence order, in substitution for those mentioned in para (a);
(c) the local authority, if the child is in care, in addition to those mentioned in para (a); and
(d) where neither (b) nor (c) applies but a residence order was in force immediately before the child reached the age of 16, that of the person with whom the child lived, or was to live, as the result of the order, in substitution for those mentioned in para (a).

The reason for two paragraphs concerning residence orders is that in exceptional cases a residence order can be made that will continue after the child has reached the age of 16 (CA 1989, s 9(6)). This is catered for in para (b) and the normal case in para (d).

It will be seen, therefore, that in the absence of circumstances mentioned in paras (b) to (d), only the mother's consent will be necessary unless the father has acquired parental responsibility by court order or agreement.

## Guardianship

Before the CA 1989, the term guardianship had different meanings and the position was confusing. Section 5 of the CA 1989 now provides the only means whereby guardians can be appointed. A guardian under s 5 has parental responsibility for the child. He or she can be appointed by a court under subss (1) and (2), by a parent under subs (3) or by a guardian under subs (4).

### Appointment by the court

A court may appoint any individual, either on the application of that individual or of the court's own motion in family proceedings, if the child has no parent with parental responsibility or if a residence order which excluded the surviving parent was in force in the deceased parent's favour at the time of the death (s 5(1), (2) and (9)).

## Appointment by a parent or guardian

Appointment by a parent with parental responsibility or a guardian must be in writing and be dated and signed by the person making the appointment (s 5(5)). The appointment may be by will (ie a testamentary guardian strictly so called), or by other document. It is no longer necessary for the appointment to be by deed. Provision is also made for signature at the direction of the appointor.

The appointment will only take effect immediately on the appointor's death if the child has no surviving parent with parental responsibility, or unless, immediately before the death, a residence order excluding the surviving parent was in force in the appointor's favour at the time of the death. If there was no such residence order and there was a surviving parent with parental responsibility, the appointment only takes effect when that parent dies or loses parental responsibility (s 5(7) and (8)). Further rules are provided in s 6 of the CA 1989 concerning the revocation of guardianship and disclaimer.

Applying these rules to unmarried couples simply involves the application of the general principles in the Act. If no order or agreement under s 4 is in force giving the father parental responsibility, then the mother must appoint him to be the child's guardian if she wishes him to have parental responsibility after her death. The father will not be able to make an effective appointment unless he has parental responsibility under s 4 or he is already the child's guardian under s 5. Even if the father does not have parental responsibility at the time he executes his will, there is presumably nothing wrong in principle with purporting to make the appointment. The will speaks only from death and he might acquire parental responsibility after executing the will. To avoid any doubt about the will being made under some misapprehension as to the law, the appointment might be prefaced by words such as: 'If, at the date of my death, I have the power to appoint a testamentary guardian in respect of my child X then I APPOINT … '

Section 5(10) permits the appointment of two or more persons acting jointly.

It was seen *above* that a guardian need not be appointed by will. In virtually all cases, however, there is value in making a will so that other matters can be dealt with. It will be remembered from Chapter 9 that a cohabitant is not within the next of kin for the purposes of intestate succession and so express dispositions of property are essential. It is conceivable, however, that a non-testamentary appointment is adequate where the will is otherwise up to date or, perhaps, where the necessary witnesses for a will are not available.

## Residence and contact

Section 8 of the CA 1989, along with the related provisions in ss 9 and 10, are at the core of the private law of children. In family proceedings which (for purposes relevant to this book, include proceedings under the CA 1989, the Family Homes and Domestic Violence Bill and the Adoption Act 1976), and in proceedings 'under the inherent jurisdiction of the High Court in relation to children', a court may make a s 8 order (s 8(3) and (4)). A s 8 order means a contact order, a prohibited steps order, a residence order, a specific issue order and any order varying or discharging one of the above (s 8(1) and (2)). An unmarried father can seek the full range of s 8 orders without leave of court, whether he has parental responsibility or not.

A 'prohibited steps order' means an order that no step that could be taken by a parent in meeting his or her parental responsibility for a child, and which is of a kind specified in the order, shall be taken by any person without the consent of the court. A 'specific issue order' means an order giving directions for the purpose of determining a specific question which has arisen, or which may arise, in connection with any aspect of parental responsibility for a child. These two orders, which are not discussed further here, are useful means of resolving disputes that may arise between unmarried parents. Residence and contact orders are, however, of central importance.

### Residence orders

A residence order is an order settling the arrangements to be made as to the person with whom a child is to live. It is intended to be flexible enough to accommodate a much wider range of situations than the old orders. It may be made in favour of more than one person (s 11(4)) and, if these people are not living together, it may specify the periods that the child is to spend in each household (*see* eg *A v A* (1994) Fam Law 431). However, a shared residence order should not be made solely to confer parental responsibility on someone who cannot acquire it in any other way, such as a stepfather, unless it reflects the underlying reality of the children's living arrangements (*see N v B* [1993] 1 FCR 231).

If a residence order provides that a child is to live with one parent, but both parents have parental responsibility, it will cease to have effect if the parents live together for a continuous period of more than six months (s 11(5)).

No court may make any s 8 order (and therefore a residence order) that is to have effect for a period that will end after the child has reached the age of 16 unless it is satisfied that the circumstances of the case are exceptional (s 9(6)).

*The father may apply for residence order without leave*

An unmarried father is entitled to apply for any s 8 order without leave of the court (s 10(4)). If the court makes a residence order in his favour then it must also make an order under s 4 giving him parental responsibility if he would not otherwise have it in respect of the child (s 12(1)). Furthermore, the parental responsibility order cannot be brought to an end at any time while the residence order remains in force (s 12(4)). This means that an unmarried father can have a parental responsibility order without having a residence order but the reverse is not the case.

It should be clear that a residence order is not normally necessary while unmarried parents live together with the child. If the parents wish parental responsibility to be shared then it can be achieved by agreement under s 4 or, if there is some particular reason for doing it this way, by court order. Even on the breakdown of the relationship there may be no need for a residence order. If the father had no parental responsibility, the mother has the power to determine where the child will live. If they share parental responsibility, then they may agree on the child's residence. It will be remembered that under the principle of non-intervention the court must not make an order unless it considers that doing so would be better for the child than making no order at all (s 1(5)).

In cases where the father concedes that the child is to reside with mother, he might still apply for parental responsibility to give him some standing with regard to the child. The mother should then consider whether, if the parental responsibility order is made, she wishes to have a residence order in her favour. Without one, the child's residence with her will be a matter of continuing agreement with the father and she may want greater security.

*When residence order will be granted*

What will always be relevant and can never be overlooked is the welfare principle in s 1(1) of the Act, the presumption against delay in subs (2) and the particular circumstances listed in subs (3). The reader is referred to a specialist text on children law for a full account of how the welfare principle is to be applied.

Where the dispute has been between two unmarried parents there is no sign in recent cases that an unmarried father has fared any differently from a married one (*see* eg *Re C* [1981] 2 FLR 163; *D v M* [1982] 3 All ER 897; *W v L* (1987) 17 Fam Law 130; *B v T* [1989] 2 FLR 31; and *Re S* [1991] 2 FLR 388). However, some judges do take into consideration the view that young children should ordinarily be with their mothers (*Re W* [1990] 2 FLR 86; *Re W* [1992] 2 FLR 332; but the consideration seems to start losing force by the time the children are two years old: *see Re S, above*).

*Father v third parties*

Where the dispute has been between an unmarried father and third parties, recent cases suggest that the father has fared well (and this may be in line with a seeming tendency in child law generally to favour parents over non-parents). In *Re K* [1990] 2 FLR 64, for example, a young child went to live with his aunt and uncle following the death of his mother. The father, with whom the mother had lived, sought care and control in wardship and this was granted in the Court of Appeal. Fox LJ quoted Lord Templeman in *Re KD* [1988] 2 FLR 139 at 141A:

> The best person to bring up a child is the natural parent. It matters not whether the parent is wise or foolish, rich or poor, educated or illiterate, provided the child's moral and physical health is not endangered.

According to Fox LJ, the right approach does not involve asking the question where will the child get the better home. The question is whether it has been demonstrated that the welfare of the child positively demands the displacement of the parental right. He went on (at 68B):

> The word 'right' is not really accurate in so far as it might connote something in the nature of a property right (which it is not) but will serve for present purposes. The 'right', if there is one, is more that of the child.

Similarly, in *Re O* [1992] 1 FLR 77, an unmarried father was seeking custody of a child who had been placed by the mother with foster carers with a view to adoption. In explaining why the father should be given first consideration as the caring parent, Butler-Sloss LJ said:

> If it were a choice of balancing the known defects of every parent ... against the idealised perfect adopters, in a very large number of cases, children would immediately move out of the family circle and towards adopters. That would be social engineering ...

It should be stressed, however, that these decisions pre-date the CA 1989, so that the range of orders available to the court was narrower than it is now.

## Contact orders

A contact order means an order requiring the person with whom a child lives, or is to live, to allow the child to visit or stay with the person named in the order, or for that person and the child otherwise to have contact with each other (CA 1989, s 8(1)). A contact order is more of a direct replacement for the old access order than a residence order is a direct replacement for a custody order.

There is no compulsion on the person with the benefit of the order to maintain contact with the child and, as a consequence of the *Gillick* decision (*above*), a mature child can presumably not be forced to allow contact to take place. Furthermore, no contact order is to have effect for a period which will end after the child has reached the age of 16 unless the court is satisfied that the circumstances of the case are exceptional (s 9(6)).

In line with a policy of having orders that are more flexible, contact might take the form of telephone calls and letters. There is a general power for the court to include directions and impose conditions as to how the order is to be carried into effect and complied with (s 11(7)).

A contact order that requires one parent to allow the other parent to have contact with the child ceases to have effect if the parents live together for a continuous period of more than six months (s 11(6)).

An unmarried father who already has parental responsibility for the child, whether by court order or agreement with the mother, does not initially need a contact order. Even where the mother has a residence order, the father and child are not thereby precluded from having contact with each other. Given the principle of non-intervention (*above*) it is by no means clear that the courts will routinely order contact in the same way that they used to grant an order for reasonable access to one parent at the same time as granting custody to the other.

*Father may apply for contact order without leave*

An unmarried father without parental responsibility may apply for a contact order without leave of the court (s 10(4)). It was held under the old law that the court had jurisdiction to make a finding of paternity in an access application (*Davies v Davies* (1983) 13 Fam Law 111). Indeed, an access order was not to be granted unless paternity had been determined. This rule was extended to apply also to an order for interim access (*Re O* [1985] FLR 716) and will presumably continue under the new law.

*When contact will be granted*

The starting-point is that the welfare principle and other matters contained in s 1 of the CA 1989 must be considered from first to last. However, a number of specific principles have been developed in relation to contact applications.

The most important of these is that contact is the right of the child, not the parents (*M v M* [1973] 2 All ER 81; *Re S* [1990] 2 FLR 166, CA). It is doubtful whether this view could withstand detailed jurisprudential scrutiny, as was implicitly acknowledged by the House of Lords in *Re KD* [1988] 2 FLR 139. Nevertheless, as Lord Oliver said in that case, it is perfectly clear that any 'right' vested in a parent must yield to the dictates of the welfare of the child: but the welfare of the child is thought to lie in maintaining contact wherever possible. Thus, in *Re H* [1992] 1 FLR 148, it was held that the question to be asked was whether there was any cogent reason why contact should be refused. It was not necessary to show positive benefits flowing from contact, since that would be assumed (*see also Re F* [1993] 2 FLR 830). Contact should be denied in only exceptional cases, for example, where the child would be at risk of abuse from the applicant, or where the stability of the child's new family unit would be severely threatened (eg *Re J* [1994] 1 FLR 729).

In the last edition of this book, it was suggested that the courts have drawn no obvious distinction between applications by unmarried and married fathers for contact with their children. Since then, however, a pattern has emerged from the cases which suggests that the presumption in favour of contact will be more easily rebutted where the applicant is an unmarried father than where he is married. There has certainly been no official statement to this effect, and it is unlikely that an explicit distinction between parents according to marital status could properly survive an appeal based on the welfare principle. Nevertheless, the pattern is striking. For example, it seems that arguments based on the hostility to contact of either the mother or her new partner, or the risk of destabilising the family unit, will be more successful where the applicant is an unmarried father (compare, for example, *Re SM* [1991] 2 FLR 333 (disruption of new relationship); *Re D* [1991] 2 FLR 333 (mother's implacable hostility) and *Re H* [1993] 1 FLR 484 (stepfather's implacable hostility), all unsuccessful applications by unmarried fathers; with *Re H* [1992] 1 FLR 148 (contact despite mother's opposition on grounds of disruption to children); *Re F* [1993] 2 FLR 830 (father's appeal allowed even though mother implacably opposed); *Re R* [1993] 2 FLR 762 (father's appeal allowed even though child had no memory of him), all of which were successful applications by married fathers).

The proposition that marital status is a significant factor in contact disputes is advanced only tentatively, since all of these cases are reports of appeals, which means that this is a necessarily selective sample of judicial thinking. Further, as with all contact and residence appeals, the appellate court will allow the lower court a 'generous ambit within which reasonable disagreement is possible' (*G v G (Minors: Custody Appeal)*

[1985] 2 FLR 894). In addition, a recent case disturbs this pattern, and may point the way to future developments. In *Re P* [1994] 2 FLR 374, an unmarried father's application was allowed despite some evidence that continued contact with the father was affecting the mother's mental health, that he had had no contact with the child for the two years before the application, and that he had been violent towards the mother in the past.

## Adoption

Cohabitants cannot jointly adopt a child, whether a child of one of them or neither of them, because s 14(1) of the Adoption Act 1976 (AA 1976), as inserted by s 88 of and Sched 10, para 4 to the CA 1989, only permits adoption by one person or by a married couple.

Adoption is sometimes an issue following the breakdown of a cohabiting relationship: for example, the mother has married and now wishes to adopt a child of the relationship jointly with her husband or the mother is willing to agree to the adoption of the child by third parties but the putative father objects. Both of these situations have featured in reported cases and they are the focus of this section. Reference to specialist texts on children law should be made for the general requirements for an adoption order and for other cases which might conceivably arise: for example where the mother or the father of the child is the sole applicant for an adoption order.

### When father may refuse consent

An unmarried father will have *locus standi* to withhold consent to adoption only if he has parental responsibility for the child (s 72 of the AA 1976, as amended by Sched10, para 30(7) to the CA 1989) or if he has been appointed a guardian of the child (*see above*). It follows that if the father has parental responsibility, either by virtue of a court order or an agreement with the mother, then his agreement to the adoption is required *qua* parent. It follows also that a father without parental responsibility may seek to thwart an adoption application either by applying for a residence order (which cannot be granted without a parental responsibility order, *see above*) or by seeking a parental responsibility order on its own. The application by the father and the application for the adoption should be heard together rather than *seriatim* (*Re G* [1980] 1 FLR 109; *Re G* [1992] 1 FLR 642; *G v G* [1993] 2 WLR 837). The same principle applies to contact applications brought by an unmarried father (*see below*).

If the father obtains a residence order then that is presumably the end of the matter. If he obtains a parental responsibility order on its own then he will be made respondent to the proceedings (r 15(2) of the Adoption Rules 1984) and the court will have to consider whether his agreement should be dispensed with on one of the grounds set out in s 16(2) (assuming, of course, that it is in the child's welfare that the adoption order be made at all *Re D* (1991) Fam Law 28).

## Judicial attitudes to fathers making pre-emptive applications

In the past, and certainly prior to the introduction of the (now replaced) parental rights and duties order in s 4 of the FLRA 1987, courts have looked with disfavour upon fathers who were making applications in order to defeat an adoption. It is clear that the welfare principle was applied in only the most erratic way and that the courts were more concerned with what they called the 'stigma of bastardy' than with the particular circumstances of the case (*see* eg *Re Adoption Application 41/61 No 1* [1962] 3 All ER 533; *Re O* [1965] Ch 23 and *Re E(P)* [1969] 1 All ER 323). On the other hand, some emphasis was placed on the blood tie between father and child (*see* eg *Re C(MA)* [1966] 1 WLR 646), although this is not self-evidently an application of the welfare principle either.

Such reported cases as there have been recently suggest that the welfare principle is applied more systematically, although the result in each case depends very much on its facts. In *Re N* [1990] 1 FLR 58, for example, the father applied in wardship for care and control of the child so as to defeat an adoption application. Wardship was continued, care and control was given to the foster parents with access to the father. No criticism was made of the father's strategy. (*See also Re M* (1991) Fam Law 136.)

Another case involved the father applying for a parental rights and duties order under s 4 of the FLRA 1987 (now replaced by CA 1989, s 4). Although it related to an application to free the children for adoption, it is relevant to adoption applications generally. The rules at the time concerning freeing were those in s 18(7) of the AA 1976 (as amended by FLRA 1987, s 7(1)). The subsection provided that a freeing order could not be made unless the court was satisfied, in relation to any person claiming to be the child's father, that either he had no intention of applying for one of the listed orders (FLRA 1987, s 4 parental rights and duties order, custody, legal or actual custody or care and control) or, if he did apply, the application would be likely to be refused.

*Re H (No 2)* [1991] 1 FLR 214 (referred to *above*, because it contains general criteria for deciding a parental responsibility application) was the culmination of complicated litigation, the details of which are no longer relevant. The father applied for an order under s 4 of the FLRA 1987 in connection with the local authority's application to free his two children for adoption. He acknowledged that he did not want custody and merely wished to be a party to the adoption proceedings on the limited question of access. The trial judge refused to make the order on the grounds that the purpose of a s 4 order was to confer all the parental rights on a deserving father and granted the authority's application. The Court of Appeal held that the judge was wrong about s 4. An order under s 4 was not intended only to operate if all the parental rights that were to be granted to the father were immediately capable of being exercised by him. Even if the father was given parental rights and duties but his agreement to the freeing of the children was dispensed with immediately thereafter, there was still some purpose in making the order. The parent of a child free for adoption has certain rights to receive progress reports and to apply for the revocation of the order if the child was not placed for adoption within 12 months. In the result, the s 4 order was made as well as the freeing order.

On the question of freeing orders, Sched 10, para 6 to the CA 1989 has now inserted a new s 18(7) of the AA 1976 as follows:

> (7) Before making an order under this section in the case of a child whose father does not have parental responsibility for him, the court shall satisfy itself in relation to any person claiming to be the father that—
> (a) he has no intention of applying for—
> (i) an order under section 4(1) of the Children Act 1989, or
> (ii) a residence order under section 10 of that Act, or
> (b) if he did make any such application, it would be likely to be refused.

## Contact applications in adoption proceedings

An unmarried father may seek a contact order in adoption proceedings. If made, this would not confer parental responsibility on him and would therefore not put him in a position where he could withhold his consent to the adoption. However, it may persuade the court to exercise its discretion to make him a party to the proceedings (*see below*); and would enable him to have contact following the adoption (although contact orders are likely to be very rare in the absence of agreement by the adopters: per Lord Ackner in *Re C* [1988] 2 FLR 159, at 167). Where the father is applying for contact in freeing proceedings, and where prospective adopters have been identified, the court must take evidence from the prospective adopters as to their attitude towards future contact (*Re C* [1992] 1 FLR 115).

A contact application should be heard at the same time as the adoption application (*G v G, above*). The fact that an unmarried father may seek contact after an adoption does not alter this rule, since once an adoption order has been made the father becomes a legal stranger to the child and would require leave to apply for a contact order (*G v G, above*; *M v C and Calderdale Metropolitan Borough Council* [1993] 1 FLR 505).

### Position of father without parental responsibility

If the father does not have parental responsibility and is not seeking it, his position may nevertheless be relevant in adoption proceedings. He is to be joined as a respondent to the proceedings if he is liable to contribute to the child's maintenance by virtue of any order or wagreement (Adoption Rules 1984 (AR 1984), r 15(2)(h)). Under r 15(3) he might be joined in the court's discretion. There is no presumption in favour of joining an unmarried father without parental responsibility as a party; and even if he is joined, that does not, of course, give him an automatic right to prevent the adoption (*Re B* (1991) Fam Law 136; *G v G, above*). Only if he has parental responsibility can he seek to do that. There is no obligation to include details of an unmarried father without parental responsibility on the form of originating application for an adoption order (AR 1984, Sched 1, Form 6; *see Re L* [1991] 1 FLR 171).

In freeing applications, however, the AR 1984—but not the Magistrates' Courts (Adoption) Rules 1984—seem open to the interpretation that an unmarried father *without* parental responsibility should be joined as a respondent to an application, because he is a 'parent' in the CA 1989 sense, which is the sense which applies in the relevant paragraphs of the AR 1984.

Irrespective of r 15(2) or (3), where the identity of the father is known to the placing agency, it is obliged so far as it considers reasonably practical and in the interests of the child to provide a counselling service and give him information about adoption in the same way as it must do in relation to the parent of a legitimate child (Adoption Agency Regulations 1983 (AAR 1983), reg 7(3)). The agency should also obtain details relating to the father for inclusion in the child's case record (AAR 1983, Sched, Pts III and IV).

In addition, an authority preparing a Schedule II report should include specified particulars concerning each parent, including their views in relation to the adoption (r 4.4 and Sched 2, para 2j of the AR 1984). This duty is to be carried out 'so far as is practicable', which has been held to mean that the duty will not apply where ascertaining the father's wishes and feelings would have detrimental results to the child (*Re P* (1994) Fam Law 310). This may apply in cases where, for example, the man is unaware of the child's existence and, if he were informed, the mother would withdraw her agreement to the adoption. However, it is normally thought to be better for the child to face up to the father being informed sooner rather than later (*Re P, above*).

Finally, if the court decides not to make an adoption order it can still make a residence order. It may be, therefore, that the father is successful both in resisting the adoption *and* in having the child reside with him, or only in resisting the adoption. In the latter case, a contact order might nevertheless be made in the father's favour.

## Children in care

A child is either being looked after by a local authority because he or she is in need of accommodation (CA 1989, s 20) or because a care order has been made under s 31. (Child assessment orders, emergency protection orders and supervision orders are not considered here.) As with adoption, much of the complexity relevant for present purposes has hitherto concerned the standing of the unmarried father.

If a child is in accommodation under s 20, then a person with parental responsibility may at any time remove the child (s 20(8)) unless, presumably, there is an order to the contrary; for example, because someone else has a residence order. An unmarried father without parental responsibility cannot remove the child but he might seek an order under s 4 or enter into an agreement with the mother so that he has the necessary power. There is no requirement to give the local authority notice of the proposed removal. The position concerning care orders requires more detailed consideration.

### Care orders

Section 31(2) of the CA 1989 provides that:

> A court may only make a care order ... if it is satisfied—
> (a) that the child concerned is suffering, or is likely to suffer, significant harm; and
> (b) that the harm, or likelihood of harm, is attributable to—
> (i) the care given to the child, or likely to be given to him if the order were not made, not being what it would be reasonable to expect a parent to give to him; or
> (ii) the child's being beyond parental control.

In addition to these conditions, the welfare principle and other matters contained in s 1 of the Act apply. Under r 4.7 of and Sched 3 to the Family Proceedings Rules 1991 a parent with parental responsibility is to be made a respondent to an application for a care order and, even if he has no parental responsibility, he is to be given notice of them (so that he could request to be joined under r 4.7(3)).

The effect of a care order is that it becomes the duty of the local authority to receive the child into its care and to keep the child in its care while the order remains in force (s 33(1)). The authority acquires parental responsibility for the child, although others with parental responsibility do not thereby lose it. The authority has the power to determine the extent to which a parent or guardian may meet her or his parental responsibility for the child but it may not exercise this power unless satisfied that it is necessary to do so in order to safeguard or promote the child's welfare (s 33(3) and (4)).

A care order can be discharged by an order of the court under s 39(1). An application for discharge can only be made by:

(a) a person with parental responsibility for the child;
(b) the child himself; or
(c) the local authority designated by the care order.

This means that an unmarried father without parental responsibility cannot apply directly for the discharge of a care order. He could, however, apply for a parental responsibility order under s 4 or acquire parental responsibility by agreement with the mother. This would then give him standing to apply for the discharge of the order. Unless a father has parental responsibility or was a party to the original care proceedings, he will not be entitled to receive notice of a discharge application.

The only other way that a care order can be brought to an end is by the making of a residence order (s 91(1)). Thus a father (or mother) could seek a residence order as a way of taking the child out of care. As was seen above, an unmarried father does not need parental responsibility to apply for a residence order but if he is successful then a parental responsibility order must also be made.

## Contact with children in care

The starting-point is that the authority shall allow the child reasonable contact with parents, any guardian and any person in whose favour a residence order was in force immediately before the care order was made. If the authority (or the child) is not content with this then *it* (or the child) must make an application to the court for an order authorising the authority to refuse to allow the contact (s 34(4)). Nevertheless, any of those listed *above* can apply for an order if they are dissatisfied with the amount of contact that is being allowed (s 34(3)).

It will be seen that reference is made simply to parents in s 34(1). This means that a child is still entitled to have contact with her or his unmarried father who lacks parental responsibility. There is no longer any need for the father to apply for an order to give him *locus standi*.

In an effort to avoid disputes arising, the court is directed *before* making a care order to consider the arrangements that the authority has made or proposes to make for affording contact with a child and invite the parties to the proceedings to comment on those arrangements (s 34(11)).

This should help to focus people's minds on the issue right at the outset. Nevertheless, an order under the section can be made either at the same time as the care order or later.

## Financial relief and support for children

This area is now dominated by the Child Support Act 1991. The Act applies irrespective of the marital status of a child's parents, and is thus of direct concern to cohabitants with children. The most significant feature of the Act is that it removes the courts' jurisdiction to make orders for child maintenance and places the functions of assessment, collection and enforcement of child support in the hands of the Child Support Agency. This implies a greatly reduced role for the courts. However, the courts retain a jurisdiction to make orders for lump sums and property transfers, as well as the power to order child maintenance in cases not covered by the Act. Further, the transfer to the Agency of those cases in which there was a maintenance agreement or court order in force on 5 April 1993 has been deferred indefinitely. Such cases remain within the court system for the time being. It is also possible to make an agreement leading to a consent order that will have the effect of ousting the Agency. The courts retain the power to vary or revoke these agreements or orders. There are a number of other functions left to the courts, such as determinations of paternity for the purposes of the Act.

We consider the Act first, followed by the remnants of the court-based system.

### Child Support Act 1991

The Child Support Act 1991 (CSA 1991) received the Royal Assent on 25 July 1991 and came into force on 5 April 1993. There is a substantial body of delegated legislation issued under the Act, much of which has already been heavily amended.

The main features of the CSA 1991 were foreshadowed in a White Paper, *Children Come First*, in 1990. The Act was passed against the background of increasing awareness of the low incidence of child maintenance orders, low compliance rates and the heavy reliance by sole parents on social security. In a Department of Social Security survey it was found that only about 39 per cent of sole parents had ever received maintenance and only 29 per cent were receiving regular payments. On the other hand, 72 per cent of lone mothers were claiming income support and 85 per cent had received it at some time since becoming a lone parent. In 1981, 50 per cent of lone parents claiming income support were also receiving maintenance payments. In 1988 the figure was only 23 per cent.

These figures may simply reflect the fact that for many years there have been disincentives to claiming maintenance for children. Every pound received simply reduces income support by one pound. Going to court can be costly, slow and troublesome. Compliance is notoriously low and enforcement difficult. The caring parent, assumed in this chapter to be the mother, may want nothing further to do with a father who has disappeared from the lives of her children. She may fear that maintenance action will revive or exacerbate the difficulties or violence in the relationship. The Act seeks to overcome these disincentives by taking enforcement of child support out of the hands of individual parents with care, vesting that responsibility in the Child Support Agency.

The Act has been controversial since its inception. Opposition to it has been intense, especially from groups representing fathers against whom Agency assessments have been made. This, combined with two critical reports from the Social Security Select Committee of the House of Commons, has forced the government to introduce two substantial tranches of amendments: the first, introduced by amending regulations, in February 1994; the second, foreshadowed by a White Paper (*Improving Child Support*, Cmnd 2745) issued in January 1995, which took the form of amendments to regulations (The Child Support and Income Support (Amendment) Regulations 1995, hereafter the 1995 Regulations) and to the primary legislation itself in the shape of the Child Support Act 1995.

Criticism of the original Act has come from different quarters. From the caring parent's point of view, any child support received simply reduces entitlement to income support pound for pound (as before). There is no proposal to introduce a maintenance disregard (although one has been introduced for Family Credit). This means that a caring parent on benefit will gain nothing through the recovery of child support on her behalf. Indeed, it raises the possibility that a caring parent who is lifted off income support by child support could end up worse off through loss of 'passported benefits', such as free school meals and dental treatment (although she would have an incentive to work in such cases, given that entitlement to child support would not be reduced by her earnings except indirectly through the operation of the formula). On the positive side, though, she will not have to go to court either for the order or for enforcement. At the same time, the Act may mean that the father is brought back into the lives of her and the children, for good or ill.

From the 'absent parent's' point of view (not our preferred term, but the one used in the statute), there have been a number of criticisms levelled at the Act. The main one has been the size of maintenance assessments arrived at under the statutory formula, which has in turn led to complaints of hardship to these men and their second families (the cost of supporting whom was not originally recognised by the formula). Allied to this have been complaints about the inflexibility of the formula, and especially its failure to recognise factors such as the costs of travel to work or of contact visits, combined with the absence of any discretion to deal with genuine cases of hardship.

Another concern stemmed from the fact that, as originally conceived, maintenance assessments under the Act and property orders under the Matrimonial Causes Act 1973 were independent of each other. No account could be taken of, say, a custodial mother being awarded the former matrimonial home when the absent father's maintenance liability was being calculated. It was thought that practices on divorce would change with the result that the housing security of some women would suffer. Because there are no adjustive powers on the breakdown of a cohabiting relationship, this is one problem which would not have affected cohabitants. It was seen above (in Chapter 7, and further *below*), however, that there is a power to settle the home for the benefit of a child (Sched 1, para 1(2)(*d*)) and, in so far as that power is used, the CSA 1991 might have reduced its frequency.

Finally, it has become clear that there are serious managerial problems in the Agency itself. In particular, it has proved incapable of dealing quickly, accurately and efficiently with processing maintenance assessments, and its forensic abilities, especially when dealing with self-employed absent parents, have been doubted.

The government responded to these criticisms by amending the formula in early 1994 so as to reduce the level of assessments in certain cases (especially, it seemed, at the top and bottom ends of the income spectrum); but pressure for more fundamental change remained, resulting in the White Paper of January 1995. This proposed a number of further changes:

(a) a discretion, exercisable by the Agency, to depart from the assessment in cases of hardship, or to take account of pre-April 1993 property transfers (discussed *below*);
(b) changes to the formula itself, including new allowances for the absent parent, and an overall ceiling on child support of 30 per cent of the absent parent's normal net income (discussed *below*);
(c) the introduction of a 'Child Maintenance Bonus' for caring parents in receipt of child support who leave income support for full-time employment; and
(d) a number of administrative changes, including deferment of the

take-on of certain types of case so as to ease the load on the Agency. We discuss transitional arrangements under a separate heading later.

What follows is only a brief account of the main provisions. There will be no detailed discussion of the formula itself, only an outline of the principles underlying it. Specialist works should be consulted as necessary. The administrative procedures, bureaucratic structure, powers of the officers, collection methods and enforcement provisions are not considered here. It should be noted in this connection, however, that s 2 imposes on the Secretary of State and any child support officer a duty to have regard to the welfare of any child likely to be affected by his decision when exercising any discretionary power conferred by the Act. This duty is enforceable, if at all, through judicial review (*see B v Secretary of State for Social Security* (1995) *The Times*, 30 January, 'the *Biggin* case').

*The duty to maintain and the basic principles*

The duty to maintain is set out in s 1(1): 'For the purposes of this Act, each parent of a qualifying child is responsible for maintaining him.'

The definition of a 'qualifying child' for the purposes of the Act is complex. In simplified form, a person is a *child* if he or she is an unmarried person under the age of 16 or under the age of 19 and receiving full-time non-advanced education (s 55(1) and (2)).

A child is a '*qualifying* child' if one or both parents are absent (s 3(1)). An absent parent is one who is not living in the same household as the child, provided that the child has her or his home with a person who is 'a person with care' (s 3(2)). A person with care is a person with whom the child has his home, provided that the person usually provides day-to-day care for the child (whether exclusively or in conjunction with any other person) and who does not fall within a prescribed category of person (s 3(3)). Local authorities and foster parents have been prescribed for these purposes. The Secretary of State cannot prescribe, *inter alia*, parents or guardians under s 3(3). 'Day-to-day care' means care of not less than 104 nights in total during the 12-month period ending with the week in which a maintenance inquiry form is sent to the absent parent (reg 1(2) of the Child Support (Maintenance Assessments and Special Cases) Regulations 1992, hereafter AR 1992, as amended).

The normal situation when a child will be a qualifying child, therefore, is where the child's parents have separated and the child is living only with one of them. It is irrelevant that the parent with care has repartnered.

An absent parent is taken to have met his responsibility to maintain the child by making such periodical payments of maintenance of such amount, and at such intervals, as are determined under the Act (s 1(2)). In particular, where a maintenance assessment is in force under the Act, then the absent parent must comply with it (s 1(3)). Payments required under a maintenance assessment are referred to as 'child support maintenance' (s 3(6)).

Subject to cases where the parent with care is receiving income support, family credit or disability working allowance (discussed *below*), and subject also to the transitional provisions (also discussed *below*), either the absent parent or the person with care can apply for a maintenance assessment (s 4(1)). Where the assessment is made, the Secretary of State may, if either party applies, arrange for the collection of the maintenance and enforcement of the obligation (s 4(2); *see* the Child Support (Collection and Enforcement) Regulations 1992).

Provision is made in s 5 for cases where more than one person has care of a qualifying child. The basic idea is that a person with parental responsibility is to apply. In the common case of a custodial mother who has repartnered, she will make the application because her new partner will not normally have parental responsibility.

If a parent with care is receiving income support, family credit or disability working allowance, she can be required to authorise the Secretary of State to recover child support maintenance from the absent parent (s 6(1)) and is prevented from applying under s 4 (s 4(10), inserted by s 18 of the CSA 1995). The parent with care cannot, however, be required so to authorise the Secretary of State if the Secretary of State considers that there are reasonable grounds for believing that the parent or any child living with her would be at risk of suffering harm or undue distress (s 6(2); *see* the CSA Policy Guidelines on the Application of the Duty to Co-operate).

The parent with care must give the Secretary of State such information as he, the Secretary of State, considers necessary to enable the absent parent to be traced and to enable child support maintenance to be assessed and recovered (s 6(9)). The obligation does not apply in prescribed circumstances or where the Secretary of State, in prescribed circumstances, waives it (s 6(10); *see* the Child Support (Information, Evidence and Disclosure) Regulations 1992, Pt II). Failure without good cause to comply with an obligation under s 6 can lead to a 'reduced benefit direction' under s 46(5), meaning a direction that income support, family credit or disability working allowance can be reduced by such an amount, and for such a period, as is specified in the direction. The maximum amount and period are prescribed in regulations (*see* the Child Support (Maintenance Assessment and Procedure) Regulations 1992,

Part IX). It is this provision which gave rise to considerable controversy when the Bill was being debated because it enables a woman who refuses to name the father of her child to be penalised.

Before giving a reduced benefit direction the child support officer must consider whether, having regard to any reasons given by the parent, there are reasonable grounds for believing that, if she were to be required to comply with the requirement there would be a risk of her or any children living with her suffering harm or undue distress as a result of complying (s 46(3)). If the child support officer considers that there are such reasonable grounds then he shall take no further action.

Section 8 of the CSA 1991 is the crucial section dealing with the future place of the courts in child maintenance. Subject to the transitional provisions (discussed *below*), in any case where a child support officer would have jurisdiction to make a maintenance assessment, no court is to exercise any power which it would otherwise have to make, vary or revive any maintenance order in relation to the child and absent parent concerned (s 8(3)). This is subject to five exceptions.

(1) A court may make an order where there is already a written maintenance agreement and the order the court makes is, in all material respects, in the same terms as the agreement, ie 'consent orders' (s 8(5)).

(2) If a maintenance assessment determined by 'the alternative formula' (discussed *below*) is in force, a court can exercise its powers to order the absent parent to pay extra maintenance (s 8(6)).

(3) In shortened form, the court can exercise its powers to order the payment of expenses incurred in connection with the instruction of a child at an educational establishment or whilst the child is undergoing training for a trade, profession or vocation (s 8(7)).

(4) The court can exercise its maintenance powers if the order is made solely for the purposes of meeting expenses attributable to a child's disability (s 8(8) and (9)).

(5) A court can still exercise its powers to make an order against a person with care.

The role of the courts is obviously greatly reduced, but it is not eliminated altogether. The courts' jurisdiction is only ousted where a Child Support Officer would have jurisdiction under the Act: thus, the courts are not ousted where the Agency has no jurisdiction. Therefore, court orders will still be necessary if maintenance is sought against step-parents under, for example, s 23 of the Matrimonial Causes Act 1973 or Sched 1, para 4(2) to the CA 1989. And they can still be sought in respect of children over the age of 18 who, for example, are undergoing higher education (MCA 1973, s 29(3) and Sched 1, para 2 to the CA

1989). In addition, under changes announced in the 1995 White Paper, and implemented by s 18 of the CSA 1995, the courts will retain jurisdiction to vary or revoke written agreements made before 5 April 1993, as well as any court orders. This is discussed further *below* in the context of transitional arrangements.

Maintenance agreements concerning periodical payments will remain possible after the CSA 1991 but nothing can prevent an application for a maintenance assessment and any provision in the agreement which purports to prevent it is void (s 9(2)–(4)). This is discussed further *below*.

*Maintenance assessments under the statutory formula*

The amount of child support maintenance to be fixed by assessment is determined under Sched 1, Pt 1 to the Act (s 11(2)). This creates the framework for the child assessment formula. The details of the formula can be found in the Assessment Regulations 1992 (as amended, especially by the 1995 Regulations). Provision is also made for interim maintenance assessments (s 12). We start first with a description of the principles underlying the statutory formula, which will include a description of the changes announced in the 1995 White Paper (embodied mainly in the 1995 Regulations). We will then look at the proposal in the White Paper to build in a discretion to depart from the formula in certain cases.

The starting point is the 'maintenance requirement'. This represents the minimum amount assumed to be necessary for the maintenance of the child or children (Sched 1, para 1). It is arrived at by aggregating the following figures: the adult carer's income support personal allowance; the income support allowance for each child (which depends on the age of the child, although the figures are reduced for older children); family premium and lone parent premium. Child benefit is then deducted from this figure (Sched 1, para 1(2)–(5); AR 1992, reg 3(1)).

Both parents, where they have sufficient income, will be expected to contribute to the maintenance requirement from their 'assessable income'. Assessable income is net income (calculated in accordance with the Assessment Regulations) less exempt income (also calculated in accordance with the Regulations) (para 5(1) and (2)). The exempt income is the amount necessary to cover daily expenses, based on income support rates, reasonable housing costs and the costs of any of the parent's other children with whom the parent is living. The 1995 White Paper proposed to enlarge exempt income in three ways, which have all been implemented by the 1995 regulations. First, the housing costs of the absent parent's new partner and stepchildren will be added to the calculation of an absent parent's exempt income (*see* reg 50 of the 1995 Regulations, revoking reg 17 of the AR 1992). Secondly, there will be an allowance for those with high travel-to-work costs (*see* Sched 3B, AR 1992 as inserted by the 1995 Regulations). Thirdly, the White Paper proposed a 'broadly based allowance' in exempt income to take account of property transfers made before 5 April 1993 (*see* Sched 3A to the AR 1992). This is to deal with the complaint that the Act in its original form was retrospective in effect and took no account of property transfers made before the Act came into force. The proposal is for a standard allowance according to the value of the transfer, with transfer values being banded. The higher the value of the transfer, the greater the allowance. This presupposes, of course, that it is known what the parties owned in the first place so that the value of a transfer can be calculated. To deal with this, there is a presumption that ex-partners were entitled each to half the total value of the property transferred. As we saw in Chapter 8, this may be an optimistic assumption in many cases involving cohabitants (and, for that matter, is not always accurate where married couples are concerned). The White Paper merely acknowledges that the proposal for standard banded allowances 'will not take account fully of the special rules governing the transfer of property and capital in cases where the parents were not married' (although why the rules of express and implied trusts are considered 'special' for these purposes is not clear). The absent parent will have to prove both that a transfer has taken place and what its value was. Under the system of 'departures' proposed in the 1995 White Paper (described *below* and now contained in ss 1–9 of the CSA 1995), it will be possible in these cases for either party to apply for a departure where these banded allowances produce exemptions that are either too high or too low.

In what follows, we assume that the parent with care will not have income bringing her above the exempt level and that liability rests solely on the absent parent. Once one has the absent parent's assessable income, 50 per cent is deducted as child support (AR 1992, reg 5). If one-half of assessable income is less than the maintenance requirement for the children, then the absent parent simply pays half of his assessable income as child support maintenance (para 2(2)).

Where one-half of the assessable income *exceeds* the maintenance requirement for the children then a more complex calculation is undertaken (paras 3 and 4; AR 1992, reg 6). Maintenance does continue beyond the maintenance requirement because, it will be recalled, the maintenance requirement is only the *minimum* amount considered necessary for the children. In essence, one calculates the amount of income needed to meet the maintenance requirement (ie that amount which, when halved, is equal to the maintenance requirement). The balance of the assessable income, subject to the upper limit mentioned *below*, then has a lower rate applied to it. This was originally a flat rate of 25 per cent, but since the February 1994 changes it was reduced to 15 per cent for one child, 20 per cent for two children and 25 per cent for three. This means that the children continue to receive maintenance from the absent father over and above the minimum requirements but they take fewer pence in the pound.

The formula has what might be called lower and upper limits. At the lower end, a liable parent is always to be left with a protected level of income so that he can meet inescapable financial obligations (para 6; AR 1992, reg 11). In these circumstances, his obligations to his partner or stepchildren may be taken into account. The protected level of income is set by reference to income support levels, including their housing costs, and an additional £30 per week margin plus 15 per cent of his remaining net income. The effect is that he stops paying his assessed amount at the point when his weekly income would be taken below his protected level of earnings.

There are, or will be, two upper limits to assessments under the formula. The first, proposed in the 1995 White Paper, will apply in all cases and will ensure that an absent parent will not be assessed to pay more than 30 per cent of his net income (*see* reg 46 of the 1995 Regulations). It is thought that this will lower an assessment in about 20 per cent of cases. Another upper limit applies where liability has been calculated according to the additional element, discussed *above*. The upper limit is set by the 'alternative formula' (Sched 1, para 4(3); AR 1992, reg 6(2)). It operates by putting a ceiling on the income that can be deducted as child support. The White Paper proposed a reduction in the level at which the ceiling is fixed (*see* reg 43 of the 1995 Regulations). Once this ceiling has been reached, it will be recalled that this is one of the occasions when a court is still permitted, by s 8(6), to make an order for maintenance.

Finally, there is a minimum amount which must be paid as child support, even if the formula would produce an assessment lower than the minimum (Sched 1, para 7). This has been prescribed as 5 per cent of the income support personal allowance for a person aged not less than 25 (AR 1992, reg 13). Some cases are exempt from the obligation to pay the minimum amount (*see* AR 1992, reg 26).

The 1995 White Paper proposes to introduce, by amending legislation, a limited discretion to allow departures from assessments in exceptional circumstances. The discretion will be exercised initially by the Agency itself, subject to appeal to the Child Support Appeal Tribunal (and higher, if necessary, on points of law). This change requires new primary legislation, hence the need for the Child Support Act 1995. The relevant provisions are contained in ss 1–9 and Sched 1 to the CSA 1995 (inserting a new s 28A–H and Sched 4A and 4B into the CSA 1991). For the most part, these provisions provide only a framework which will be fleshed out later by regulations.

The grounds for an application are as follows:

(a) the absent parent may apply on the ground that he faces additional expenses not taken account of in the formula *and* that he would face hardship if he had to pay the amount assessed under the formula. The expenses to be taken into account and the definition of hardship will all be defined (*see* Sched 4B, para 2 );

(b) a parent with care will also be able to apply where the assessment is unrealistically low, for example, where the absent parent has a low income but substantial assets, where the absent parent's housing costs are excessive, where his housing costs (which, as we saw *above*, include the costs of housing a new partner and stepchildren) are being met, or should be met, wholly or in part by a new partner or where the absent parent has abused the new travel-to-work costs allowance in exempt income (*see* Sched 4B, para 4); and

(c) there will be special treatment accorded under the system of departures to those cases where there was a maintenance agreement entered into, or a capital or property settlement made, before 5 April 1993, so as to reduce the retrospective effect of the Act (Sched 4B, para 3; *see also* the crude system of banded allowances when calculating exempt income, discussed above).

In each case, the Secretary of State must have regard to the following principles before making a departure order:

(a) that parents should be responsible for maintaining their children whenever they can afford to do so (s 28E(2)(*a*));

(b) that a parent owes an equal duty of support to all his children (s 28E(2)(*b*)); and

(c) it must be just and equitable to make an order having particular regard to the financial circumstances of the parents and the welfare of any child likely to be affected by the direction (s 28F).

It is expected that the new departures system will be introduced in the financial year 1996/7.

*Transitional provisions*

Not all cases have been taken on by the Agency straight away: indeed, some have now been postponed indefinitely. The following is an attempt to summarise the current position (which is based on proposals in the

1995 White Paper, the 1995 Act and ministerial announcements):

(1) Where there was a court order or written agreement in force on 5 April 1993: here, the courts retain the power to vary or revoke the order or agreement (*see* s 18(3) of the CSA 1995, amending s 8 of the CSA 1991). If an agreement or order were revoked, it is open to the caring parent to apply to the Agency for an assessment; but it has been held that it is inappropriate for a court to revoke an agreement simply to enable the parent with care to have access to the Agency (*B v M* (1994) Fam Law 370). The original intention was that these cases would be taken on by the Agency over a period starting in 1996; but in the 1995 White Paper, the government announced that it intends to postpone indefinitely the take-on of these cases by the Agency. Indeed, s 18(1) of the CSA 1995 amends s 4 of the CSA 1991 to prevent an application for an assessment being made where there was a written maintenance agreement in force on 5 April 1993, or where there is a court order currently in force. This means that the courts' powers of variation and revocation in these cases will remain for the foreseeable future.

(2) Where there was no court order or written agreement in force on 5 April 1993: here, the caring parent can either apply to the Agency for an assessment, or can make a written agreement with the absent parent. The only thing that she cannot do is to apply to court for an order which the other party has not agreed in writing. On its own, a written agreement would not prevent the caring parent from later applying to the Agency; but if it were converted into a court order under s 8(5) (*see above*), then the Agency would be excluded until the order is revoked: s 4(10) of the CSA 1991, as inserted by s 18 of the CSA 1995, provides that an application under s 4 cannot be made while there is a court order in force, whether that order pre- or post-dates 5 April 1993 (unless the order in question was made under s 8(7) or (8) of the CSA 1991 to cover the costs of education or disability: *see above*).

(3) Where the parent with care is on benefit: it will be remembered that, if this is the case, she can be required to make an application under s 6 of the Act. Once an assessment is made, any court order will be superseded; before then, a court may vary or revoke a court order. The government made it clear from the very beginning that it intended to give the highest priority to these 'benefit cases'. However, in December 1994 it was announced that the take-on of two categories of benefit case would be deferred: namely, those cases where the parent with care was on benefit

before 5 April 1993 and those cases where the Agency wrote to the parent with care before 1 July 1994 and either she has not replied or she has not given all the necessary information.

The objective is to give priority to those cases which have arisen since April 1993 to enable the Agency to provide a better service.

*Disputes about parentage*

The word 'parent' is not defined very helpfully in s 54 of the CSA 1991. It means any person who is in law the mother or father of the child. Section 26, however, deals with disputes about parentage. Where there is a dispute about parentage, a child support officer must not make a child support assessment unless the case falls within one of those set out in s 26(2). In England and Wales, a person is a parent if he or she has adopted the child; is treated as such by s 30 of the Human Fertilisation and Embryology Act 1990 (*see above*); is declared as such by a declaration under s 56 of the Family Law Act 1986 (*see above*); is declared as such by a declaration under s 27 of the CSA 1991 (*see above*); or if a man has been found or adjudged to be the father in court proceedings and that finding or adjudication still subsists. It seems, therefore, that a married father need only deny paternity and the child support officer cannot make an assessment. This is because the presumption of legitimacy is not expressed to apply and so the officer cannot assume that the husband of a married mother is the father of the child. Of course, the husband is very likely to be penalised in costs if he unreasonably forces proceedings, but it is nevertheless a strange state of affairs and contrasts with the Australian legislation (which was partly a model for the Act); *see* s 29(2) of the Child Support (Assessment) Act 1989 (Aus).

If a case does not fall into any of these categories, then there is a procedure for seeking declarations of parentage from a court (s 27; *see above*). The power to order blood tests under s 20 of the FLRA 1969 is available in these proceedings and tests will be ordered unless the court is satisfied that it is against the child's best interests to do so (*see Re E* (1994) Fam Law 539 and *above*). The costs of testing may be borne by the Agency in some cases.

## Financial relief under the Children Act 1989

Section 15 of CA 1989 provides that Sched 1 governs the situation concerning financial relief for children. The Schedule consists primarily of the re-enactment, with consequential amendments and minor modifications, of provisions in the Guardianship of Minors Acts 1971 and 1973, the Children Act 1975 and ss 15 and 16 of the FLRA 1987. (The provisions in the Matrimonial Causes Act 1973 and the Domestic Proceedings and Magistrates' Courts Act 1978 are not replaced but they have no bearing on unmarried families anyway.) In effect, the CA 1989 preserves the position as it existed after the FLRA 1987 abolished affiliation proceedings, brought financial relief for all children within the 1971 Act and broadened the powers in that Act. The operation of these powers must be considered in the light of the CSA 1991.

## Maintenance agreements

Schedule 1 to the CA 1989 enables a court to vary a maintenance agreement (para 10). The significance of this power is much reduced in the wake of the CSA 1991. Although the Act preserves the right of individuals to make maintenance agreements (s 9(2) of the CSA 1991), an agreement will not prevent the Agency making an assessment (s 9(3)), unless it was in force on 5 April 1993 (*see above*). Once made, an assessment renders the agreement unenforceable for so long as the assessment remains in force (s 10(2)). The courts have also lost the power to vary the terms of maintenance agreements by either inserting or increasing an obligation to pay periodical child maintenance (s 9(5)). However, the courts retain full power to vary (or revoke) written agreements that were in force on 5 April 1993. A maintenance agreement will not be affected by the CSA 1991 in so far as it deals with transfers of property or lump sums, although these are of limited variability.

Private maintenance agreements may well have been common in the days of affiliation proceedings: perhaps entered into by the putative father in order to avoid an affiliation summons. They are unquestionably valid (*Jennings v Brown* (1842) 9 M&W 496) and, although they are best made in a deed, the courts will strive to find consideration (*Ward v Byham* [1957] 1 WLR 496). The consideration is generally stated to be the mother's promise not to institute affiliation proceedings (*Jennings v Brown*, *above*) but that promise does not actually prevent her from doing so (*Follitt v Koetzow* (1860) 2 E&E 730). Whilst there may, theoretically, have been enforcement problems involving public policy rules where the document was drafted unwisely, it is inconceivable that these could now be raised, given that statute has provided a procedure for the judicial alteration of those maintenance agreements that comply with certain requirements; *see below*. A maintenance agreement does not operate to shift any income tax liability from the payer to the payee (*see* Chapter 4).

For the purposes of Sched 1 to the CA 1989, a maintenance agreement is defined by para 10 as:

> any agreement in writing made in respect of a child, whether before or after the commencement of this section, being an agreement which—

(a) is or was made between the father and mother of the child; and
(b) contains provision in respect of the making or securing of payments, or the disposition or use of any property, for the maintenance or education of the child.

Where the agreement was made in writing before 5 April 1993, if either party is domiciled or resident in England and Wales then he or she may apply to the High Court, a county court or a magistrates' court for an order under para 10. If the court is satisfied that, because of a change in circumstances or because the agreement does not contain proper financial arrangements with respect to the child, the agreement should be altered so as to make different financial arrangements, then the court may by order vary or revoke the financial arrangements as may appear to it to be just having regard to all the circumstances. An obvious yardstick to be employed on a variation application is the assessment that would be arrived at under the CSA formula. The agreement thereupon has effect as if any alteration made by the order had been made by agreement between the parties and for valuable consideration.

The magistrates' court's powers are more limited than those of a county court or the High Court, quite apart from certain residence requirements, because it can only insert, increase, reduce or terminate periodical payments. Whatever the court, the normal rules on duration of a periodical payments order (discussed *below*) apply to the agreement as varied.

The powers concerning maintenance agreements can be expected to be attractive to those unmarried parents who wish to bring a pre-April 1993 agreement up to date, but who do not wish to apply to the CSA for an assessment. Furthermore, cohabitants may now be encouraged to make private arrangements, rather than use the courts, because they know that the terms are not immutable; but it should be borne in mind that an agreement, unless enshrined in a consent order or made before 5 April 1993, will not be binding in the Child Support Agency.

There is an incentive to provide for the continuation of the maintenance agreement after the death of one of the parties because para 11 lays down circumstances where the High Court or a county court can vary the terms within six months from the date on which representation in regard to the estate of the deceased is first taken out. In such circumstances, the alteration is treated as if it had been made immediately before the death, by agreement and for valuable consideration. This power would presumably survive a Child Support assessment, since, although an assessment would supersede an agreement during the parties' lifetime, the child would cease to be a 'qualifying child' and the Agency would lose its jurisdiction, with the result that the agreement becomes enforceable once more.

## Orders under Sched 1 to the CA 1989

Schedule 1 to the CA 1989 confers powers to order financial provision to or for the benefit of children. The main provision is contained in para 1. Orders can be made against either or both of the child's parents. In so far as these powers concern periodical maintenance for children, the powers of the court will be curtailed by the CSA 1991 in ways already discussed.

*The powers of the court*

We deal first with the powers of the High Court or a county court. On the application of a parent or guardian of a child, or of any person in whose favour a residence order is in force, the court may make one or more of the orders listed in para 1(2) against either or both parents of the child. For the purposes of Sched 1 as a whole, a 'parent' includes both a biological parent *and* a step-parent married to the mother who has treated the child as a 'child of the family' (para 16(2)). It does not include an unmarried step-parent (*J v J* [1993] 2 FLR 56).

In shortened form, the available orders are:

(a) periodical payments by one to the other for the benefit of the child, or to the child;
(b) secured periodical payments;
(c) a lump sum;
(d) a transfer of property to the other parent for the benefit of the child, or to the child;
(e) a settlement of property for the benefit of the child.

There are marked similarities, therefore, with the powers contained in ss 23 and 24 of the Matrimonial Causes Act 1973. As Ward J has put it, '[a] purposive interpretation of the Act leads to the conclusion that the claims of children whose parents are unmarried should be dealt with in similar manner to the claims where the parents are (or were) married' (in *A v A* [1994] 1 FLR 657). Nevertheless, some important differences remain between proceedings under Sched 1 and those under ss 23–5 of the MCA 1973, not the least of which is that the sole beneficiary of the Sched 1 powers is the child.

On making, varying or discharging a residence order the court may exercise any of its powers under the Schedule even though no application for financial relief had been made to it (para 1(6)).

The magistrates' court is limited to making the orders in points (a) and (c) *above* and the amount of any lump sum required to be paid by a magistrates' court shall not exceed £1,000 or such larger amount as is prescribed from time to time, (paras 1(*b*) and 5(2)).

In certain circumstances a child who has attained the age of 18 may apply under para 2 for a periodical payments or lump sum order against either or both parents. A court will only have power to order periodical payments if the child in question is not a 'qualifying child' for the purposes of the CSA 1991.

Orders under paras 1 and 2 are subject to two kinds of time limits. First, there are limits relating to the age of the child in para 3. These are the limits familiar in divorce and matrimonial proceedings so that normally the order should be expressed to terminate on the child's seventeenth birthday with a further cut-off point of 18. Even this will not apply if the child is undergoing educational instruction or vocational training or there are special circumstances.

The second kind of time limit relates to the parents' cohabitation. Under para 3(4) a periodical payments order against one parent in favour of the other ceases to have effect if the parents live together for a period of more than six months.

The courts have new powers, conferred under the CSA 1991, to backdate periodical payments ordered under Sched 1 (Sched 1, para 3(5)–(8), inserted by the Maintenance Orders (Backdating) Order 1993) or to backdate a variation or discharge of an order. The new powers are designed to deal with three types of case. The first is where a court makes an order for periodical payments under one of the exceptions set out in s 8 of the CSA 1991, discussed earlier. Here the court can backdate the periodical payments order to the date of the assessment, even if that predates the date of the application for the order. The application must be made within six months of the making of the assessment, and the order can be backdated either to the date of the assessment or to the date six months before the order was made, whichever is the later, or to a later date. The second is where a CSA assessment has been in force but is either cancelled or otherwise ceases to have effect under the terms of the CSA 1991. Provided that an application is made under Sched 1 within six months of the assessment ceasing to apply, the court may backdate an order for periodical payments to the date on which the assessment was cancelled or ceased to have effect, or to a later date.

The third is where an assessment is made with respect to some but not all of a number of children who may be named in an order. If the amount payable in respect of each child is not separately specified, the order remains enforceable, but the paying parent may wish to have it reviewed in the light of the assessment. Thus, there is a power to vary or discharge a periodical payments order where the order has been made in favour of more than one child, where the amounts payable to each child are not separately specified and where an assessment is made with respect to some but not all of the children named in the order (Sched 1, para 6.9). The court may direct that the variation or discharge should take effect from the date of the assessment, or any later date.

*Relevant criteria*

As one would expect, there is a list of matters to which the court must have regard in exercising its powers under Sched 1. This means that the child's welfare is *not* the governing criterion (s 105(1) of the CA 1989: *see K v K* [1992] 2 FLR 220); nor is it even the 'first consideration' as it is under s 25 of the MCA 1973. Nevertheless, the courts seem willing to take account of the child's welfare as one of the circumstances when making an order (per Ward J in *A v A, above*).

Paragraph 4 requires the court to have regard to all the circumstances of the case including, in shortened form:

(a) the income and resources, present and future, of the persons mentioned in subpara (4);
(b) the needs and obligations, present and future, of the persons mentioned in subpara (4);
(c) the financial needs of the child;
(d) the income and resources of the child;
(e) any physical or mental disability of the child.

The persons mentioned in subpara (4) are, basically, the parents, the applicant and any other person in whose favour the court proposes to make the order. There is no mention here of 'the standard of living enjoyed by the parties' as there is in s 25(1) of the MCA 1973, 'no doubt because it is recognised that mother and father may never have lived together as a family' (per Ward J in *A v A, above*). Reference to the needs of the parents suggests that, whilst formally one unmarried parent has no right to personal maintenance from the other, the court may include an element for personal support even though the child is intended to be the ultimate beneficiary. This was acknowledged in cases under the Affiliation Proceedings Act 1957 (*Haroutunian v Jennings* (1977) 7 Fam Law 10) and was expressly approved for the purposes of Sched 1 by Ward J in *A v A, above*.

*Use of the powers in practice*

Now that the powers to make orders for periodical payments have been largely superseded by the CSA 1991, it is expected that the majority of orders made under Sched 1 will be for the settlement or transfer of property to or 'for the benefit of' children. The phrase 'for the benefit of' the child is not confined to financial benefit, nor does it limit the court to making orders that vest a beneficial interest in the child. It will be enough if the caring parent is given a beneficial interest with a view to providing a home for the children (*K v K, above*). Nor must the benefit be confined exclusively to the child named in the order: there will inevitably be some benefit to the caring parent, and the child is not prevented from spending any income she or he might receive on other family members (per Ward J in *A v A, above*).

As a result, these powers have the potential to reduce some of the disadvantages that cohabitants face through not being able to make use of an adjustive jurisdiction. It has been held, for example, that a court may order the transfer of a tenancy from one joint tenant to another under these provisions (always assuming that this is justified in the particular circumstances of the case in the light of the specified factors: *see K v K, above* and *Pearson v Franklin* [1994] 1 FLR 246). As already discussed in Chapter 7, there may be significant advantages in securing occupation by this means as against the other methods described in that chapter.

Where the parties' assets extend beyond a tenancy, the courts' traditional reluctance to make capital orders in favour of children on divorce (*see*, eg *Chamberlain v Chamberlain* [1974] 1 All ER 33 and *Lilford v Lord Glyn* [1979] 1 All ER 441) applies also to applications under Sched 1. The underlying principle is that 'property adjustment orders should not ordinarily be made to provide benefits for the child after he has obtained his independence' (per Ward J in *A v A, above*). For example, the court has the power to settle the home which might be used to enable the custodial parent and child to remain in occupation: but since the order must be to or for the benefit of *the child*, and since the benefits conferred on the child cannot last beyond independence, the order is likely to be for occupation during the child's minority only.

Thus, in *T v S (Financial Provision for Children)* (1994) Fam Law 11, a district judge ordered under Sched 1 that a house be purchased for the occupation of the mother and children, to be held on trust for sale with sale postponed until the youngest child reached 21 or finished full-time secondary education, when the benefit would pass to the surviving children in equal shares. The father successfully appealed against the final part of this order, Johnson J ordering instead that the property should revert to the father on execution of the trust for sale (*see also H v P* (1993) Fam Law 515, where a judge ordered a capital sum to be settled for the benefit of the child, during his minority or until he ceased full-time education, with the sole purpose of enabling the mother to buy accommodation for herself and the child).

The only exception to this general rule that children should not benefit beyond independence would be where there are 'exceptional circumstances' which justify making such an order (Sched 1, para 3(2)(*b*)).

Chapter 11

# Cohabitation Contracts, Trust Deeds and Other Formal Agreements

## General

At various points in the book we have discussed the relevance to the parties' legal position of an agreement or understanding between them. In Chapter 8, for example, we saw that an agreement as to sharing the ownership of the home, followed by contributions, may lead to a finding that the home is held on a constructive trust. Agreement can also be relevant in determining the ownership of personal property (Chapter 8 also) and in creating an enforceable testamentary obligation (Chapter 9). It is also possible to make effective agreements as to the sharing of parental responsibility and, by agreement or unilaterally, appoint a testamentary guardian for children (Chapter 10). The purpose of this chapter is to explore further aspects of formal, express agreements between the parties and to draw together the relevant law.

It is natural that some parties will wish to regulate their relationship, or the consequences of its breakdown, through a formal, private agreement. The topics to be covered might include the allocation of domestic responsibilities, the ownership of property as at the date of the agreement, the ownership of after-acquired property, the use of money during the relationship, responsibility for, residence of and contact with children, post-separation maintenance and the consequences of the death of one or both of the parties.

It is common to refer to the use of 'cohabitation contracts' to give effect to agreements on these matters, but a contract is only one of a range of mechanisms that might be appropriate. Equally relevant might be a formal declaration of trust in the conveyance or transfer, a separate declaration of trust, mutual wills, an arrangement with a third party (such as a bank), a unilateral instruction to a third party (such as a nomination addressed to the trustees of a pension fund) or a registered parental responsibility agreement.

One of the themes to emerge in this chapter is that a contract, strictly so-called, may not always be an appropriate or sufficiently flexible mechanism to use. Where a choice exists, a trust may be preferable. Furthermore, although there are clear psychological and practical advantages to the parties in having a comprehensive, single document which deals with all relevant matters, it might be more advisable in the particular circumstances to use a range of documents, including a declaration of trust, a contract, a will and a power of attorney.

The emphasis in this chapter is on the kinds of things about which the parties might make their own provision and the different mechanisms through which the provision can be effective. We leave it to the legal adviser to construct the package that seems appropriate in the circumstances. It should be stressed, however, that contracts and express trusts have rarely been the subjects of litigation in the context of cohabiting relationships and clients should be advised accordingly.

Even when the form and substance of the agreement has been decided upon, there may be limitations on the effectiveness of any particular strategy. Public policy rules may still cast a shadow over some of the terms, the agreement may be open to challenge on the grounds of undue influence or misrepresentation, or legislation may exist which could interfere with the achievement of the parties' plans. For example, the Inheritance (Provision for Families and Dependants) Act 1975 (*see* Chapter 9) allows a surviving or former spouse, or a child of the deceased, to attack the terms of a will. In the case of a party who has previously been married, a spouse or former spouse might yet invoke the court's adjustive powers in the Matrimonial Causes Act 1973, unless that possibility has been precluded by an order, agreement or remarriage. This may have the effect of reducing the resources of one of the cohabitants and thereby defeat the assumptions underlying the arrangement.

In short, there are practical and legal impediments to the parties creating a conclusive and comprehensive charter for their relationship.

Any account of the possibilities of private ordering for cohabitants is bound to be incomplete because the circumstances of cohabiting parties are diverse. We might be dealing with a couple who desire a relationship of considerable commitment, but who are unable or unwilling to resort to formal marriage for this purpose, or we might be dealing with people who want to retain maximum independence and separation of resources. The latter might particularly be the case where one or both of the parties have a family by a previous relationship, or where divorce proceedings are not completed. For example, in *Frary v Frary* [1993] 2 FLR 696, a case on 'production appointments' discussed in Chapter 2, the parties had entered into an agreement which provided that:

(a) he was a licensee in her house;
(b) they would share outgoings as agreed between them from time to time;
(c) he would acquire no beneficial interest in the house;
(d) they were not to be classed as dependants within the Inheritance (Provision for Family and Dependants) Act 1975; and
(e) a subsequent marriage between them would not revoke the agreement.

This agreement might not have been effective to achieve all of its aims, but the point is simply that this is a quite different kind of agreement from one made by a couple who propose to purchase a house together and to have children.

## Public policy and other factors which inhibit the making or enforcement of agreements

### Public policy rules

There is still some residual doubt about the enforceability of contracts made between cohabitants. The problem stems from rules of public policy; in particular those rules that render contracts void or unenforceable on the grounds of sexual immorality or prejudicial effect on the institution of marriage. Sexual immorality is the more potent vitiating factor and a classic statement of the relevant rule can be found in the judgment of Lord Wright in *Fender v St John Mildmay* [1938] AC 1 (at 42):

> The law will not enforce an immoral promise, such as a promise between a man and woman to live together without being married or to pay a sum of money or to give some other consideration in return for immoral association.

There seems to be no objection to the parties making a contract once they have separated, provided consideration can be found which is not past or provided the agreement is in a deed. By the same token, there might be no objection to a contract being made during the currency of the relationship, any supposed damage to public morals already being done.

Voidness for prejudice to the marital state is relatively rare in modern times. Barton suggests that relevant grounds for voidness might be that a contract between cohabitants could hamper their freedom to marry third parties or, if one or both of them is already married, that the contract might exacerbate the marital breach (*see* C Barton, *Cohabitation Contracts* (Gower 1985), p 43). Both these arguments seem insubstantial today and, it is suggested, the first court to decide on the enforceability of a modern cohabitation contract will concentrate on sexual immorality.

It is arguable that too many decisions have been made in cohabitant cases relying in some way on the parties' agreement or assumption for the courts now to go back. In the trust cases, the policy considerations taken into account in *Diwell v Farnes* [1959] 2 All ER 379 no longer feature overtly in judicial reasoning. Similarly, as we saw in Chapter 7, the Court of Appeal has on a number of occasions found an implied contractual licence (*see* eg *Tanner v Tanner* [1975] 3 All ER 776) and even when none has been found (eg *Horrocks v Forray* [1976] 1 All ER 737) immorality has not been given as the reason. We have also seen that the courts are now prepared to hold that a cohabitant was a member of a deceased tenant's family for the purposes of succession to a statutory tenancy whereas in 1950 such a construction of the phrase had been regarded by the Court of Appeal as an abuse of the English language.

In some jurisdictions the courts have faced up to the issue and declared that the purpose of the contract is no longer to be regarded as immoral. Judges in Australia and the United States have done this provided that the agreement was not solely for sexual purposes (in Australia *see Andrews v Parker* [1973] Qd R 93 and *Seidler v Schallhofer* [1982] 2 NSWLR 80; and in the USA *see Marvin v Marvin* (18 Cal 3d 668 and 557 P 2d 106 (1976)). The legislatures in New South Wales, the Northern Territory and Ontario have now tackled the problem head-on by making provision for written contracts between unmarried couples (*see* the De Facto Relationships Act 1984 (NSW) and 1991 (NT) and the Family Law Reform Act 1978 (Ont)). In June 1991 a Private Member's Bill was introduced into the House of Commons which would have permitted cohabitation contracts to regulate financial arrangements between the couple (Cohabitation (Contract Enforcement) Bill 1991). As with most private member's bills its prospects were bleak and it failed. Nevertheless, its passage would probably be in line with the European Community Council of Ministers' recommendation (R(88)3) that member states should not preclude cohabitation contracts from dealing with property merely on the ground that the parties are not married to each other. In 1992 the Scottish Law Commission recommended that contracts between cohabitants concerning property and financial matters should not be void solely because the parties were living together.

Whilst it cannot seriously be imagined that a court in England and Wales in the 1990s would hold void a contract between cohabitants because of the alleged immorality of their relationship, it is suggested nevertheless that the safest course is for any agreement to avoid express reference to sexual relations. Ironically the curious situation will then exist where an identical agreement between spouses in contemplation of future divorce proceedings is still void as being prejudicial to the institution of marriage (*Wilson v Wilson* [1948] 1 HLC 538).

### Undue influence and misrepresentation

Negotiations and agreements between the parties are thought not to be *uberrimae fidei*; *see Wales v Wadham* [1977] 1 WLR 199 at 218D. There is therefore apparently no obligation on the parties to make a full and frank disclosure of all relevant matters, provided their silence does not, on the facts, amount to a misrepresentation. In the absence of any express or implied term creating such a duty, the general common law rules and equitable principles making agreements void or voidable apply. The reader is referred to Chapter 8 for a discussion of recent case law on undue influence within cohabiting relationships.

Whatever the document used, whether it be a contract, declaration of trust or one which records both, it is prudent to include a clause to the effect that the parties acknowledge they have been separately advised, assuming this to be the case, and that they have entered into the agreement voluntarily. This will go some way to negative a claim in undue influence.

### Ethical difficulties in one lawyer advising both parties

It can be tempting for a legal adviser to agree to act for both parties when they present themselves as being in agreement on all matters of substance. The indications are that this can only lead to trouble, for the parties and the adviser. A court is likely to find that there was a real possibility of a conflict of interest arising between the parties so that the lawyer could not discharge her or his fiduciary and contractual obligations of confidentiality and loyalty to each of them.

One expedient in use is for the lawyer formally to act for only one of the parties, for the other party to be acting in person, but for all concerned to meet together. The indications are that this will not protect the lawyer. A fiduciary duty can still arise towards the other party even though there is no retainer. The Family Court of Australia has certainly decided to this effect (*Simmonds v Simmonds* [1991] FLC 92–219). Much will depend on the facts. Where no fiduciary duty arises in equity, it seems clear that a sufficient relation of proximity can still arise between the solicitor and non-client so that a duty of care is owed. Carelessly failing to carry out the client's instructions, particularly where it is now beyond the client's power to put matters right, or carelessly advising the non-client on matters of law may render the solicitor liable in negligence (*Hemmens v Wilson Browne* [1994] 2 FLR 101). The more direct contact the solicitor has had with the non-client, the more possible it is that negligence could be found.

## The range of relevant mechanisms: contracts, trusts, wills etc

The focus in this chapter is on express terms in formal instruments and, by and large, a practitioner should have no difficulty in complying with the relevant formation rules. Under the subheadings below, we offer reminders of the main rules and deal with some areas where difficulties might be encountered.

### Contract

In Chapter 9, whilst discussing agreements for testamentary provision, we saw the problems that can arise with informal attempts to create contractual obligations between cohabitants. Leaving aside the possibility that the parties might unwisely agree to particular terms or might infringe public policy rules (*see above*), the agreement might still lack legal effect through failure to comply with legal requirements. The words of the document might inadvertently fail to rebut the presumption which can arise in domestic agreements that the parties did not intend to create legal relations. The agreement might be expressed so vaguely that it is held to be void for uncertainty. Where the terms concern the sale or other disposition of an interest in land, the requirements in s 2 of the Law of Property (Miscellaneous Provisions) Act 1989 (that the contract must be signed by or on behalf of each party and must incorporate all the express terms in one agreement) might be breached. Where the agreement does not provide for an exchange or act of reliance regarded as sufficient at common law to amount to consideration, then the agreement will be unenforceable unless it is made in a deed. To be a deed it should comply with the requirements in s 1(2) of the 1989 Act. A deed is advisable on the other grounds. If the agreement provides in terms for a gift of chattels a deed will overcome any argument that there has been insufficient delivery of the chattels for property to pass. For example, where the parties agree that all chattels owned by either of them shall henceforth be held jointly, this might operate as a series of gifts of half-shares in the chattels and give rise to complex arguments about delivery. A deed bypasses such arguments (although, as will be suggested *below*, a more prudent method is to declare a trust over the relevant property and rely on equity rather than the common law).

Once aware of these possible problems, the draftsperson can take appropriate steps to overcome them. The agreement should be made in a deed. It should mention expressly either that the parties do intend to create legal relations or that they intend the agreement to be binding in honour only. Care should be taken to specify precisely the obligations being created and the property being affected. The agreement should be broken into as many separate clauses as possible and a severance clause included so that the foregoing clauses are regarded as independent and if any of them is found to be void the validity of the remainder is not affected. Precedents of these contracts are now available, *see* in particular D Lush, *Cohabitation and Co-Ownership Precedents* (Family Law, 1993) and J Bowler, J Jackson and E Loughridge, *Living Together Precedents* (Sweet & Maxwell, 1994, 2nd edn).

Even when technical problems have been overcome and a contract has been drafted which reflects the agreement of the parties, the contract remains a device of uncertain utility. The remedy for breach is usually an award of damages, calculated on particular principles which might not reflect the loss subjectively suffered by the aggrieved party. Furthermore, there is no general contractual obligation on parties to perform the contract in good faith. An alternative is sometimes to create obligations under a trust. This gives rise to a fiduciary obligation on each party towards the other and imports a series of obligations specific to trustees. Furthermore, the remedies to restrain or redress a breach of trust may be more suitable to a domestic relationship.

## Trusts

By virtue of s 53(1)(*b*) of the Law of Property Act 1925 'a declaration of trust respecting any land or any interest therein must be manifested and proved by some writing signed by some person who is able to declare such trust or by his will.' Although a declaration of trust over personal property can be made orally (*see* eg *Paul v Constance* [1977] 1 All ER 195, discussed in Chapter 8, which concerned money in a bank account), the assumption in this chapter is that the parties wish to reduce their agreement to writing.

There is no requirement that the declaration of trust be under seal. It is in fact quite common for a declaration as to the beneficial interest in a home to be made in the conveyance to the settlors or, in the case of registered land, in the transfer. Thus, in a typical purchase by cohabitants, the legal estate is necessarily taken as joint tenants but there may be a declaration that the beneficial interest is held as joint tenants or tenants in common in stated shares. Whilst a declaration in the conveyance or transfer is clearly better than no declaration at all, it is usually considered best to keep trusts off the title. This, in any event, is the policy of the land registration scheme and it also has a practical dimension. The original conveyance or transfer is unlikely to be available to the cohabitants if there is a mortgage on the property and although copies can obviously be kept it is best if the original is under the direct control of the parties.

If there is to be a declaration of trust separate from the conveyance or transfer, it can be contained in a more general cohabitation agreement or in an independent document created for the purpose. In the writers' view, until cohabitation agreements have been considered extensively in the courts it is advisable to reserve the declaration of trust for matters concerning the ownership, use and sale of such property as is capable of being made subject to a trust (*see below* for the difficulties in creating a trust over future property). Terms to do with lifestyle, domestic arrangements, children and financial support should be in a separate document. One reason for this is that trusts are subject to the same rules of public policy as are contracts. Equity follows the law in this regard. It is hard to imagine, given the history of case law on constructive trusts in cohabiting relationships, that a court would fail to enforce a trust document which confines itself to property, but it is taking an unnecessary risk if that document also deals with other matters, and perhaps entangles clauses over trust property with clauses about the relationship generally.

As we saw in Chapter 8, a declaration of trust which complies with the formalities in s 53(1)(*b*) is regarded by the courts as conclusive evidence of the state of the beneficial interest, in the absence of some factor which would lead to the document being set aside or rectified (*Goodman v Gallant* [1986] 1 FLR 513 at 517C). In *Pettit v Pettit* [1969] 2 All ER 385 at 405I, Lord Upjohn said:

> If that document declares not merely in whom the legal title is to vest but in whom the beneficial title is to vest that necessarily concludes the question of title as between [the parties] *for all time*, and in the absence of fraud or mistake at the time of the transaction the parties cannot go behind it at any time thereafter even on death or the break-up of the marriage. [Emphasis added.]

Of course, there is nothing to prevent the parties subsequently varying the beneficial interests, provided the variation complies with s 53(1)(*c*). This subsection requires that:

> a disposition of an equitable interest or trust subsisting at the time of the disposition, must be in writing signed by the person disposing of the same, or by his agent thereunto lawfully authorised in writing or by will.

In other words, the variation must actually *be* in writing, as opposed to being merely *evidenced* in writing.

Despite the dicta from Lord Upjohn in *Pettit*, *above*, there seems to be no case which has stated definitively that an *informal* attempt at the variation of stated beneficial interests supported by consideration or followed by detrimental reliance by the plaintiff will be ineffective. As we know, s 53(2) of the LPA provides that '[t]his section does not affect the creation or operation of resulting, implied or constructive trusts', thus creating the impression that such trusts can apply in the case of attempted dispositions of expressly declared equitable interests, and not just to informal attempts to create a trust. Suppose the parties had initially provided that the man owned 90 per cent of the beneficial interest and the woman owned 10 per cent. This was at a time when the woman was not working because of child-care responsibilities. Suppose then that the woman goes out to work and the parties clearly agree that she will pay half the mortgage and will be regarded as owning half the equity. If the woman makes her contribution to the mortgage, as agreed, for any length of time it is difficult to imagine a court allowing the man to hide behind the express declaration of the trusts. Either a fresh constructive trust would be found or the doctrine of estoppel invoked—perhaps promissory estoppel—to prevent the man from unconscionably resiling from the agreement.

## Powers of attorney

It is arguable that anyone involved in an established domestic relationship should consider giving her or his partner a power of attorney. If there is reason to suppose there is a risk of mental incapacity, perhaps because of age or the early signs of degenerative illness, consideration should be given to creating an enduring power of attorney, under the Enduring Powers of Attorney Act 1985.

A power of attorney may be of particular use to unmarried couples. Whereas third parties will often, in practice, take directions from, or accord status to, a person known to be a spouse, they may be more reluctant where there is no marriage. (Note, however, in this regard that a person who has lived with a patient as their spouse for not less than six months can qualify as a 'relative' for the purposes of Pt II of the Mental Health Act 1983, *see* s 26(6).)

In deciding whether to grant a power of attorney, consideration should be given to the particular relationship. The reason for seeking advice in the first place might be in order to *protect* the party's position in the event that the relationship breaks down; giving extensive powers to the other may not be consistent with this aim. A power of attorney can, however, be expressly limited as to the scope of matters it covers and as to the circumstances when it is terminated. In any event, one trustee for sale of land cannot appoint the only other trustee (ie the only sole co-owner) as an attorney for the purposes of selling the land, although this restriction does not apply in the case of an enduring power of attorney (*see* s 25(2) of the Trustee Act 1925, as amended, *Walia v Michael Naughton Ltd* [1985] 3 All ER 673 and s 3(3) of the Enduring Powers of Attorney Act 1985).

## Wills

There are few special factors to be borne in mind when drafting a will for a cohabitant, particularly if the relationship is substantially similar to a marriage. A will is not revoked upon the subsequent cohabitation of the testator, whereas it may be revoked by subsequent marriage (Wills Act 1837, s 17). The cohabitant of a witness to the will can be a beneficiary, whereas a spouse of a witness cannot (Wills Act 1837, s 15). Where a testator appears to give a spouse an absolute interest in property but also gives an interest in it to her or his children, there is a rebuttable presumption that the gift is an absolute one to the spouse (Administration of Justice Act 1982, s 22). In similar circumstances concerning a cohabitant, the survivor would take only a life interest, with the remainder going to the children.

Normal drafting language can be used. For wills made prior to the entry into force of s 19 of the Family Law Reform Act 1987 (4 April 1988), references to children are construed as including references to illegitimate children, unless a contrary intention appears (s 15 of the Family Law Reform Act 1969). The common formulation of a gift 'to my children and if more than one in equal shares' is therefore appropriate for unmarried testators as well as married ones. Dispositions of property after 4 April 1988 are to be construed in the light of the general principle in s 1 of the Family Law Reform Act 1987 (FLRA 1987). This is discussed further in Chapter 10. Briefly, s 1 introduced a new general principle that references to any relationship between two persons shall, unless the contrary intention appears, be construed without regard to whether or not the father and mother of either of them, or the father and mother of any person through whom the relationship is deduced, have or had been married to each other. In other words, marital status is rebuttably presumed to be irrelevant in deducing relationships and so no specific rules are required about the meaning of certain words.

If a cohabitant is to be a beneficiary in a will he or she should be named specifically, although the court can find that a testator has created her or his own dictionary. In *Re Lynch* [1943] 1 All ER 168 the testator appointed 'my wife Annie' to be his executrix and made 'my wife' a beneficiary, even though they had been living together unmarried. Elsewhere in the will he referred to her 'widowhood'. Uthwatt J held that the testator had clearly created his own meaning of 'wife' and effect was given to the obvious intention.

Further advice on the contents of a will can be found *below.*

### Licences

Where it is not the parties' intention that the ownership of the home should be shared, consideration should be given to the creation of a formal licence for the non-owner to occupy the property. Contractual and other forms of licence were discussed in Chapter 7. The relevant case law is largely concerned with informally created licences, however, and the draftsperson can only proceed on the basis of normal land law and contractual principles. Provided one is careful not to allow a *tenancy* to come into existence—and this can be achieved by calling the document a licence, denying that a tenancy is created and avoiding giving exclusive possession of any part of the property to the licensee—the main things to be covered are the consideration, if any, to be provided by the licensee and the length of any notice to determine the licence.

## Topics for agreement and methods of implementation

### Assets already owned at the time of the agreement

If the parties wish to share the ownership of property belonging to each of them at the time of the agreement—ie existing property—then a trust is essential in the case of land and probably desirable in the case of other property. This is so whether or not the legal estate is to be vested in joint names (*see*, however, Chapter 8 for a discussion of the desirability of having two trustees for sale of land and of methods by which a beneficiary can protect her or his beneficial interest against the claims of third parties). It is assumed in what follows that no third party is to be appointed as a trustee so that the cohabitants are simply declaring that they hold on trust the relevant property for themselves jointly, either as beneficial joint tenants or as tenants in common in stated shares.

*Land*

A number of precedent books now provide precedent clauses for declarations of trust over the parties' home; *see*, for example, Lush, and Bowler,

Jackson and Loughridge, *above*. There is no need actually to stipulate the precise beneficial interests if the parties wish to defer the ascertainment of them until the property is sold, with a view to calculating then how much each contributed. For a discussion of the relative advantages and disadvantages of each method, *see* Lush, *above*, pp 11–16.

It is assumed in what follows that the parties do not wish to provide *inter vivos* for successive interests in the land and that accordingly no consideration need be given to the Settled Land Act 1925 as an alternative to the trust for sale; *see below*, however, for the creation of strict settlements by will.

*Personal property*

Co-ownership of personal property is not held behind a trust for sale by operation of law and, unless it is desired to provide *inter vivos* for *successive* interests in personalty, it is not necessary to use a trust. In the case of property already owned at the time of the agreement, simple words of gift can be used to declare that the owner is giving all or a share in the property to the other. To avoid any doubts that insufficient delivery has taken place to perfect the gift, the declaration should be made in a deed. Even without a deed, however, it is possible that the arrangement is construed not as a gift but as an exchange (ie each party is giving to the other a stated share in their presently held property in a reciprocal fashion) and the shares in the property pass in contract rather than gift. If survivorship is to apply, it should be made clear that the parties are to hold as joint tenants.

The published precedents tend not to make clear the mechanism through which joint ownership of chattels is being achieved. The authors suggest that rather than rely on common law notions such as gift, exchange, or even sale, thought should be given to declaring a trust over present personalty as well as land and achieving the assignment in this way. Provided the intention is clear and unconditional, and the property is adequately described, this is sufficient to constitute the parties as trustees of the property, it puts them into a fiduciary relationship with each other as regards the property and gives rise to the widest range of remedies.

It is possible that the parties do not wish to make any change to the existing ownership of present property but they do want to govern the situation should one of them die. In these circumstances, a will should be made and consideration be given to the making of mutual wills. This would preserve freedom of alienation and dissipation until at least the death of the first of them. In any event, as was discussed in Chapter 9, the parties should each make or reconsider their wills once their relationship has reached the stage where they are thinking of formal agreements. Even if it seems that all assets have been covered by joint ownership, nominations and agreements about after-acquired property, there is always the possibility of something being overlooked and the will operates as a fallback, rather than the intestacy rules.

*Recitals*

Extensive use can be made of recitals in declarations of trust. They can be used to describe the existing and proposed relationship and they can contain statements as to the underlying purpose of the trust being created. As we saw in Chapter 7, when deciding on postponement of sale, the court will look to the underlying purpose of the trust and a recital is likely to be conclusive evidence of that. A recital can also be used to confirm that a payment was not made with the intention to give or lend but with the intention of acquiring a beneficial interest. This is safer than relying upon the presumption of resulting trust. A recital might also be used, if such is the case, to record the fact that each party has received independent legal advice prior to signing the declaration.

*The trusts*

The trusts to be declared depend, of course, upon the agreement between the parties. An express trust for sale will be declared, with the beneficial interests stated and where equality of ownership is desired the trusts will make clear whether it is as joint tenants or tenants in common. A variety of standard clauses exist which provide expressly for the postponement of sale and which, possibly out of an excess of caution, enlarge the powers of the trustees to those of a sole beneficial owner. It is certainly advisable to consult precedents, such as those by Lush (*above*), which were devised with cohabitants or at least co-residing co-owners in mind. These will give ideas on matters such as how the net proceeds of sale are to be calculated, how contributions are to be calculated, how the shares are to be expressed and how to achieve a *Mesher* or *Martin* kind of deferment of sale (*see* Chapter 2, *above*). As an introduction to the complex possibilities, *see* the discussion in Chapter 8 *above* of different methods by which the courts, unaided by any express agreement of the parties, have approached the calculation of contributions and the quantification of beneficial interests.

Legal advisers should also take instructions on the parties' wishes in the event of certain contingencies occurring. For example, there may be a simple way of expressing, perhaps in a schedule to the agreement, the parties' wishes in the event of one of them becoming insolvent, becoming unemployed, of the woman becoming incapable of working through pregnancy and child care, of one of them becoming a student, of one of them departing from the property, and so on. Again, precedent books will contain ideas as to how these contingencies might be provided for. One possibility is for a fixed shares agreement to convert automatically to a deferred ascertainment one (where the total contributions are calculated at the point of sale and the shares determined then) in the event of one of the events occurring.

If the property is being purchased with an interest-only mortgage supported by an endowment policy, a clause may be drafted which declares trusts over the proceeds of that policy but subject to the prior assignment of the policy to the mortgagee.

*Covenants*

Covenants can be included as to what the parties must and must not do in relation to the property. It is advisable to contain any covenants as to the way that the parties will behave generally in the relationship in a separate document so that any uncertainty in the latter does not contaminate straightforward covenants to do with things like lettings, repairs and insurance.

*Buying out*

Finally, it is desirable to take instructions on a clause which allows one party to buy the other out under certain stated circumstances. The court has power to order sale and division of the proceeds but it has no direct power to order one party to sell her or his share to the other. There can be indirect ways of a court achieving this end but it seems much better to make express provision. If it is to be included, careful thought needs to be given to the manner in which the property is to be valued for this purpose.

## After-acquired property

A trust cannot validly be declared over future property because a trust cannot be created over an expectancy. The parties might, however, wish to make provision at the outset as to what is to happen to property yet to be acquired. They might, for example, wish to provide that all such property will belong to them equally. This might be particularly important in the case of chattels because ordinarily the person who purchases an item becomes the owner of it (*see* Chapter 8). The purchase of land, being much less routine, is usually accompanied by express discussion at the time as to how it is to be held and the parties may not feel the need to make advance provision.

An agreement about future property might have effect as a contract to put into joint ownership after-acquired assets (preferably in a deed, to avoid any difficulties with consideration) although the use of a contract may have some disadvantages. The remedy for failure to put subsequently acquired property into joint ownership may sound only in damages unless, within certain well-known categories, damages are an inadequate remedy; and the calculation of those damages may be difficult. Furthermore, particularly in the case of assets where there are no title documents, it might well not be clear whether the defendant *has* failed to put the chattels into joint ownership. This gives rise to doubt whether an action should be for breach of contract or for detinue or conversion of the property (although *see* the comments of Waite J in *H v M*, discussed in Chapter 8, as to the appropriate procedure to follow in the latter case).

An alternative may be to rely on equity rather than the common law to achieve the same ends. Whilst it is clear that no trust can validly be created over future property, it is also clear that where a promisee has given valuable consideration for a promise that future property will be put into an existing trust then equity will not allow the promise to be defeated; *Re Ellenborough* [1903] 1 Ch 697. 'An assignment for value binds the conscience of the assignor', per Buckley J at 700. The moment the asset is acquired it will be fixed with the trusts; *Holroyd v Marshall* (1862) 10 HLC 191 at 220, per Lord Chelmsford. Assuming therefore that each party is putting something into the trust—for example, each is declaring a trust over their existing property, as discussed *above*—so that there is valuable consideration each way, a particular kind of clause suggests itself. It involves an acknowledgment by each party that their actions and promises under the trust shall be treated as valuable consideration for the promise by the other to hold future property under the trusts. This should have the effect then of fixing the property with the trusts from the moment that it is acquired, it will give rise to the normal trustee's obligations in respect of that property, and to the full range of remedies in equity for breach of trust; including, where appropriate, the award of damages under s 50 of the Supreme Court Act 1981 in lieu of or in addition to an injunction or specific performance. The clause should be followed by a provision that if, for any reason, the promise fails to be enforceable in equity, it shall nevertheless take effect as a contract under which each agrees to put after-acquired property into joint ownership. By adopting this procedure one seeks to benefit from the flexibility provided by equity whilst keeping the common law available in reserve.

The discussion so far has assumed that the parties do wish to share future property acquired by only one of them. Of course, the opposite might be so. One can certainly include in a contract or declaration of trust a statement to the effect that neither party will acquire or seek to acquire a beneficial interest in any future property or in any present property other than that which is specifically covered in the instant agreement. In the absence of any argument that the statement is void or voidable, the courts will presumably give effect to it. As far as present property is concerned it is the equivalent of an express declaration as to the beneficial interests (*see above*). It should also negative any possible finding with regard to future property that the parties intended joint ownership.

## Money

As we have seen there is no direct, enforceable obligation on one cohabitant to support the other. The cohabitation rule in social security assumes that the support will take place, as does the liable relative procedure (*see* Chapter 3). Child support under the Child Support Act 1991 is also calculated by reference to a formula which has built into it some recognition of the custodian's own needs as well as the child's. But the only way in which maintenance can be sought directly is pursuant to a contractual obligation voluntarily entered into by the defendant. Certain jurisdictions in the United States and elsewhere have been sympathetic to claims based on an *implied* contract, or one based on restitutionary principles, but there have been no comparable developments in England and Wales.

Provided that normal contractual principles regarding intention to create legal relations and certainty of terms are borne in mind (*see above*), there are no special rules. The agreement might provide for a housekeeping allowance of a set amount, perhaps adjusted for inflation or as otherwise agreed from time to time, and it might provide for maintenance after separation.

As far as the ownership of money is concerned, *see* the discussion in Chapter 8 of bank accounts. It is possible, as we saw there, to declare an express trust over a bank account. It is also possible to have a joint account, with funds provided by only one party, and to declare that the beneficial ownership of the money in the account either is or is not to be held jointly. Similarly, it is possible to make a declaration as to the ownership of property purchased from the account; either it is to be owned by the party making the withdrawal or it is to be owned jointly.

## Domestic responsibilities and lifestyle issues

Some of the precedents available have examples of elaborate clauses seeking to govern how the parties should live their life together. As far as is known, no such agreements have yet come before the courts in England and Wales. It would be important to make clear whether the terms were intended to have legal effect or whether they were binding in honour only. It is also important to include a severance clause in the agreement so that any voidness for uncertainty or public policy does not taint the remainder of the agreement. Beyond that, much is left to the ingenuity of the draftsperson, both as to the topics covered and the manner of the drafting. The parties should be advised, in writing, that this part of their agreement is the most vulnerable to challenge, from a legal point of view. In particular, a clause placing the responsibility for birth control measures on one party only would give rise to complex doctrinal and philosophical issues to do with enforcement or breach if that party was negligent or deliberately failed to comply.

**Children**

The rules and procedures governing parental responsibility agreements between unmarried parents were discussed in Chapter 10. It is very likely that a couple who have decided to seek legal advice on a cohabitation agreement would wish to share parental responsibility for the children of their relationship. Short of this, however, there is a provision in s 2(9) of the Children Act 1989 allowing a person with parental responsibility to arrange for some or all of it to be met by someone acting on her or his behalf. The section does not permit the surrender or transfer of parental responsibility and is of uncertain scope. Nevertheless, the parties might wish to record their agreement as to the manner in which the children are to be brought up and the sharing of tasks and this section provides some kind of vehicle by which the mother—who has the sole parental responsibility in the absence of a registered parental responsibility agreement or court order—can give effect to the agreement. It is not likely that a court would grant any contractual remedy for breach, nor is it clear how any damages would be calculated. The agreement would not be binding on a court when making orders about the upbringing or property of the child because the welfare principle in s 1 of the Children Act 1989 makes the child's welfare the paramount consideration. Nevertheless, the terms of any agreement might have an influence on how the welfare of the particular child was perceived or, which is probably saying the same thing, how (if at all) the court's discretion was to be exercised. It would be prudent to include in this part of any agreement an acknowledgment that the parties have been advised about the welfare principle.

It is common for provision to be made in wills about the appointment of testamentary guardians but there is no obstacle to an *inter vivos* appointment which is to take effect on death.

## Separation

The parties might wish to make express provision as to the effects of separation. Any well-drafted declaration of trust over property will probably have made some reference to this already. A separate cohabitation agreement might provide for the closure of credit card accounts and bank accounts and the termination of standing arrangements. If there is an express occupational licence, a decision should be made as to the effect of separation on it. Although probably unenforceable, provision can be made for attendance at counselling before a final decision to separate is to be made. It is quite possible that the parties will not wish there to be any express terms as to mutual support during the relationship—preferring to leave that to trust—but that a support obligation should arise following separation. It is important to try to establish and record with precision the definition of separation for these purposes, the nature of the support to be provided and the date or events on which support is to cease.

## Death

Clearly, the focus of advice on what provision to make on death will be a will, but there are other matters to be considered.

If the parties do not wish the survivor to have a claim on the deceased's estate under the Inheritance (Provision for Family and Dependants) Act 1975, then a declaration in an *inter vivos* document to this effect can be made. The declaration will not necessarily be effective because only an order by a divorce court under ss 15 and 15A will exclude the Act. Any other attempt will, strictly, be void as an attempt to oust the jurisdiction of the court. Nevertheless, the sentiments expressed in the declaration may be influential in a court's decision whether the applicant was dependent on the deceased and, if so, whether any provision should be made.

If either party is a member of an occupational or private pension scheme, the rules of the scheme should be perused and any nominations made. In most schemes, death benefits do not go through the estate.

Consideration should be given as to whether life policies on own lives should be made subject to a declaration of trust in favour of the other party, with appropriate notice to the life company, rather than allowing the proceeds to go through the estate. Presumably the central issue is revocability if the relationship breaks down. A will can be revoked unilaterally, whereas a declaration of trust cannot. On the other hand, if the settlor defaults in the payment of the premiums, so that the policy lapses, it is not clear what remedy, if any, the beneficiary under the trust would have. Declaring a trust over a policy on one's own life is a separate matter from taking out a policy on the partner's life. It has not affirmatively been established that the policyholder has an insurable interest in her or his cohabitant's life, although one imagines that there is no difficulty in this regard, particularly where there are children.

The occasion of making a will is a good one for checking that co-owned assets are held in the way desired by the parties. For example, the parties might no longer wish those assets to pass on survivorship and would prefer a severance of the joint tenancy so that their shares pass through their wills. As for the drafting of the will, precedents are plentiful. A common structure is for there to be a 'primary will' whereby the other party takes the bulk of the estate and is appointed an executor; and then a 'secondary will', or gift over, leaving the estate in trust for children in the event of the other cohabitant failing to survive for a specified period. There is, however, no surviving cohabitant exemption from inheritance tax and in the case of a client likely to leave an estate which will attract the tax (the threshold in 1994–95 being £150,000) careful consideration to *inter vivos* gifts should be given, *see* Chapter 4.

Alternatively, the client might prefer that a life interest only be given to the survivor, with a remainder to children. This is particularly likely where one or both of the parties have children by a previous relationship. The alternatives are to provide for this under a trust for sale or, in the case of land, under a Settled Land Act settlement. Although the latter are rarely used today, except where they arise unintentionally, they may have certain advantages, in particular the powers given to the tenant for life. This might avoid tension arising between the survivor and trustees who represent a former family of the deceased.

It is particularly important to consider the appointment of testamentary guardians for minor children. An unmarried father does not automatically have parental responsibility (*see* Chapter 10) and if he has not acquired it by a court order or by agreement, the mother should consider appointing him as the guardian. If the father does have parental responsibility then he too can appoint a testamentary guardian to act after his death. Even if he does not have parental responsibility at the time he makes the will, there seems nothing wrong in principle in making an appointment to operate in the event of him having it at the date of his death. Section 5(3) of the Children Act 1989 says that a parent 'who has parental responsibility for his child may appoint another individual to be the child's guardian in the event of his death'. Because the will speaks from death, the relevant time for considering whether the father has parental responsibility is the time of his death.

One significant change made by the Children Act 1989 is that the appointment of a testamentary guardian does not take effect immediately on death if the other parent with parental responsibility is still alive unless the testator had a residence order in his favour at the time of his death.

Finally, consideration should be given as to whether mutual wills should be executed. These allow for a measure of security where the wills have been carefully balanced to preserve the interests of various families because a constructive trust is imposed over the relevant property in the survivor's estate if the survivor has revoked her or his will in breach of the agreement. At the same time, mutual wills do not guard against the *inter vivos* disposition or dissipation of the property by the survivor.

# Index